THE BASEBALL BOOK 1989

THE BASEBALL BOOK 1989

ANDREW THOMAS

Macdonald
Queen Anne Press
In association with
Major League Baseball

A Queen Anne Press BOOK

© Andrew Thomas 1989

First published in Great Britain in 1989 by
Queen Anne Press, a division of
Macdonald & Co (Publishers) Ltd
66-73 Shoe Lane
London EC4P 4AB

A member of Maxwell Pergamon Publishing Corporation plc

Jacket photographs – *Front:* David Cone, New York Mets (B. Schwartzman/All-Sport) and Kirk Gibson, Los Angeles Dodgers (Linda Hecht).
Back: Wrigley Field (Linda Hecht)

All rights reserved. No part of this publication may be reproduced, stored in a retrieval system, or transmitted, in any form or by any means, without the prior permission in writing of the publisher, nor be otherwise circulated in any form of binding or cover other than that in which it is published and without a similar condition including this condition being imposed on the subsequent purchaser.

British Library Cataloguing in Publication Data
Thomas, Andrew, 1951–
  The baseball book 1989
  1. Baseball
  I. Title
  796; 357

ISBN 0-356-17109-4

Printed and bound in Great Britain by
Purnell Book Production Ltd, Paulton

PICTURE CREDITS
All-Sport: 43; 68, 77, 78, 86 (C. Bernhardt), 69 (John Biever), 95 (P. Brouillet), 60 (Brian Drake), 44 (S. Dunn, 124 (G. Gojkovich), 85, 87 (Steve Goldstein), 37, 62 (Otto Greule), 99, 116 (Will Hart), 100T (Diane Johnson), 96 (Allen Kaye), 38, 105 (T. Inzerillo), 65 (Brian Masck), 52, 115 (Mike Powell), 29, 45 (K. Schlea), 82, 94 (B. Schwartzman), 64, 90 (Keith Simonian), 88 (Don Smith), 63 (Allen Steele), 72, 73, 91 (Rick Stewart), 107 (Budd Symes); Associated Press: 118; Bodleian Library: 125; FW: 92 (John Biever), 25 (Robert Beck), 57, 74, 83, 84, 97, 98 (C. Bernhardt), 109 (J. Daniel), 35B (D. Dunn), 17, 21, 32, 40, 104 (S. Dunn), 70 (Bill Frakes), 2-3 (Otto Greule), 58 (Robert Hagan), 6, 66, 67, 106 (J. Rattaliata), 22 (Mitch Reibel), 59 (Rick Stewart), 36 (Dave Stock), 108 (John Swart); Linda Hecht: 1, 14, 15, 16, 18, 19, 23, 24, 26, 27, 28, 30, 31, 33, 34, 35, 39, 41, 42, 47, 48, 49, 53T, 55, 56, 61, 71, 76, 79, 80, 81, 89, 93, 110; Lenscape Inc.: 75; National Baseball Library: 102; Sporting Pictures UK: 100B (John biever); John Swart: 46

Contents

Introduction	7
Major League Baseball Map	8
Spring Training	10
Organised Baseball and a review of MLB 1987–88	11

THE NATIONAL LEAGUE 13
East Division
Chicago Cubs	14
Montreal Expos	17
New York Mets	20
Philadelphia Phillies	23
Pittsburgh Pirates	26
St Louis Cardinals	29

West Division
Atlanta Braves	32
Cincinnati Reds	35
Houston Astros	38
Los Angeles Dodgers	41
San Diego Padres	44
San Francisco Giants	47
National League Winners	50
National League Records	51
Most Valuable Player Awards	52
Cy Young/Rookie of the Year	53

THE AMERICAN LEAGUE 54
East Division
Baltimore Orioles	55
Boston Red Sox	58
Cleveland Indians	61
Detroit Tigers	64
Milwaukee Brewers	67
New York Yankees	70
Toronto Blue Jays	73

West Division
California Angels	76
Chicago White Sox	79
Kansas City Royals	82
Minnesota Twins	85
Oakland Athletics	88
Seattle Mariners	91
Texas Rangers	94
American League Winners	97
American League Records	98
Most Valuable Player Awards	99
Cy Young/Rookie of the Year	100
All-Star Game	101
National Baseball Hall of Fame	102
Seven future Hall of Famers	104
ALCS 1988	111
ALCS/NLCS Records and Results	112
NLCS 1988	113
The World Series.1988	114
World Series Results	117
World Series Records	118
1988 Players Off the Pitch	119
British-Born Major Leaguers	120
Abbreviations used	120
The Minor Leagues 1988	121
NCAA College Baseball	122
IBA Amateur Baseball and Tee Ball	123
Olympic Baseball and Little League	124
CEBA European Baseball and Britain in Europe	125
British Baseball Results	126
All-Time MLB Records and AFN Europe Radio Frequencies	127
1989 AL/NL Standings Grids	127
ALCS/NLCS/World Series Grids	128

Mike Schmidt, 542 career home runs since 1972.

Introduction

As recently as 1985, the prospect of a book about baseball, published in Britain, seemed unlikely. However, during the past three years there has been a rapid increase in public awareness of the game.

Baseball's acceptance by the IOC as a full medal sport at the Barcelona Olympics in 1992, ever-increasing coverage of professional Major League Baseball on network, cable (and, soon, satellite) television, and reports in newspapers and magazines are supporting this surge of interest.

No longer do the British think of baseball as an overgrown version of rounders. The subtleties, skills and excitement of the game, the glamour and hype of its presentation by the American media, can increasingly be seen and appreciated on our own screens.

Young people in particular have taken to baseball. This interest is reflected in chain stores which now sell a wide range of unisex leisurewear bearing baseball logos.

In early 1986, *A Guide to Baseball*, the first introductory paperback was published, followed a year later by *The Baseball Book 1987-88*, a more lavish companion volume that assumed some knowledge about the game. This updated 1989 edition includes extra information and many new features, designed to complement those in the second book, such as MLB's history and development, or background information about each Major League ballpark, or baseball's history in Britain.

Interest in baseball around the world has never been greater. The game's growing popularity in every continent makes its inclusion in the Olympics a logical progression. The International Baseball Association has 68 member federations including the USSR and China, and expects to reach 100 countries and 100 million players by the turn of the century.

In Europe this year, Britain will be playing in the European Pool A Championships in Paris. But on the world stage, the amateur highlight promises to be the Inter-Continental Cup in Puerto Rico, where the 1988 Olympic champions, the USA, will face keen opposition from Cuba (who boycotted Seoul), and Japan.

Baseball's appeal to all nationalities may be illustrated by its development in the USA. When Alexander Cartwright codified the game in 1845, the country's total population was barely 20m but by the time the National League started in 1876 massive immigration had swelled it to 50m. The two major leagues drew 10m fans for the first time in 1928, that was 8 per cent of the population of 122m. Despite the continued influx of people from all over the world, the 26m spectators who attended ballparks in 1968 represented 13 per cent of the population. Twenty years later, this total had doubled to a record 53m fans, 20 per cent of the 1988 US and Canadian populations.

The fairytale success of the Los Angeles Dodgers in the 1988 World Series is sure to make beautiful Dodger Stadium a popular attraction for British tourists taking in Disneyland and the Hollywood film studios. However, the team's chances of repeating its success are not great. In 112 NL seasons, only 33 clubs have retained pennants. Oakland may fare better in the AL, where 36 teams have defended their titles in 87 years.

Away from the playing field, MLB developments during 1989 will include the start of Bart Giamatti's five-year term as Commissioner of Baseball. Giamatti has been President of Yale University and, more recently, President of the National League. Three topics that will take up much of the new commissioner's time will be confirming details of the four-year $1,100m CBS and $400m ESPN cable TV contracts, a new Basic Agreement between the owners and the players' association, to avoid any lockout in 1990, and some advance on the tentative plans for expansion.

Toronto will be hoping to mark the opening of its new indoor stadium, The SkyDome, by playing Canada's first World Series. And what more appropriate opponent for the Blue Jays than Montreal! It's highly unlikely, and would be a TV advertiser's nightmare, but few would have said the Dodgers could improve from 73–89, and 17 games behind San Francisco in 1987, to win the World Series in 1988.

Those glorious uncertainties, the excitement that returns each Spring, the optimism that *this* will be our team's year, they are all part of the game's appeal. And once it grabs you, baseball never lets go.

Andrew Thomas   January 1989

Major League Baseball

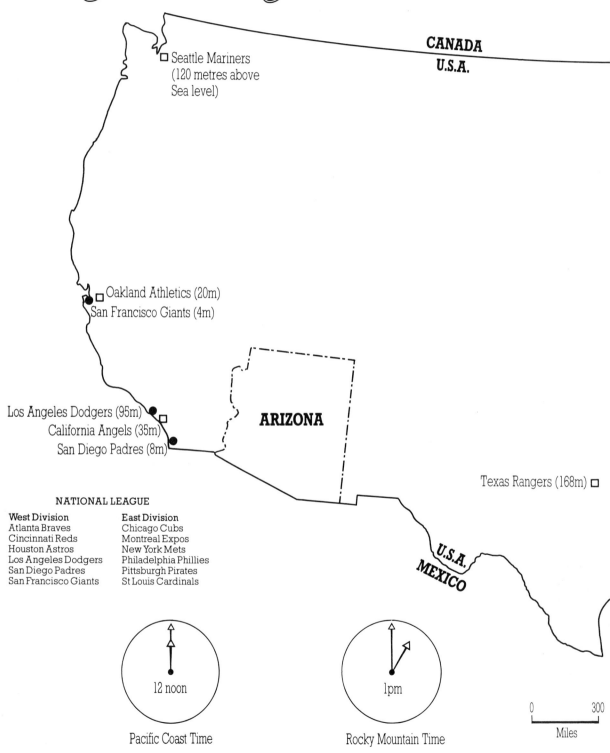

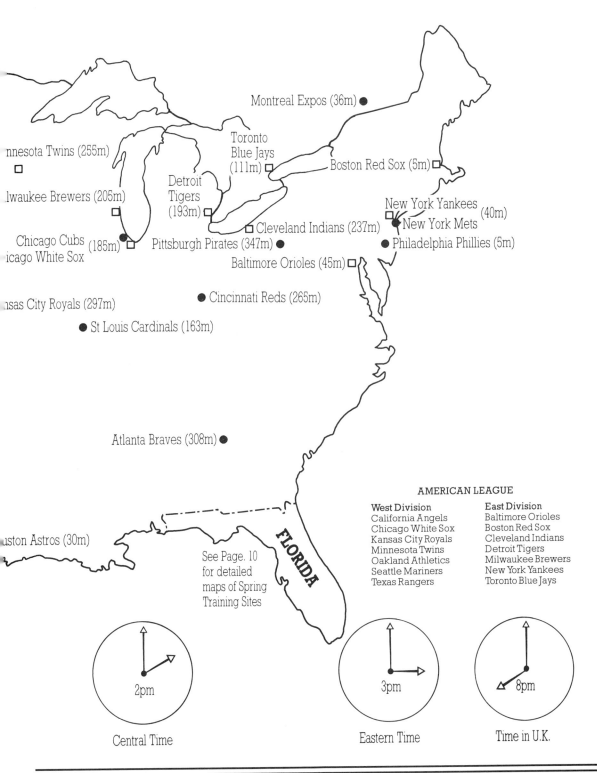

MAJOR LEAGUE BASEBALL

Spring Training

In mid-February, each Major League club summons its pitchers, catchers and injured players to the franchise's baseball complex in the southern 'sun belt' of the USA. A week later, the full Major League squads of up to 100 players report for spring training.

From the first week in March, until the regular season begins in early April, the 26 clubs play about 20 games against teams in the area, which attract about 2m spectators. (These games are against clubs from the same or rival Major League, college teams, or farm clubs.) Spring training games not only help player evaluation but also generate pre-season media interest and many millions of dollars of tourist revenue for Florida and Arizona.

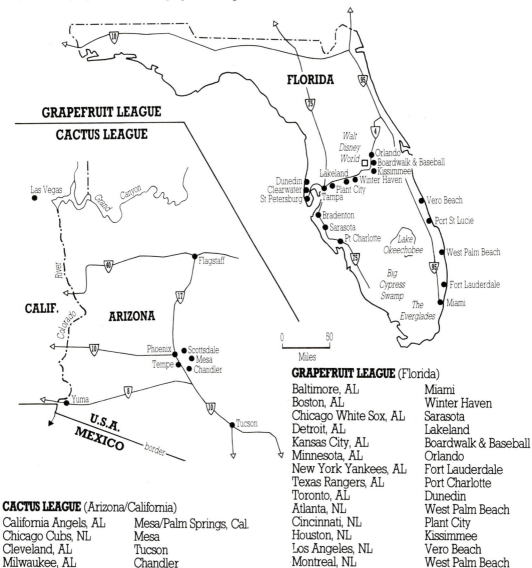

CACTUS LEAGUE (Arizona/California)

California Angels, AL	Mesa/Palm Springs, Cal.
Chicago Cubs, NL	Mesa
Cleveland, AL	Tucson
Milwaukee, AL	Chandler
Oakland, AL	Phoenix
San Diego, NL	Yuma
San Francisco, NL	Scottsdale
Seattle, AL	Tempe

GRAPEFRUIT LEAGUE (Florida)

Baltimore, AL	Miami
Boston, AL	Winter Haven
Chicago White Sox, AL	Sarasota
Detroit, AL	Lakeland
Kansas City, AL	Boardwalk & Baseball
Minnesota, AL	Orlando
New York Yankees, AL	Fort Lauderdale
Texas Rangers, AL	Port Charlotte
Toronto, AL	Dunedin
Atlanta, NL	West Palm Beach
Cincinnati, NL	Plant City
Houston, NL	Kissimmee
Los Angeles, NL	Vero Beach
Montreal, NL	West Palm Beach
New York Mets, NL	Port St Lucie
Philadelphia, NL	Clearwater
Pittsburgh, NL	Bradenton
St Louis, NL	St Petersburg

Organised Baseball

MLB COMMISSIONERS
Kenesaw M. Landis (54) 12 January 1923 to 25 November 1944
Albert B. Chandler (47) 24 April 1945 to 15 July 1951
Ford C. Frick (57) 8 October 1951 to 14 December 1965
William D. Eckert (56) 15 December 1965 to 4 February 1969
Bowie K. Kuhn (42) 4 February 1969 to 30 September 1984
Peter V. Ueberroth (46) 1 October 1984 to 31 March 1989
A. Bartlett Giamatti (50) 1 April 1989 –

Postal Address:
Office of the Commissioner, Major League Baseball, 350 Park Avenue, NEW YORK, New York 10022, USA

Organised Baseball includes the activities of the 12 National League and 14 American League franchises of Major League Baseball as well as 3-AAA, 3-AA, 6-A, and 3-Rookie A minor leagues of professional baseball.

The following diary lists a selection of events 1987–88, from the end of the 1987 Twins-Cardinals World Series, through the winter leagues to spring training, the 1988 regular season, NL/AL playoffs, to the 1988 World Series. It gives some indication of the events that shape a Major Leaguer's year. In 1988, a player who was at every regular season game for the Oakland Athletics, would have travelled 38,400 miles (not to mention spring training, the All-Star Game and the playoffs).

For those battling injury, lack of form, or just the misfortune of being at the wrong club at the wrong time, there were the unsettling worries associated with being traded, sent down to or called up from, the minor leagues (620 such transactions by the 26 franchises during the year), or the sadness of being released.

REVIEW OF MLB 1987–88

1987
October: 84th World Series: Minnesota beat St Louis 4–3. Eligible players had from 5–15 days after the World Series in which to file for free agency.
November: End of season individual awards made. NL umpire, Dick Stello, was killed in a car accident. Former Atlanta slugger, Bob Horner, returned from playing for Yakult Swallows in Japan and signed for St Louis.
December: MLB 86th Winter Meetings, at Dallas, Texas. Free agents who signed for new clubs included Chili Davis (California Angels) and Brett Butler (San Francisco Giants). The Chicago Cubs traded top relief pitcher Lee Smith to Boston in exchange for pitchers Al Nipper and Calvin Schiraldi.

1988
8 January: The last day for clubs to re-sign players who are free agents.
Willie Stargell was elected to the National Baseball Hall of Fame at Cooperstown, New York. He was only the 17th player elected in his first year of eligibility.
Cincinnati has been replacing its AstroTurf, so the Hall of Fame was sent the section of carpet where the ball landed after Pete Rose's record 4,192nd hit.
St Louis slugger, Jack Clark, signed for the Yankees.
1–20 February: Salary arbitration for 108 players.
Kirk Gibson traded from Detroit to Los Angeles Dodgers.
19 February: The earliest date pitchers, catchers and injured players were allowed to report for spring training in Florida and Arizona. Full squads reported from 24 February.
Billy Martin returned as manager of the New York Yankees, for the fifth time.
4 March: Spring training games began in the Cactus League and Grapefruit League. Umpires were enforcing the new balk rule for pitchers, and smaller strike zone for batters.
Pam Postema started a one month tour of NL games in her unsuccessful attempt to become the first woman NL umpire.
11 March: The last day for contract renewals in time for the new season.
29 March: The last date to request waivers to release a player without having to pay his salary for 1988. The 1988 salary bill exceeded $300m, at $433,000 per player, not including bonuses. 73 received more than $1m, nine more than $2m.
3 April: The last day of spring training games. Winter rosters had to be reduced to 25 (24 active) players.
4 April: Opening Day of the 1988 AL & NL regular seasons. Pitchers had such trouble with the balk rule in these early weeks that a new season record was set in April.

Managerial changes already involved Gene Mauch (Angels), who retired after 26 seasons (fourth on the all-time list), and Cal Ripken Sr, sacked by Baltimore (replaced by Frank Robinson), but the Orioles still lost 21 in a row.

1 May: Clubs able to re-sign free agents.
Cincinnati manager, Pete Rose, was suspended for 30 days and fined $10,000 for bumping NL umpire, Dave Pallone.
15 May: Clubs able to re-sign players released last year.
21 May: The 150,000th NL game since 1876 was played at Candlestick Park, between the Giants and Montreal. Chuck Tanner was sacked as manager by Atlanta (replaced by Russ Nixon), and Larry Bowa was fired by San Diego (replaced by general manager, Jack McKeon).
23 May–29 June: All-Star balloting at ballparks.
1–3 June: Summer free agent draft, 1,432 players selected including Jim Abbott, 20, the brilliant pitcher who has only one hand, signed by the California Angels.
More managerial changes. Seattle fired veteran manager, Dick Williams (replaced by Jim Snyder), New York Yankees sacked Billy Martin (replaced by Lou Piniella). Peter Ueberroth confirmed he would not be seeking a second five-year term as commissioner.
Cal Ripken Jr played his 1000th consecutive game (fifth on the all-time list).
July: NL umpire, Lee Weyer, died of a heart attack.
12 July: Mid-season All-Star Game won by the AL, 2–1. Boston fired manager, John McNamara (replaced by Joe Morgan).
24 July: The Mets retired uniform No.41, for 3-time NL Cy Young Award winner, Tom Seaver.
31 July: Willie 'Pops' Stargell, 47 (OF/1B Pirates 1962–82), was inducted into the Hall of Fame.
1 August: Hall of Fame Game (Cubs-Indians).
Bob Boone (Angels) broke the 40-year-old AL record for the most games as a catcher.
8 August: In the first night game at Wrigley Field, the Cubs beat the NY Mets. The planned first game on the previous evening (against Philadelphia) had been rained out.
Pitcher, Nolan Ryan, passed 4,700 career strikeouts.
13 August: Orioles owner, Edward Bennett Williams, died. Boston's winning streak at home ended after 24 games. The NY Mets called up super-rookie, Gregg Jefferies, 21, from their AAA-Tidewater farm club.
31 August: The deadline for player eligibility for the post-season playoffs.
1 September: Fred Lynn, traded from Baltimore to the Tigers, did not reach Detroit by midnight. However, the illogical rule was later changed so that he could play in the playoffs, if Detroit qualified.
Major League rosters expanded to 40 players, by bringing up prospects from the minor leagues.
Mike Schmidt had shoulder surgery, so ending his season with a total of 542 career home runs.
8 September: NL president, Bart Giamatti, was elected the next Commissioner of Major League Baseball.
16 September: Tom Browning pitched a 'perfect game' (only the 14th in Major League history), for Cincinnati against Los Angeles.

Jose Canseco became the first ML player ever to hit 40 home runs and get 40 stolen bases in a season. Wade Boggs collected his 200th hit for the sixth consecutive year.
The season ended as it began, with managers being fired. California Angels sacked Cookie Rojas, the Phillies let Lee Elia go, Houston fired Hal Lanier, Seattle fired Jim Snyder and the White Sox sacked Jim Fregosi.
28 September: Dodgers pitcher, Orel Hershiser, set a new NL record with a streak of 59 scoreless innings. Penny-pinching Pittsburgh sacked their successful general manager, Syd Thrift.
October: After a record haul of home runs in 1987, the homer total for 1988 was down by 28 per cent, to 3,180. However, MLB attendances, which have doubled in the last 20 years, set a record for the sixth time in seven seasons, with over 53m. Jack Clark traded to Padres, Tommy Herr to Phillies, Shane Rawley to Twins, and Bert Blyleven to the Angels.

Final Standings of 1988 Regular Season

AL East	W	L	Pct.	GB	Home	Away	Div.
Boston Red Sox	89	73	.549	—	53–28	36–45	44–34
Detroit Tigers	88	74	.543	1	50–31	38–43	42–63
Milwaukee Brewers	87	75	.537	2	47–34	40–41	37–41
Toronto Blue Jays	87	75	.537	2	45–36	42–39	47–31
New York Yankees	85	76	.528	3½	46–34	39–42	39–39
Cleveland Indians	78	84	.481	11	44–37	34–47	39–39
Baltimore Orioles	54	107	.335	34½	34–46	20–61	25–53

AL West	W	L	Pct.	GB	Home	Away	Div.
Oakland Athletics	104	58	.642	—	54–27	50–31	47–31
Minnesota Twins	91	71	.562	13	47–34	44–37	44–34
Kansas City Royals	84	77	.522	19½	44–36	40–41	43–34
California Angels	75	87	.463	29	35–46	40–41	36–42
Chicago White Sox	71	90	.441	32½	40–41	31–49	37–41
Texas Rangers	70	91	.435	33½	38–43	32–48	34–44
Seattle Mariners	68	93	.422	35½	37–44	31–49	31–46

NL East	W	L	Pct.	GB	Home	Away	Div.
New York Mets	100	60	.625	—	56–24	44–36	57–33
Pittsburgh Pirates	85	75	.531	15	43–38	42–37	49–41
Montreal Expos	81	81	.500	20	43–38	38–43	45–45
Chicago Cubs	77	85	.475	24	39–42	38–43	40–50
St Louis Cardinals	76	86	.469	25	41–40	35–46	39–51
Philadelphia Phillies	65	96	.404	35½	38–42	27–54	40–50

NL West	W	L	Pct.	GB	Home	Away	Div.
Los Angeles Dodgers	94	67	.584	—	45–36	49–31	53–37
Cincinnati Reds	87	74	.540	7	45–35	42–39	50–40
San Diego Padres	83	78	.516	11	36–44	47–34	49–41
San Francisco Giants	83	79	.512	11½	45–36	38–43	47–43
Houston Astros	82	80	.506	12½	44–37	38–43	44–46
Atlanta Braves	54	106	.338	39½	28–51	26–55	27–63

ALCS: Oakland Athletics beat Boston Red Sox, 4–0.
NLCS: Los Angeles Dodgers beat New York Mets, 4–3.
85th World Series: Los Angeles beat Oakland, 4–1.
Eligible players have from 5–15 days after the World Series ends in which to file for free agency.
5–13 November: MLB All-Stars (managed by Sparky Anderson) toured Japan for a seven-game series. Thirteen MLB clubs and six All-Star squads have toured Japan since 1931. 1989 minimum salary $68,000.
December: MLB 87th Winter Meetings at Atlanta, Georgia.

The National League

WEST DIVISION	EAST DIVISION
Atlanta Braves	Chicago Cubs
Cincinnati Reds	Montreal Expos
Houston Astros	New York Mets
Los Angeles Dodgers	Philadelphia Phillies
San Diego Padres	Pittsburgh Pirates
San Francisco Giants	St Louis Cardinals

The National League was organised in 1876, at the Grand Central Hotel in New York City, out of the public's 'loss of confidence' (there was rampant gambling and bribery) in the National Association of Professional Baseball Players, formed five years earlier. The first NL game (Boston v. Philadelphia) was between franchises from traditional baseball cities, but neither club survives. One club soon folded, while the other had to relocate in another city some years later. The uncertain economic climate and strong competition between clubs and rival leagues for players and fans is reflected by the 27 NL clubs in 20 cities which became 'extinct' between 1876 and 1965.

In 1969 the NL expanded to 12 franchises and divided into an East and West Division.

From early April until early October, each club plays 162 games. The other 5 teams in the same division are played 18 times (9 at home and 9 games away), whereas the 6 clubs in the other division are played only 12 times (6 at home and 6 games away).

The traditional rivalry between the Dodgers and Giants (West) is so strong because it is vital for teams to do well against clubs in their own division. They play 90 games against those 5 teams, but only 72 games with the other 6 clubs. In 1988, the 12 franchises played 972 games: 68 per cent were at night, 50 per cent on artificial turf, and 33 per cent indoors. (AL figures on page 54.)

At the end of the regular season the winners of each division play off in the best of 7 games NLCS for the league pennant. The winner then plays the American League champion in the World Series.

In 1989, a designated hitter (dh) will be permitted for both teams in the AL club's ballpark, but not for those games played in the NL stadium. (See page 128 for details.)

NATIONAL LEAGUE PRESIDENTS

Morgan G. Bulkeley	1876
William A. Hulbert	1876 to 1882
Arthur H. Soden	1882
Col. A. G. Mills	1882 to 1884
Nicholas E. Young	1884 to 1902
Harry C. Pulliam	1902 to 1909
John A. Heydler	July 1909 to Dec. 1909
Thomas J. Lynch	1909 to 1913
John K. Tener	1913 to 1918
John A. Heydler	1918 to 1934
Ford C. Frick	1934 to 1951
Warren C. Giles	1951 to 1969
Charles S. Feeney	1970 to 1986
A. Bartlett Giamatti	1986 to 1989

NATIONAL LEAGUE 1876–1988

Present Franchise		Games	Won	Lost	Tied	Pct
Atlanta	1966–88	3659	1710	1943	6	.468
Chicago	1876–1988	16587	8527	7908	152	.519
Cincinnati	1890–1988	15213	7640	7450	123	.506
Houston	1962–88	4315	2081	2230	4	.483
Los Angeles	1958–88	4939	2695	2239	5	.546
Montreal	1969–88	3175	1530	1643	2	.482
New York	1962–88	4311	1986	2317	8	.462
Philadelphia	1883–1988	15981	7389	8481	111	.466
Pittsburgh	1887–1988	15594	7988	7480	126	.516
St Louis	1892–1988	14851	7482	7334	125	.508
San Diego	1969–88	3178	1392	1784	2	.438
San Francisco	1958–88	4937	2540	2392	5	.515
Totals		106830	52960	53201	669	.499

Distances in miles		SF	SD	StL	Pit	Phi	NY	Mon	LA	Hou	Cin	Chi	Atl
Atlanta	W	2590	2125	565	750	770	860	1290	2275	895	470	710	
Chicago	E	2200	2180	300	465	755	850	865	2175	1175	300		
Cincinnati	W	2415	2225	345	290	585	665	850	2260	1105			
Houston	W	2020	1995	820	1395	1500	1595	1900	1565				
LA	W	415	135	1915	2620	2920	3025	3040					
Montreal	E	3100	3045	1165	965	465	375						
New York	E	3050	2850	970	370	95							
Philadelphia	E	2940	2900	900	300								
Pittsburgh	E	2145	2480	600									
St Louis	E	2170	1880										
San Diego	W	530											
San Francisco	W												

Chicago Cubs

NATIONAL LEAGUE EAST DIVISION

Team Colours: Royal blue, scarlet and white
Postal Address: 1060 West Addison Street, Chicago, Illinois 60613, USA
Telephone: (312) 281 5050
History of Franchise: Chicago Cubs 1876– (Known as White Stockings 1876–93, Colts 1894–97, Orphans 1898. Officially became the Cubs in 1907)
NL Honours: 1876, 80, 81, 82, 85, 86, 1906, 07, 08, 10, 18, 29, 32, 35, 38, 45
WS Honours: 1907, 1908
Retired Uniforms: 14–Ernie Banks, 26–Billy Williams

RECENT CUBS TOTALS
(NL Rankings out of 12):

	1988 (Rk)	1987 (Rk)	1986 (Rk)	1985 (Rk)
Games W/L Pct:	.475(9)	.472(9)	.438(11)	.478(8)
Pitching ERA:	3.84(10)	4.55(11)	4.49(12)	4.16(11)
Batting Ave:	.261(1)	.264(4)	.256(3)	.254(7)
Home Runs:	113(3)	209(1)	155(1)	150(1)
Fielding Pct:	.980(3)	.979(7)	.980(2)	.979(6)
Total Errors:	125(4)	130(7)	124(2)	134(7)
Stolen Bases:	120(9)	109(12)	132(9)	182(2)

Pitcher Rick Sutcliffe, W–117, L–92 in 12 years with the Dodgers, Indians and Cubs.

SEASON RECORDS SINCE 1969

Year	Position	W	L	Pct	GB/GA	Attendance
1969	Second	92	70	.568	−8	1,674,993
1970	Second	84	78	.519	−5	1,642,705
1971	Third	83	79	.512	−14	1,653,007
1972	Second	85	70	.548	−11	1,229,163
1973	Fifth	77	84	.478	−5	1,351,705
1974	Sixth	66	96	.407	−22	1,015,378
1975	Fifth	75	87	.463	−17½	1,034,819
1976	Fourth	75	87	.463	−26	1,026,217
1977	Fourth	81	81	.500	−20	1,439,834
1978	Third	79	83	.488	−11	1,525,311
1979	Fifth	80	82	.494	−18	1,648,587
1980	Sixth	64	98	.395	−27	1,206,776
1981	Sixth/fifth	38	65	.369		565,637
1982	Fifth	73	89	.451	−19	1,249,278
1983	Fifth	71	91	.438	−19	1,479,717
1984	First	96	65	.596	+6½	2,107,655
1985	Fourth	77	84	.478	−23½	2,161,534
1986	Fifth	70	90	.438	−37	1,859,102
1987	Sixth	76	85	.472	−18½	2,035,130
1988	Fourth	77	85	.475	−24	2,089,034

After 74 years of day games, Wrigley Field became the last Major League ballpark to install lights in 1988.

WRIGLEY FIELD

Location: Addison Street, N. Clark Street, Waveland Avenue and Sheffield Avenue
Cost: $250,000
First NL game: 20 April 1916
Hand operated scoreboard rebuilt 1937. Known as Weeghman Park and Cubs Park until 1926, it's the Cubs' 5th ballpark. The long-awaited first night game at Wrigley Field (8 August 1988 v. Phillies) was rained out (as first scheduled ML night game was in 1935) after 3½ innings, so the Cubs 6–4 Mets was the official debut, on 9 August.
Record crowd: 46,965 (31 May 1948) dh v. Pitts
Record season attendance: 2,161,534 (1985)
Stadium ranked: No. 2 NL hitters park
Ave total runs/game (NL Rk) 1986 & 1987:
At Chicago 9.65(1), Away 8.76(7)

Weather	Apr.	May	Jun.	Jul.	Aug.	Sept.	Oct.
Temp (deg. C):	10	15	21	24	23	19	13
Rainfall (cm):	9.6	8.6	10.1	10.3	7.9	7.6	6.6
Rainy days:	11	12	11	9	9	9	9

1988 tickets: $3.50 bleachers, to $10.50 box
Newspapers: (see White Sox AL), *Chicago Tribune, Southtown Economist*
Radio: WGN 720AM (68stns)
TV: WGN Ch9 Superstation (Harry Caray, Steve Stone, Dave Nelson, DeWayne Staats)
Chicago hotels used by NL clubs: (see W. Sox AL) Hyatt (Phi, LA, Atl, Hou), Westin (other 7 clubs)

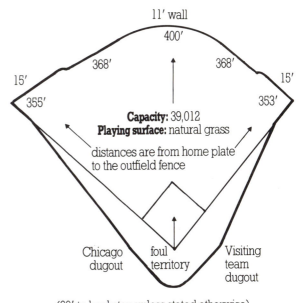

(60′ to backstop unless stated otherwise)

1988 SEASON

Chairman: John Madigan
VP/Baseball Operations: Jim Frey
Manager: Don Zimmer
1988 Cubs Roster: 17% purchased/free agents, 39% acquired by trades, 44% drafted by Cubs

1988 Spring Training Site: HoHoKam Park, Mesa, Arizona (since 1979)
1988 Minor League farm club teams: AAA–Iowa (AmA); AA–Pittsfield (E); A–Winston-Salem Spirits (C), Peoria Chiefs (MW), Charleston Wheelers (SA), Geneva (NY-P); Rookie–Wytheville (Ap)

1988 home games: 73 day, 8 night
1988 away games: 26 day, 55 night
1988 games: 48 on turf, 114 on grass
147 outside, 15 indoors

LEADING CUBS (1988 REGULAR SEASON):

Batters	AtBats	Runs	Hits	HRs	RBIs	Ave
Rafael Palmeiro	580	75	178	8	53	.307
Andre Dawson	591	78	179	24	79	.303
Mark Grace	486	65	144	7	57	.296
Vance Law	556	73	163	11	78	.293
Darrin Jackson	188	29	50	6	20	.266
Ryne Sandberg	618	77	163	19	69	.264
Mitch Webster	523	69	136	6	39	.260
Damon Berryhill	309	19	80	7	38	.259
Manny Trillo	164	15	41	1	14	.250
Shawon Dunston	575	69	143	9	56	.249

Pitchers	W-L	Saves	Inns	BBs	SOs	ERA
Al Nipper	2-4	1	80.0	34	27	3.04
Greg Maddux	18-8	0	249.0	81	140	3.18
Jamie Moyer	9-15	0	202.0	55	121	3.48
Les Lancaster	4-6	5	85.2	34	36	3.78
Rick Sutcliffe	13-14	0	226.0	70	144	3.86
Pat Perry	4-4	1	58.2	16	35	4.14
Jeff Pico	6-7	1	112.2	37	57	4.15
Rich Gossage	4-4	13	43.2	15	30	4.33
Calvin Schiraldi	9-13	1	166.1	63	140	4.38
Kevin Coffman	2-6	0	67.0	54	24	5.78

Rafael Palmeiro, hit by a pitch during his best ML season so far, was traded to Texas for 1989.

16 **CHICAGO CUBS** 1988 SEASON

Montreal Expos

NATIONAL LEAGUE EAST DIVISION

Team Colours: Royal blue, scarlet and white
Postal Address: PO Box 500, Station M, Montreal, Quebec H1V 3P2, Canada
Telephone: (514) 253 3434
History of Franchise: Montreal Expos 1969–
Honours: Yet to win NL or World Series

RECENT EXPOS TOTALS
(NL Rankings out of 12):

	1988 (Rk)	1987 (Rk)	1986 (Rk)	1985 (Rk)
Games W/L Pct:	.500(8)	.562(3)	.484(7)	.522(5)
Pitching ERA:	3.08(3)	3.92(6)	3.78(6)	3.55(5)
Batting Ave:	.251(3)	.265(3)	.254(5)	.247(8)
Home Runs:	107(6)	120(10)	110(11)	118(7)
Fielding Pct:	.977(9)	.976(10)	.979(3)	.981(3)
Total Errors:	142(9)	147(10)	133(4)	121(3)
Stolen Bases:	189(4)	166(4)	193(2)	169(3)

Outfielder Tim Raines, 544 stolen bases in 10 years with the Expos.

SEASON RECORDS SINCE 1969

Year	Position	W	L	Pct	GB/GA	Attendance
1969	Sixth	52	110	.321	−48	1,212,608
1970	Sixth	73	89	.451	−16	1,424,683
1971	Fifth	71	90	.441	−25½	1,290,963
1972	Fifth	70	86	.449	−26½	1,142,145
1973	Fourth	79	83	.488	−3½	1,246,863
1974	Fourth	79	82	.491	−8½	1,019,134
1975	Fifth	75	87	.463	−17½	908,292
1976	Sixth	55	107	.340	−46	646,704
1977	Fifth	75	87	.463	−26	1,433,757
1978	Fourth	76	86	.469	−14	1,427,007
1979	Second	95	65	.594	−2	2,102,173
1980	Second	90	72	.556	−1	2,208,175
1981	Third/first	60	48	.556		1,534,564
1982	Third	86	76	.531	−6	2,318,292
1983	Third	82	80	.506	−8	2,320,651
1984	Fifth	78	83	.484	−18	1,606,531
1985	Third	84	77	.522	−16½	1,502,494
1986	Fourth	78	83	.484	−29½	1,128,981
1987	Third	91	71	.562	−4	1,850,324
1988	Third	81	81	.500	−20	1,478,659

Pitcher Tim Burke, 48 saves in four years with Montreal.

OLYMPIC STADIUM

Location: 4545 Pierre de Coubertin Street, Sherbrooke Street, Pie IX Boulevard, Viau Street
Cost: Canadian $770m
First NL game: 15 April 1977
Expos played at Jarry Park 1969–76
The Kelvar and canvas roof weighing 65 tons is supported by steel cables from an inclined 552ft tower. It takes 45 minutes to lower or raise the roof. A 90 passenger cable car takes visitors up to the top observation decks.
Record crowd: 59,282 (16 Sept 1979) v. St Louis
Record season attendance: 2,320,651 (1983)
A pitchers park ranked: No. 8 for NL hitters
Ave total runs/game (NL Rk) 1986 & 1987:
At Montreal 8.73(6), Away 9.08(2)
Weather April–October outside Olympic Stadium:
6–21 degrees C; 7.4–8.7cm rainfall
1988 tickets: $1 bleachers, to $12 box
Newspapers: *Montreal Gazette, Le Journal de Montreal*
Radio: CFCF 600AM (9stns), Canadian Forces Network, W. Germany/Holland
TV: CBMT Ch6 (45stns), CBFT Ch2 (20stns). Cable: TSN (Dave VanHorne, Jim Fanning, Ken Singleton, Jim Hughson)
Montreal hotel used by all NL clubs: Sheraton

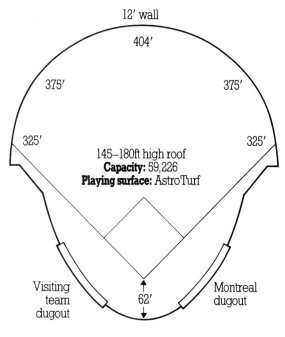

145–180ft high roof
Capacity: 59,226
Playing surface: AstroTurf

1988 SEASON

Chairman: Charles R. Bronfman
GM/VP Baseball Operations: Bill Stoneman
Manager: Buck Rodgers
1988 Expos Roster: 40% purchased/free agents, 35% acquired by trades, 25% drafted by Expos

1988 Spring Training Site: Municipal Stadium, West Palm Beach, Florida
1988 Minor League farm club teams: AAA–Indianapolis Indians (AmA); AA–Jacksonville (S); A–West Palm Beach (FS), Rockford (MW), Jamestown (NY-P); Rookie–Bradenton (GC)

1988 home games: 14 day, 67 night
1988 away games: 31 day, 50 night
1988 games: 120 on turf, 42 on grass
75 outside, 87 indoors

LEADING EXPOS (1988 REGULAR SEASON):

Batters	AtBats	Runs	Hits	HRs	RBIs	Ave
Andres Galarraga	609	99	184	29	92	.302
Hubie Brooks	588	61	164	20	90	.289
Rex Hudler	216	38	59	4	14	.273
Mike Fitzgerald	155	17	42	5	23	.271
Tim Raines	429	66	116	12	48	.270
Tom Foley	377	33	100	5	43	.265
Tim Wallach	592	52	152	12	69	.257
Dave Martinez	447	51	114	6	46	.255
Nelson Santovenia	309	26	73	8	41	.236
Luis Rivera	371	35	83	4	30	.224

Pitchers	W-L	Saves	Inns	BBs	SOs	ERA
Pascual Perez	12-8	0	188.0	44	131	2.44
Jeff Parrett	12-4	6	91.2	45	62	2.65
Dennis Martinez	15-13	0	235.1	55	120	2.72
Andy McGaffigan	6-0	4	91.1	37	71	2.76
Joe Hesketh	4-3	9	72.2	35	64	2.85
Bryn Smith	12-10	0	198.0	32	122	3.00
John Dopson	3-11	0	168.2	58	101	3.04
Brian Holman	4-8	0	100.1	34	58	3.23
Tim Burke	3-5	18	82.0	25	42	3.40
Neal Heaton	3-10	2	97.1	43	43	4.99

First baseman Andres Galarraga was one of Montreal's successes in 1988.

New York Mets

NATIONAL LEAGUE EAST DIVISION

Team Colours: Royal blue, orange and white
Postal Address: William A. Shea Stadium, Roosevelt Avenue & 126th Street, Flushing, New York 11368, USA
Telephone: (718) 507 6387
History of Franchise: New York Mets 1962–
NL Honours: 1969, 1973, 1986
WS Honours: 1969, 1986
Retired Uniforms: 14–Gil Hodges, 37–Casey Stengel, 41–Tom Seaver

RECENT METS TOTALS
(NL Rankings out of 12):

	1988 (Rk)	1987 (Rk)	1986 (Rk)	1985 (Rk)
Games W/L Pct:	.625(1)	.568(2)	.667(1)	.605(2)
Pitching ERA:	2.91(1)	3.84(3)	3.11(1)	3.11(3)
Batting Ave:	.256(2)	.268(1)	.263(1)	.257(4)
Home Runs:	152(1)	193(3)	148(3)	134(3)
Fielding Pct:	.981(1)	.978(9)	.978(5)	.982(2)
Total Errors:	115(1)	137(9)	138(7)	115(2)
Stolen Bases:	140(5)	159(6)	118(10)	117(7)

First baseman Keith Hernandez, 2,106 hits in 15 years with St Louis and the Mets.

SEASON RECORDS SINCE 1969

Year	Position	W	L	Pct	GB/GA	Attendance
1969	First	100	62	.617	+8	2,175,373
1970	Third	83	79	.512	−6	2,697,479
1971	Third	83	79	.512	−14	2,266,680
1972	Third	83	73	.532	−13½	2,134,185
1973	First	82	79	.509	+1½	1,912,390
1974	Fifth	71	91	.438	−17	1,722,209
1975	Third	82	80	.506	−10½	1,730,566
1976	Third	86	76	.531	−15	1,468,754
1977	Sixth	64	98	.395	−37	1,066,825
1978	Sixth	66	96	.407	−24	1,007,328
1979	Sixth	63	99	.389	−35	788,905
1980	Fifth	67	95	.414	−24	1,178,659
1981	Fifth/fourth	41	62	.398		701,910
1982	Sixth	65	97	.401	−27	1,320,055
1983	Sixth	68	94	.420	−22	1,103,808
1984	Second	90	72	.556	−6½	1,829,482
1985	Second	98	64	.605	−3	2,751,437
1986	First	108	54	.667	+21½	2,762,417
1987	Second	92	70	.568	−3	3,027,121
1988	First	100	60	.625	+15	3,047,724

20 NEW YORK METS NATIONAL EAST

Pitcher Ron Darling, W–73, L–41 in six years, attended Yale University.

WILLIAM A. SHEA STADIUM

Location: Roosevelt Avenue & 126th Street
First NL game: 17 April 1964
Mets played at Polo Grounds 1962–63
Videoscreen: DiamondVision, and $2m scoreboard
Record crowd: 57,397 (16 Oct 1969) WS v. Balt.
Record season attendance: 3,047,724 (1988)
A pitchers park ranked: No. 11 for NL hitters
Ave total runs/game (NL Rk) 1986 & 1987:
At New York 8.47(8), Away 9.32(1)

Weather	Apr.	May	Jun.	Jul.	Aug.	Sept.	Oct.
Temp (deg. C):	11	17	22	25	24	20	15
Rainfall (cm):	8.4	8.8	7.6	9.3	10.1	8.4	7.3
Rainy days:	11	11	10	12	10	9	9

1988 tickets: $1 seniors, to $11 box
Newspapers: *New York Daily News*, *New York Post* (see NY Yankees AL)
Radio: WFAN 1050AM
TV: WWOR Ch9. Cable: SportsChannel (Bob Murphy, Gary Thorne, Ralph Kiner, Tim McCarver, Steve Zabriskie, Fran Healy, Rusty Staub)
New York hotel used by all NL clubs: Grand Hyatt (see NY Yankees AL)

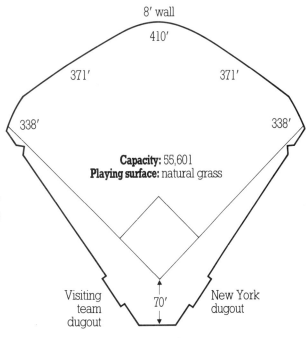

NEW YORK METS WILLIAM A. SHEA STADIUM

1988 SEASON

Chairman: Nelson Doubleday Jr
President/CEO: Fred Wilpon
VP/General Manager: Frank Cashen
Manager: Dave Johnson
1988 Mets Roster: 8% purchased/free agents, 46% acquired by trades, 46% drafted by Mets

1988 Spring Training Site: St Lucie County Sports Complex, Port St Lucie, Florida
1988 Minor League farm club teams: AAA–Tidewater Tides (Int); AA–Jackson (T); A–St Lucie (FS), Columbia (SA), Little Falls (NY-P); Rookie–Kingsport (Ap), Sarasota (GC)

1988 home games: 30 day, 51 night
1988 away games: 29 day, 52 night
1988 games: 48 on turf, 114 on grass
147 outside, 15 indoors

LEADING METS (1988 REGULAR SEASON):

Batters	AtBats	Runs	Hits	HRs	RBIs	Ave
Gregg Jefferies	109	19	35	6	17	.321
Wally Backman	294	44	89	0	17	.303
Mookie Wilson	378	61	112	8	41	.296
Kevin McReynolds	552	82	159	27	99	.288
Dave Magadan	314	39	87	1	35	.277
Keith Hernandez	348	43	96	11	55	.276
Lenny Dykstra	429	57	116	8	33	.270
Darryl Strawberry	543	101	146	39	101	.269
Gary Carter	455	39	110	11	46	.242
Howard Johnson	495	85	114	24	68	.230
Kevin Elster	406	41	87	9	37	.214

Pitchers	W-L	Saves	Inns	BBs	SOs	ERA
Randy Myers	7-3	26	68.0	17	69	1.72
David Cone	20-3	0	231.1	80	213	2.22
Terry Leach	7-2	3	92.0	24	51	2.54
Roger McDowell	5-5	16	89.0	31	46	2.63
Bob Ojeda	10-13	0	190.1	33	133	2.88
Sid Fernandez	12-10	0	187.0	70	189	3.03
Dwight Gooden	18-9	0	248.1	57	175	3.19
Ron Darling	17-9	0	240.2	60	161	3.25

Shea Stadium, built on landfill once called Fishhook Murphy's Dump.

22 NEW YORK METS 1988 SEASON

Philadelphia Phillies

NATIONAL LEAGUE EAST DIVISION

Team Colours: Crimson and white
Postal Address: PO Box 7575, Philadelphia, Pennsylvania 19101, USA
Telephone: (215) 463 6000
History of Franchise: Philadelphia Phillies 1883– (Worcester Brown Stockings 1880–82, moved and renamed Phillies, but were sometimes called the Quakers. Known as Blue Jays 1944–45)
NL Honours: 1915, 50, 80, 83
WS Honours: 1980
Retired Uniforms: 1–Richie Ashburn, 32–Steve Carlton, 36–Robin Roberts

RECENT PHILLIES TOTALS
(NL Rankings out of 12):

	1988 (Rk)	1987 (Rk)	1986 (Rk)	1985 (Rk)
Games W/L Pct:	.404(11)	.494(6)	.534(3)	.463(9)
Pitching ERA:	4.14(12)	4.18(7)	3.85(7)	3.68(8)
Batting Ave:	.239(12)	.254(10)	.253(7)	.245(11)
Home Runs:	106(7)	169(5)	154(2)	141(2)
Fielding Pct:	.976(11)	.980(4)	.978(5)	.978(8)
Total Errors:	145(11)	121(4)	137(6)	139(8)
Stolen Bases:	112(11)	111(11)	153(6)	122(6)

Outfielder Phil Bradley, who played well in the NL after five seasons with Seattle, was traded to Baltimore for 1989.

SEASON RECORDS SINCE 1969

Year	Position	W	L	Pct	GB/GA	Attendance
1969	Fifth	63	99	.389	−37	519,414
1970	Fifth	73	88	.453	−15½	708,247
1971	Sixth	67	95	.414	−30	1,511,233
1972	Sixth	59	97	.378	−37½	1,343,329
1973	Sixth	71	91	.438	−11½	1,475,934
1974	Third	80	82	.494	−8	1,808,648
1975	Second	86	76	.531	−6½	1,909,233
1976	First	101	61	.623	+9	2,480,150
1977	First	101	61	.623	+5	2,700,070
1978	First	90	72	.556	+1½	2,583,389
1979	Fourth	84	78	.519	−14	2,775,011
1980	First	91	71	.562	+1	2,651,650
1981	First/third	59	48	.551		1,638,932
1982	Second	89	73	.549	−3	2,376,394
1983	First	90	72	.556	+6	2,128,339
1984	Fourth	81	81	.500	−15½	2,062,696
1985	Fifth	75	87	.463	−26	1,830,350
1986	Second	86	75	.534	−21½	1,933,355
1987	Fourth	80	82	.494	−15	2,100,110
1988	Sixth	65	96	.404	−35½	1,990,041

Versatile Von Hayes, 1,007 hits in eight years with the Phillies.

VETERANS STADIUM

Location: Broad Street and Pattison Avenue
Cost: $50m
First NL game: 10 April 1971
Phillies had 7 ballparks from 1883–1970
Philadelphia Athletics played in first-ever NL game (22 April 1876 v. Boston) but the team folded.
Videoscreen: Panasonic colour video replay
Record crowd: 63,816 (3 July 1984) v. Cinc.
Record season attendance: 2,775,011 (1979)
Other stadium users: NFL Eagles, NCAA Temple Owls
Stadium ranked: No. 3 NL hitters park
Ave total runs/game (NL Rk) 1986 & 1987:
At Philadelphia 9.35(4), Away 8.51(8)

Weather	Apr.	May	Jun.	Jul.	Aug.	Sept.	Oct.
Temp (deg. C):	12	17	22	25	24	20	14
Rainfall (cm):	8.4	8.6	9.3	10.3	10.3	7.6	6.3
Rainy days:	11	11	10	11	11	8	8

1988 tickets: $4 general, to $9 box
Newspapers: *Philadelphia Enquirer, Philadelphia News*
Radio: WCAU 1200AM (29stns)
TV: WTAF Ch29 (Richie Ashburn, Harry Kalas, Andy Musser, Chris Wheeler, Garry Maddox)
Philadelphia hotels used by NL clubs: Sheraton (StL, Cin, Atl, Pit), Hershey (7 others)

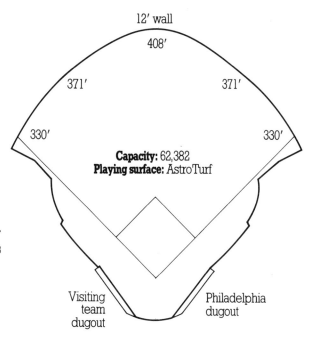

24 PHILADELPHIA PHILLIES VETERANS STADIUM

1988 SEASON

President/General Partner: Bill Giles
VP/Player Personnel: Woody Woodward (to 7 June), Lee Thomas
Manager: Lee Elia (to 23 September), Nick Leyva
1988 Phillies Roster: 9% purchased/free agents, 28% acquired by trades, 63% drafted by Phillies

1988 Spring Training Site: Carpenter Complex, Jack Russell Stadium, Clearwater, Florida (since 1947)
1988 Minor League farm club teams: AAA–Maine Guides (Int); AA–Reading (E); A–Clearwater (FS), Spartanburg (SA), Batavia (NY-P); Rookie–Martinsville (Ap)

1988 home games: 20 day, 61 night
1988 away games: 25 day, 56 night
1988 games: 120 on turf, 42 on grass
147 outside, 15 indoors

LEADING PHILLIES
(1988 REGULAR SEASON):

Batters	AtBats	Runs	Hits	HRs	RBIs	Ave
Ricky Jordan	273	41	84	11	43	.308
Bob Dernier	166	19	48	1	10	.289
Mike Thompson	378	53	109	2	33	.288
Von Hayes	367	43	100	6	45	.272
Phil Bradley	569	77	150	11	56	.264
Mike Schmidt	390	52	97	12	62	.249
Juan Samuel	629	68	153	12	67	.243
Chris James	566	57	137	19	66	.242
Lance Parrish	424	44	91	15	60	.215
Steve Jeltz	379	39	71	0	27	.187

Pitchers	W-L	Saves	Inns	BBs	SOs	ERA
Greg Harris	4-6	1	107.0	52	71	2.36
Kent Tekulve	3-7	4	80.0	22	43	3.60
Kevin Gross	12-14	0	231.2	89	162	3.69
Steve Bedrosian	6-6	28	74.1	27	61	3.75
Mike Maddux	4-3	0	88.2	34	59	3.76
Shane Rawley	8-16	0	198.0	78	87	4.18
Don Carman	10-14	0	201.1	70	116	4.29
Bruce Ruffin	6-10	3	144.1	80	82	4.43
David Palmer	7-9	0	129.0	48	85	4.47

Pitcher Steve Bedrosian has 97 saves in his three years with the Phillies, after only 41 in five seasons at Atlanta.

Pittsburgh Pirates

NATIONAL LEAGUE EAST DIVISION

Team Colours: Black, gold and white
Postal Address: PO Box 7000, Pittsburgh, Pennsylvania 15212, USA
Telephone: (412) 323 5000
History of Franchise: Pittsburgh Pirates 1887– (Original club, formed 1876, called Alleghenies until 1889, Innocents 1890, and Pirates 1891–)
NL Honours: 1901, 02, 03, 09, 25, 27, 60, 71, 79
WS Honours: 1909, 25, 60, 71, 79
Retired Uniforms: 1–Billy Meyer, 4–Ralph Kiner, 8–Willie Stargell, 9–Bill Mazeroski, 20–Pie Traynor, 21–Roberto Clemente, 33–Honus Wagner, 40–Danny Murtaugh

RECENT PIRATES TOTALS
(NL Rankings out of 12):

	1988 (Rk)	1987 (Rk)	1986 (Rk)	1985 (Rk)
Games W/L Pct:	.531(4)	.494(6)	.395(12)	.354(12)
Pitching ERA:	3.47(8)	4.20(8)	3.90(8)	3.97(10)
Batting Ave:	.247(7)	.264(4)	.250(10)	.247(8)
Home Runs:	110(5)	131(7)	111(10)	80(12)
Fielding Pct:	.980(3)	.980(4)	.978(5)	.978(6)
Total Errors:	125(4)	123(5)	143(10)	133(6)
Stolen Bases:	119(10)	140(7)	152(7)	110(8)

Mike LaValliere, 369 games as a catcher in five years with the Phillies, Cards and Pirates.

SEASON RECORDS SINCE 1969

Year	Position	W	L	Pct	GB/GA	Attendance
1969	Third	88	74	.543	−12	769,369
1970	First	89	73	.549	+5	1,341,947
1971	First	97	65	.599	+7	1,501,132
1972	First	96	59	.619	+11	1,427,460
1973	Third	80	82	.494	−2½	1,319,913
1974	First	88	74	.543	+1½	1,110,552
1975	First	92	69	.571	+6½	1,270,018
1976	Second	92	70	.568	−9	1,025,945
1977	Second	96	66	.593	−5	1,237,349
1978	Second	88	73	.547	−1½	964,106
1979	First	98	64	.605	+2	1,435,454
1980	Third	83	79	.512	−8	1,646,757
1981	Fourth/sixth	46	56	.451		541,789
1982	Fourth	84	78	.519	−8	1,024,106
1983	Second	84	78	.519	−6	1,225,916
1984	Sixth	75	87	.463	−21½	773,500
1985	Sixth	57	104	.354	−43½	735,900
1986	Sixth	64	98	.395	−44	1,000,917
1987	Fourth	80	82	.494	−15	1,161,193
1988	Second	85	75	.531	−15	1,865,713

Outfielder Barry Bonds, 65 home runs in three seasons with the Pirates.

THREE RIVERS STADIUM

Location: 600 Stadium Circle at junction of Ohio, Allegheny, Monongahela Rivers
Cost: $55m
First NL game: 16 July 1970
Videoscreen: 30′×33′ DiamondVision
Record crowd: 54,089 (11 April 1988) v. Phila.
Record season attendance: 1,865,713 (1988)
Pirates had 3 stadiums between 1887–1970
Other stadium user: NFL Steelers
Stadium ranked: No. 4 NL hitters park
Ave total runs/game (NL Rk) 1986 & 1987:
At Pittsburgh 8.98(5), Away 8.49(9)

Weather	Apr.	May	Jun.	Jul.	Aug.	Sept.	Oct.
Temp (deg. C):	10	16	20	22	21	18	12
Rainfall (cm):	8.6	9.0	8.8	9.6	8.1	6.3	6.3
Rainy days:	13	13	12	12	10	9	10

1988 tickets: $1 children, to $9.50 box
Newspapers: *Pittsburgh Press, Pittsburgh Post-Gazette*
Radio: KDKA 1020AM (38stns). Broadcast first-ever ML game, Pirates–Phillies, 5 August 1921
TV: KDKA Ch2 (6stns). Cable: TCI (Lanny Frattare, Jim Rookes, John Sanders, Steve Blass)
Pittsburgh hotels used by NL clubs: Hyatt (Hou), Hilton (LA), Westin (Mon, Cin), Vista (7 others)

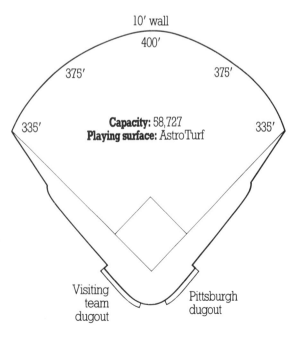

PITTSBURGH PIRATES THREE RIVERS STADIUM

1988 SEASON

Chairman/CEO: Douglas D. Danforth
VP/General Manager: Syd Thrift (fired 4 October), Larry Doughty
Manager: Jim Leyland
1988 Pirates Roster: 35% purchased/free agents, 44% acquired by trades, 21% drafted by Pirates

1988 Spring Training Site: Pirate City, McKechnie Field, Bradenton, Florida (since 1969)
1988 Minor League farm club teams: AAA–Buffalo Bisons (AmA); AA–Harrisburg Senators (E); A–Salem Buccaneers (Car), Augusta (SA), Watertown (NY-P); Rookie–Bradenton (GC), Princeton (Ap)

1988 home games: 16 day, 65 night
1988 away games: 21 day, 60 night
1988 games: 120 on turf, 42 on grass
147 outside, 15 indoors

LEADING PIRATES (1988 REGULAR SEASON):

Batters	AtBats	Runs	Hits	HRs	RBIs	Ave
Andy Van Slyke	587	101	169	25	100	.288
Barry Bonds	538	97	152	24	58	.283
Bobby Bonilla	584	87	160	24	100	.274
Ken Oberkfell	476	49	129	3	42	.271
Glenn Wilson	126	11	34	2	15	.270
Sid Bream	462	50	122	10	65	.264
Jose Lind	611	82	160	2	49	.262
Mike LaValliere	352	24	92	2	47	.261
R. J. Reynolds	323	35	80	6	51	.248
Rafael Belliard	286	28	61	0	11	.213

Pitchers	W-L	Saves	Inns	BBs	SOs	ERA
Bob Walk	12-10	0	212.2	65	81	2.71
Dave LaPoint	4-2	0	52.0	10	19	2.77
Jeff Robinson	11-5	9	124.2	39	87	3.03
Doug Drabek	15-7	0	219.1	50	127	3.08
John Smiley	13-11	0	205.0	46	129	3.25
Jim Gott	6-6	34	77.1	22	76	3.49
Bob Kipper	2-6	0	65.0	26	39	3.74
Mike Dunne	7-11	0	170.0	88	70	3.92
Brian Fisher	8-10	1	146.1	57	66	4.61

Versatile Andy Van Slyke, 726 hits in 832 games in six years with St Louis and the Pirates.

28 PITTSBURGH PIRATES 1988 SEASON

St Louis Cardinals

NATIONAL LEAGUE EAST DIVISION

Team Colours: Scarlet, navy blue and white
Postal Address: Busch Memorial Stadium, 250 Stadium Plaza, St Louis, Missouri 63102, USA
Telephone: (314) 421 4040
History of Franchise: (St Louis Cardinals 1876–77, 1885–86), St Louis Browns/Perfectos formed 1892–, became known as Cardinals 1899–
NL Honours: 1926, 28, 30, 31, 34, 42, 43, 44, 46, 64, 67, 68, 82, 85, 87
WS Honours: 1926, 31, 42, 44, 46, 64, 67, 82
Retired Uniforms: 6–Stan Musial, 14–Ken Boyer, 17–Dizzy Dean, 20–Lou Brock, 45–Bob Gibson, 85–August A. Busch Jr

RECENT CARDINALS TOTALS
(NL Rankings out of 12):

	1988 (Rk)	1987 (Rk)	1986 (Rk)	1985 (Rk)
Games W/L Pct:	.469(10)	.586(1)	.491(6)	.623(1)
Pitching ERA:	3.47(8)	3.91(5)	3.37(4)	3.10(2)
Batting Ave:	.249(4)	.263(6)	.236(12)	.264(1)
Home Runs:	71(12)	94(12)	58(12)	87(11)
Fielding Pct:	.981(1)	.982(1)	.981(1)	.983(1)
Total Errors:	121(3)	116(1)	123(1)	108(1)
Stolen Bases:	234(1)	248(1)	262(1)	314(1)

Pitcher Todd Worrell, 106 saves in four years with St Louis.

SEASON RECORDS SINCE 1969

Year	Position	W	L	Pct	GB/GA	Attendance
1969	Fourth	87	75	.537	−13	1,682,583
1970	Fourth	76	86	.469	−13	1,628,729
1971	Second	90	72	.556	−7	1,604,671
1972	Fourth	75	81	.481	−21½	1,196,894
1973	Second	81	81	.500	−1½	1,574,012
1974	Second	86	75	.534	−1½	1,838,413
1975	Third	82	80	.506	−10½	1,695,394
1976	Fifth	72	90	.444	−29	1,207,036
1977	Third	83	79	.512	−18	1,659,287
1978	Fifth	69	93	.426	−21	1,278,175
1979	Third	86	76	.531	−12	1,627,256
1980	Fourth	74	88	.457	−17	1,385,147
1981	Second/second	59	43	.578		1,010,247
1982	First	92	70	.568	+3	2,111,906
1983	Fourth	79	83	.488	−11	2,317,914
1984	Third	84	78	.519	−12½	2,037,448
1985	First	101	61	.623	+3	2,637,563
1986	Third	79	82	.491	−28½	2,471,817
1987	First	95	67	.586	+3	3,072,121
1988	Fifth	76	86	.469	−25	2,892,629

Dorrel Norman Elvert 'Whitey' Herzog, W–1,162, L–1,002 in 16 seasons managing the Rangers, Angels, Royals, and St Louis.

BUSCH MEMORIAL STADIUM

Location: Broadway, Walnut Street, Spruce Street
First NL game: 12 May 1966
St Louis used 4 stadiums before 1966
Videoscreen: 1983 Stewart-Warner 22'×30' board
Record crowd: 55,347 (20, 21, 22 October 1987) three WS games v. Minnesota
Record season attendance: 3,072,122 (1987)
Busch Stadium was formerly used by the NFL St Louis Cardinals who moved to Phoenix, 1988
Stadium ranked neutral: No. 6 NL hitters park
Ave total runs/game (NL Rk) 1986 & 1987:
At St Louis 8.33(10), Away 8.35(10)

Weather	Apr.	May	Jun.	Jul.	Aug.	Sept.	Oct.
Temp (deg. C):	14	19	24	26	25	21	15
Rainfall (cm):	9.8	9.8	11.1	9.3	7.3	7.3	7.1
Rainy days:	11	11	11	9	8	8	8

1988 tickets: $4 bleachers, to $10.50 box
Newspapers: *St Louis Post-Dispatch*, *St Louis Globe-Democrat*
Radio: KMOX 1120AM (125stns)
TV: KPLR Ch11. Cable: CENCOM (Jack Buck, Mike Shannon, Ken Wilson, Al Hrabosky)
St Louis hotels used by NL clubs: Adam's Mark (Phi, Atl, Pit, SD), Marriott (7 others)

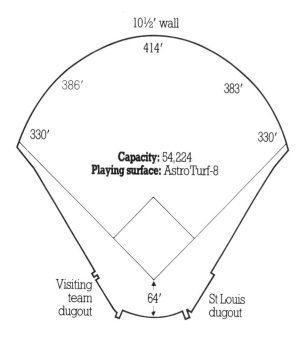

ST LOUIS CARDINALS BUSCH MEMORIAL STADIUM

1988 SEASON

Chairman/President/CEO: August A. Busch Jr
VP/General Manager: Dal Maxvill
Manager: Whitey Herzog
1988 Cardinals Roster: 12% purchased/free agents, 38% acquired by trades, 50% drafted by Cardinals

1988 Spring Training Site: Busch Complex, Al Lang Stadium, St Petersburg, Florida (since 1946)
1988 Minor League farm club teams: AAA–Louisville Redbirds (AmA); AA–Arkansas Travelers (T); A–St Petersburg (FS), Springfield (MW), Savannah (SA), Hamilton (NY-P); Rookie–Johnson City (Ap)

1988 home games: 23 day, 58 night
1988 away games: 39 day, 42 night
1988 games: 120 on turf, 42 on grass
147 outside, 15 indoors

LEADING CARDINALS (1988 REGULAR SEASON):

Batters	AtBats	Runs	Hits	HRs	RBIs	Ave
Willie McGee	562	73	164	3	50	.292
Pedro Guerrero	364	40	104	10	65	.286
Jose Oquendo	451	36	125	7	46	.277
Ozzie Smith	575	80	155	3	51	.270
Geronimo Pena	505	55	133	10	51	.263
Vince Coleman	616	77	160	3	38	.260
Bob Horner	206	15	53	3	33	.257
Terry Pendleton	391	44	99	6	53	.253
Tom Brunansky	523	69	128	22	79	.245
Denny Walling	234	22	56	1	21	.239
Luis Alicea	297	20	63	1	24	.212

Pitchers	W-L	Saves	Inns	BBs	SOs	ERA
John Costello	5-2	1	49.2	25	38	1.81
Joe Magrane	5-9	0	165.1	51	100	2.18
Ken Dayley	2-7	5	55.1	19	38	2.77
Scott Terry	9-6	3	129.1	34	65	2.92
Todd Worrell	5-9	32	90.0	34	78	3.00
Jose Deleon	13-10	0	225.1	86	208	3.67
Larry McWilliams	6-9	1	136.0	45	70	3.90
Danny Cox	3-8	0	86.0	25	47	3.98
Greg Mathews	4-6	0	68.0	33	31	4.24
Randy O'Neal	2-3	0	53.0	10	20	4.58

Outfielder Tom Brunansky soon adjusted to the NL, after 913 games with the Angels and Twins.

Atlanta Braves

NATIONAL LEAGUE WEST DIVISION

Team Colours: Navy blue, scarlet and white
Postal Address: PO Box 4064, Atlanta, Georgia 30302, USA
Telephone: (404) 522 7630
History of Franchise: Boston Braves 1876–1952, Milwaukee Braves 1953–65, Atlanta Braves 1966– (Known as Red Caps 1876–82, Beaneaters 1883–1906, Doves 1907–08, Pilgrims 1909–11, Bees 1936–40)
Honours (since 1966): Yet to win NL or World Series
Retired Uniforms: 21–Warren Spahn, 35–Phil Niekro, 41–Eddie Mathews, 44–Hank Aaron

RECENT BRAVES TOTALS
(NL Rankings out of 12):

	1988 (Rk)	1987 (Rk)	1986 (Rk)	1985 (Rk)
Games W/L Pct:	.338(12)	.429(11)	.447(10)	.407(10)
Pitching ERA:	4.09(11)	4.63(12)	3.97(10)	4.19(12)
Batting Ave:	.242(11)	.258(9)	.250(10)	.246(11)
Home Runs:	96(9)	152(6)	138(9)	126(5)
Fielding Pct:	.975(12)	.982(1)	.978(5)	.976(9)
Total Errors:	151(12)	116(1)	141(9)	159(11)
Stolen Bases:	95(12)	135(8)	93(12)	72(11)

Zane Smith deserves a break, having pitched in 142 games in five years for lowly Atlanta.

SEASON RECORDS SINCE 1969

Year	Position	W	L	Pct	GB/GA	Attendance
1969	First	93	69	.574	+3	1,458,320
1970	Fifth	76	86	.469	−26	1,078,848
1971	Third	82	80	.506	−8	1,006,320
1972	Fourth	70	84	.455	−25	752,973
1973	Fifth	76	85	.472	−22½	800,655
1974	Third	88	74	.543	−14	981,085
1975	Fifth	67	94	.416	−40½	534,672
1976	Sixth	70	92	.432	−32	818,179
1977	Sixth	61	101	.377	−37	872,464
1978	Sixth	69	93	.426	−26	904,494
1979	Sixth	66	94	.413	−23½	769,465
1980	Fourth	81	80	.503	−11	1,048,411
1981	Fourth/fifth	50	56	.472		535,418
1982	First	89	73	.549	+1	1,801,985
1983	Second	88	74	.543	−3	2,119,935
1984	Second	80	82	.494	−12	1,724,892
1985	Fifth	66	96	.407	−29	1,350,137
1986	Sixth	72	89	.447	−23½	1,387,181
1987	Fifth	69	92	.429	−20½	1,217,402
1988	Sixth	54	106	.338	−39½	848,089

Gerald June Perry, 571 games in six years for the Braves.

ATLANTA-FULTON COUNTY STADIUM

Location: 521 Capitol Avenue at junction of Interstate Highways 20, 75 & 85
Cost: $18m
First NL game: 12 April 1966
Videoscreen: Mitsubishi DiamondVision
Record crowd: 53,775 (8 April 1974) v. LA
Record season attendance: 2,119,935 (1983)
Other stadium user: NFL Atlanta Falcons
Stadium ranked: No. 1 NL hitters park
Ave total runs/game (NL Rk) 1986 & 1987:
At Atlanta 9.64(2), Away 8.32(11)

Weather	Apr.	May	Jun.	Jul.	Aug.	Sept.	Oct.
Temp (deg. C):	16	20	24	26	26	22	17
Rainfall (cm):	11.6	9.3	9.3	12.3	8.8	8.1	6.3
Rainy days:	10	10	11	13	12	8	7

1988 tickets: $1 children, to $9.50 club
Newspapers: *Atlanta Journal, Atlanta Constitution*
Radio: WSB 750AM
TV/Cable: WTBS Ch17 (Skip Caray, Ernie Johnson, Pete VanWieren, Billy Sample)
Atlanta hotels used by NL clubs: Hyatt (LA, Hou), Ritz-Carlton (Phi), Marriott (other 8 clubs)

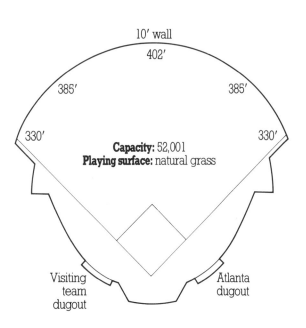

1988 SEASON

Chairman/President/CEO: Ted Turner
General Manager: Bobby Cox
Managers: Chuck Tanner (to 22 May), Russ Nixon
1988 Braves Roster: 28% purchased/free agents, 28% acquired by trades, 44% drafted by Braves

1988 Spring Training Site: Municipal Stadium, West Palm Beach, Florida (since 1963)
1988 Minor League farm club teams: AAA–Richmond (Int); AA–Greenville (S); A–Durham Bulls (Car), Burlington (MW), Sumter (SA); Rookie–Pulaski (Ap), Bradenton (GC), Idaho Falls (P)

1988 home games: 17 day, 64 night
1988 away games: 24 day, 57 night
1988 games: 42 on turf, 120 on grass
  147 outside, 15 indoors

LEADING BRAVES (1988 REGULAR SEASON):

Batters	AtBats	Runs	Hits	HRs	RBIs	Ave
Gerald Perry	547	61	164	8	74	.300
Ron Gant	563	85	146	19	60	.259
Dion James	386	46	99	3	30	.256
Ozzie Virgil	320	23	82	9	31	.256
Andres Thomas	606	54	153	13	68	.252
Albert Hall	231	27	57	1	15	.247
Bruce Benedict	236	11	57	0	19	.242
Jody Davis	257	21	59	7	36	.230
Dale Murphy	592	77	134	24	77	.226
Terry Blocker	198	13	42	2	10	.212

Pitchers	W-L	Saves	Inns	BBs	SOs	ERA
Chris Alvarez	5-6	3	102.1	53	81	2.99
Paul Assenmacher	8-7	5	79.1	32	71	3.06
Charlie Puleo	5-5	1	106.1	47	70	3.47
Pete Smith	7-15	0	195.1	88	124	3.69
Rick Mahler	9-16	0	249.0	42	131	3.69
Zane Smith	5-10	0	140.1	44	59	4.30
Tom Glavine	7-17	0	195.1	63	84	4.56
Jim Acker	0-4	0	42.0	14	25	4.71
Bruce Sutter	1-4	14	45.1	11	40	4.76
Houston Jimenez	1-6	0	55.2	12	26	5.01

Catcher Ozzie Virgil Jr. limbers up to take batting practice.

34 ATLANTA BRAVES 1988 SEASON

Cincinnati Reds

NATIONAL LEAGUE WEST DIVISION

Team Colours: Scarlet and white
Postal Address: 100 Riverfront Stadium, Cincinnati, Ohio 45202, USA
Telephone: (513) 421 4510
History of Franchise: Cincinnati Red Stockings 1869–80, modern NL club re-formed 1890– (Joined American Association 1882–89, following liquor dispute with NL) (Known as Red Legs 1954–60)
NL Honours: 1919, 39, 40, 61, 70, 72, 75, 76
WS Honours: 1919, 40, 75, 76
Retired Uniforms: 1–Fred Hutchinson, 5–Johnny Bench

RECENT REDS TOTALS
(NL Rankings out of 12):

	1988 (Rk)	1987 (Rk)	1986 (Rk)	1985 (Rk)
Games W/L Pct:	.540(3)	.519(5)	.531(4)	.553(4)
Pitching ERA:	3.35(5)	4.24(9)	3.91(9)	3.71(9)
Batting Ave:	.246(9)	.266(2)	.254(5)	.255(5)
Home Runs:	122(2)	192(3)	144(4)	114(9)
Fielding Pct:	.980(3)	.979(7)	.978(5)	.980(4)
Total Errors:	125(4)	130(7)	140(8)	122(4)
Stolen Bases:	207(2)	169(3)	177(3)	159(4)

Catcher Bo Diaz, 950 games in 12 years with Boston, Cleveland, the Phillies and Reds.

SEASON RECORDS SINCE 1969

Year	Position	W	L	Pct	GB/GA	Attendance
1969	Third	89	73	.549	−4	987,991
1970	First	102	60	.630	+14½	1,803,568
1971	Fourth	79	83	.488	−11	1,501,122
1972	First	95	59	.617	+10½	1,611,459
1973	First	99	63	.611	+3½	2,017,601
1974	Second	98	64	.605	−4	2,164,307
1975	First	108	54	.667	+20	2,315,603
1976	First	102	60	.630	+10	2,629,708
1977	Second	88	74	.543	−10	2,519,670
1978	Second	92	69	.571	−2½	2,532,497
1979	First	90	71	.559	+1½	2,356,933
1980	Third	89	73	.549	−3½	2,022,450
1981	Second/second	66	42	.611		1,093,730
1982	Sixth	61	101	.377	−28	1,326,628
1983	Sixth	74	88	.457	−17	1,190,419
1984	Fifth	70	92	.432	−22	1,275,887
1985	Second	89	72	.553	−5½	1,834,619
1986	Second	86	76	.531	−10	1,692,432
1987	Second	84	78	.519	−6	2,185,205
1988	Second	87	74	.540	−7	2,072,528

Outfielder Eric Davis, 108 home runs and 191 stolen bases in 509 games for the Reds.

RIVERFRONT STADIUM

Location: downtown Cincinnati, Pete Rose Way to Ohio River, Walnut Street to Broadway
The Reds had played at Redland Field, later renamed Crosley Field, since 1912.
Cost: $48m
First NL game: 30 June 1970
Videoscreen: Sony
Record crowd: 56,393 (16 Oct 1975) WS v. Bos
Record season attendance: 2,629,708 (1976)
Other stadium users: NFL Bengals, NCAA Bearcats
Stadium ranked: No. 4 NL hitters park
Ave total runs/game (NL Rk) 1986 & 1987:
At Riverfront 9.61(3), Away 8.81(5)

Weather	Apr.	May	Jun.	Jul.	Aug.	Sept.	Oct.
Temp (deg. C):	13	18	23	24	23	20	14
Rainfall (cm):	9.8	10.1	9.8	10.1	7.6	6.8	5.6
Rainy days:	12	12	13	10	9	8	9

1988 tickets: $3.50 reserved, to $8.50 box
Newspapers: *Cincinnati Enquirer, Cincinnati Post*
Radio: WLWT 700AM (68stns)
TV: WLWT Ch5 (25stns) (Marty Brennaman, Joe Nuxhall, Johnny Bench, Jay Randolph)
Cincinnati hotels used by NL clubs: Hyatt (SF, St L, Phi, LA, SD), Hilton (other 6 clubs)

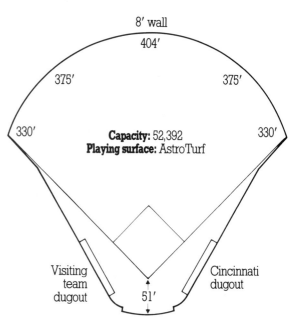

1988 SEASON

President/CEO/General Partner: Mrs Marge Schott
VP/General Manager: Murray Cook
Manager: Pete Rose
1988 Reds Roster: 19% purchased/free agents, 32% acquired by trades, 49% drafted by Reds

1988 Spring Training Site: Plant City, Florida (Hillsborough Co., since 1931)
1988 Minor League farm club teams: AAA–Nashville Sounds (AmA); AA–Chattanooga Lookouts (S); A–Cedar Rapids (MW), Greensboro Hornets (SA); Rookie–Billings Mustangs (P), Sarasota (GC)

1988 home games: 22 day, 59 night
1988 away games: 28 day, 53 night
1988 games: 112 on turf, 50 on grass
147 outside, 15 indoors

LEADING REDS (1988 REGULAR SEASON):

Batters	AtBats	Runs	Hits	HRs	RBIs	Ave
Barry Larkin	588	91	174	12	56	.296
Kal Daniels	495	95	144	18	64	.291
Eric Davis	472	81	129	26	93	.273
Chris Sabo	538	74	146	11	44	.271
Ken Griffey	243	26	62	4	23	.255
Jeff Treadway	301	30	76	2	23	.252
Paul O'Neill	485	58	122	16	73	.252
Nick Esasky	391	40	95	15	62	.243
Jeff Reed	265	20	60	1	16	.226
Bo Diaz	315	26	69	10	35	.219

Pitchers	W-L	Saves	Inns	BBs	SOs	ERA
John Franco	6-6	39	86.0	27	46	1.57
Jose Rijo	13-8	0	162.0	63	160	2.39
Frank Williams	3-2	1	62.2	35	43	2.59
Danny Jackson	23-8	0	260.2	71	161	2.73
Rob Murphy	0-6	3	84.2	38	74	3.08
Tom Browning	18-5	0	250.2	64	124	3.41
Norm Charlton	4-5	0	61.1	20	39	3.96
Ron Robinson	3-7	0	78.2	26	38	4.12
Mike Armstrong	4-7	0	65.1	38	45	5.79

Pitcher Danny Jackson made a spectacular start to his NL career, after five indifferent years with the Royals.

Houston Astros

NATIONAL LEAGUE WEST DIVISION

Team Colours: Navy blue, burnt orange, orange, yellow and white
Postal Address: PO Box 288, Houston, Texas 77001, USA
Telephone: (713) 799 9500
History of Franchise: Houston Colt 45s 1962–64, renamed Houston Astros 1965–
Honours: Yet to win NL or World Series
Retired Uniforms: 32–Jim Umbricht, 40–Don Wilson

SEASON RECORDS SINCE 1969

Year	Position	W	L	Pct	GB/GA	Attendance
1969	Fifth	81	81	.500	−12	1,442,995
1970	Fourth	79	83	.488	−23	1,253,444
1971	Fourth	79	83	.488	−11	1,261,589
1972	Second	84	69	.549	−10½	1,469,247
1973	Fourth	82	80	.506	−17	1,394,004
1974	Fourth	81	81	.500	−21	1,090,728
1975	Sixth	64	97	.398	−43½	858,002
1976	Third	80	82	.494	−22	886,146
1977	Third	81	81	.500	−17	1,109,560
1978	Fifth	74	88	.457	−21	1,126,145
1979	Second	89	73	.549	−1½	1,900,312
1980	First	93	70	.571	+1	2,278,217
1981	Third/first	61	49	.555		1,321,282
1982	Fifth	77	85	.475	−12	1,558,555
1983	Third	85	77	.525	−6	1,351,962
1984	Second	80	82	.494	−12	1,229,862
1985	Third	83	79	.512	−12	1,184,314
1986	First	96	66	.593	+10	1,734,276
1987	Third	76	86	.469	−14	1,909,902
1988	Fifth	82	80	.506	−12½	1,933,505

RECENT ASTROS TOTALS
(NL Rankings out of 12):

	1988 (Rk)	1987 (Rk)	1986 (Rk)	1985 (Rk)
Games W/L Pct:	.506(7)	.469(8)	.593(2)	.512(6)
Pitching ERA:	3.41(7)	3.84(3)	3.15(2)	3.66(7)
Batting Ave:	.244(10)	.253(11)	.255(4)	.261(2)
Home Runs:	96(9)	122(9)	125(8)	121(6)
Fielding Pct:	.978(8)	.981(3)	.979(3)	.976(9)
Total Errors:	138(8)	116(1)	130(3)	152(10)
Stolen Bases:	198(3)	162(5)	163(4)	96(10)

First baseman Glenn Davis, 110 home runs in 579 games for Houston.

Nolan Ryan, 4,775 strikeouts in 22 years with the Mets, Angels and Astros, moved to Texas for 1989.

THE ASTRODOME
(Harris County Domed Stadium)

Location: Kirby and Interstate Loop 610
Cost: $31.6m
First NL game: 12 April 1965
Houston formerly played across the car park in Colts Stadium 1962–64.
Videoscreen: 26′×27′ DiamondVision
Famous old scoreboard replaced and 10,000 seats added in $60m facelift, 1988–89.
Record crowd: 50,908 (22 June 1966) v. LA
Record season attendance: 2,278,217 (1980)
Other stadium users: NFL Oilers, NCAA Cougars
A pitchers park ranked: No. 10 for NL hitters
Ave total runs/game (NL Rk) 1986 & 1987:
At Houston 7.52(12), Away 8.22(12)
Weather April–October outside the Astrodome:
20–28 degrees C; 8.8–13.0 cm rainfall
1988 tickets: $1 children, to $10 field
Newspapers: *Houston Chronicle*, *Houston Post*
Radio: KTRH 740AM (9stns)
TV: KTXH Ch20 (5stns) Cable: HSE (Bill Brown, Milo Hamilton, Larry Dierker, Bill Ubrrell)
Houston hotels used by NL clubs: InterContinental (SF), Westin (other 10 clubs)

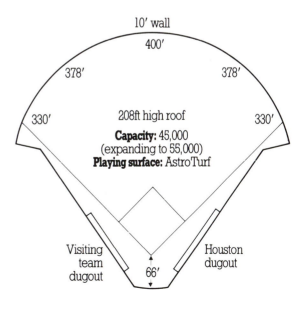

10′ wall
400′
378′   378′
330′   330′
208ft high roof
Capacity: 45,000 (expanding to 55,000)
Playing surface: AstroTurf
Visiting team dugout
Houston dugout
66′

HOUSTON ASTROS THE ASTRODOME 39

1988 SEASON

Chairman: Dr John J. McMullen
General Manager: Bill Wood
Manager: Hal Lanier (to 2 October), Art Howe
1988 Astros Roster: 24% purchased/free agents, 27% acquired by trades, 49% drafted by Astros

1988 Spring Training Site: Osceola County Stadium, Kissimmee, Florida
1988 Minor League farm club teams: AAA–Tucson Toros (Pac); AA–Columbus (S); A–Osceola (FS), Asheville Tourists (SA); Rookie–Auburn (NY-P), Sarasota (GC)

1988 home games: 20 day, 61 night
1988 away games: 24 day, 57 night
1988 games: 112 on turf, 50 on grass
75 outside, 87 indoors

LEADING ASTROS (1988 REGULAR SEASON):

Batters	AtBats	Runs	Hits	HRs	RBIs	Ave
Terry Puhl	234	42	71	3	19	.303
Rafael Ramirez	566	51	156	6	59	.276
Glenn Davis	561	78	152	30	99	.271
Billy Hatcher	530	79	142	7	52	.268
Gerald Young	576	79	148	0	37	.257
Kevin Bass	541	57	138	14	72	.255
Alex Trevino	193	19	48	2	13	.249
Bill Doran	480	66	119	7	53	.248
Buddy Bell	323	27	78	7	40	.241
Alan Ashby	227	19	54	7	33	.238

Pitchers	W-L	Saves	Inns	BBs	SOs	ERA
Juan Agosto	10-2	4	91.2	30	33	2.26
Dave Smith	4-5	27	57.1	19	38	2.67
Mike Scott	14-8	0	218.2	53	190	2.92
Larry Andersen	2-4	5	82.2	20	66	2.94
Jim Deshaies	11-14	0	207.0	72	127	3.00
Bob Knepper	14-5	0	175.0	67	103	3.14
Nolan Ryan	12-11	0	220.0	87	228	3.52
Danny Darwin	8-13	3	192.0	48	129	3.84
Joaquin Andujar	2-5	0	78.2	21	35	4.00
Bob Forsch	10-8	0	136.1	44	54	4.29

Split-fingered fastball pitcher, Mike Scott, W–95, L–83 in 10 years with the Mets and Astros.

Los Angeles Dodgers

NATIONAL LEAGUE WEST DIVISION

Team Colours: Royal blue, red and white
Postal Address: 1000 Elysian Park Avenue, Los Angeles, California 90012, USA
Telephone: (213) 224 1500
History of Franchise: Brooklyn 1890–57 (Bridegrooms 1890–98, Superbas 1899–1910, Dodgers 1911–57), Los Angeles Dodgers 1958–
NL Honours (since 1958): 1959, 63, 65, 66, 74, 77, 78, 81, 88
WS Honours (since 1958): 1959, 63, 65, 81, 88
Retired Uniforms: 1–PeeWee Reese, 4–Duke Snider, 19–Jim Gilliam, 24–Walt Alston, 32–Sandy Koufax, 39–Roy Campanella, 42–Jackie Robinson, 53–Don Drysdale

RECENT DODGERS TOTALS
(NL Rankings out of 12):

	1988 (Rk)	1987 (Rk)	1986 (Rk)	1985 (Rk)
Games W/L Pct:	.584(2)	.451(10)	.451(9)	.586(3)
Pitching ERA:	2.96(2)	3.72(2)	3.76(5)	2.96(1)
Batting Ave:	.248(5)	.252(12)	.251(9)	.261(2)
Home Runs:	99(8)	125(8)	130(7)	129(4)
Fielding Pct:	.977(9)	.975(12)	.971(12)	.974(12)
Total Errors:	142(9)	155(12)	181(12)	166(12)
Stolen Bases:	131(6)	128(9)	155(5)	136(5)

Tom Lasorda, W–1,020, L–874 in 13 years as Dodgers manager.

SEASON RECORDS SINCE 1969

Year	Position	W	L	Pct	GB/GA	Attendance
1969	Fourth	85	77	.525	−8	1,784,527
1970	Second	87	74	.540	−14½	1,697,142
1971	Second	89	73	.549	−1	2,064,594
1972	Third	85	70	.548	−10½	1,860,858
1973	Second	95	66	.590	−3½	2,136,192
1974	First	102	60	.630	+4	2,632,474
1975	Second	88	74	.543	−20	2,539,349
1976	Second	92	70	.568	−10	2,386,301
1977	First	98	64	.605	+10	2,955,087
1978	First	95	67	.586	+2½	3,347,845
1979	Third	79	83	.488	−11½	2,860,954
1980	Second	92	71	.564	−1	3,249,287
1981	First/fourth	63	47	.573		2,381,292
1982	Second	88	74	.543	−1	3,608,881
1983	First	91	71	.652	+3	3,510,313
1984	Fourth	79	83	.488	−13	3,134,824
1985	First	95	67	.586	+5½	3,264,593
1986	Fifth	73	89	.451	−23	3,023,208
1987	Fourth	73	89	.451	−17	2,797,406
1988	First	94	67	.584	+7	2,949,142

Outfielder Kirk Gibson, traded to LA in 1988 after nine years with Detroit, was the catalyst LA needed to win the World Series.

DODGER STADIUM

Location: 1000 Elysian Park Avenue, Chavez Ravine
First NL game: 10 April 1962
Dodgers played at LA Memorial Coliseum 1958–61
Only 15 rainouts ever at Dodger Stadium
Videoscreen: 35′×25′ DiamondVision 1980
Record crowd: 56,242 (24 October 1981) WS v. NYY
Record season attendance: 3,608,881 (1982)
Stadium ranked neutral: No. 7 for NL hitters
Ave total runs/game (NL Rk) 1986 & 1987:
At Los Angeles 8.65(7), Away 8.80(6)

Weather	Apr.	May	Jun.	Jul.	Aug.	Sept.	Oct.
Temp (deg. C):	17	18	20	22	23	22	20
Rainfall (cm):	3.2	0.2	–	–	–	0.5	0.7
Rainy days:	4	2	1	0	0	1	2

1988 tickets: $2 children, to $7 box
Newspapers: *Los Angeles Times, LA Herald-Examiner* (see Angels AL)
Radio: KABC 790AM (28stns)
TV: KTTV Ch11. Cable: American Spectator (Vin Scully, Don Drysdale, Ross Porter)
LA hotels used by NL clubs: (see Angels AL) Biltmore (Atl), Sheraton (NY), Hyatt (9 others)

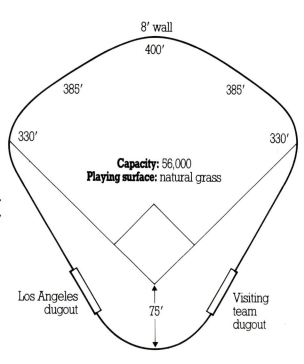

1988 SEASON

President: Peter O'Malley
Exec VP/Player Personnel: Fred Claire
Manager: Tom Lasorda
1988 Dodgers Roster: 37% purchased/free agents, 30% acquired by trades, 33% drafted by Dodgers

1988 Spring Training Site: Dodgertown, Holman Stadium, Vero Beach, Florida (since 1948)
1988 Minor League farm club teams: AAA–Albuquerque Dukes (Pac); AA–San Antonio Missions (T); A–Bakersfield (Cal), Vero Beach (FS), Salem (NW); Rookie–Great Falls (P), Sarasota (GC)

1988 home games: 20 day, 61 night
1988 away games: 25 day, 56 night
1988 games: 42 on turf, 120 on grass
　　　　　　　　147 outside, 15 indoors

LEADING DODGERS
(1988 REGULAR SEASON):

Batters	AtBats	Runs	Hits	HRs	RBIs	Ave
Mickey Hatcher	191	22	56	1	25	.293
Kirk Gibson	542	106	157	25	76	.290
Steve Sax	632	70	175	5	57	.277
Mike Marshall	542	63	150	20	82	.277
John Shelby	494	65	130	10	64	.263
Mike Scioscia	408	29	105	3	35	.257
Rick Dempsey	167	25	42	7	30	.251
Dave Anderson	285	31	71	2	20	.249
Jeff Hamilton	309	34	73	6	33	.236
Franklin Stubbs	242	30	54	8	34	.223
Alfredo Griffin	316	39	63	1	27	.199

Pitchers	W-L	Saves	Inns	BBs	SOs	ERA
Brian Holton	7-3	1	84.2	26	49	1.70
Alejundra Pena	6-7	12	94.1	27	83	1.91
Jay Howell	5-3	21	65.0	21	70	2.08
Orel Hershiser	23-8	1	267.0	73	178	2.26
John Tudor	10-8	0	197.2	41	87	2.32
Jesse Orosco	3-2	9	53.0	30	43	2.72
Tim Belcher	12-6	4	179.2	51	152	2.91
Tim Leary	17-11	0	228.2	56	180	2.91
Tim Crews	4-0	0	71.2	16	45	3.14
Ramon Martinez	1-3	0	35.2	22	23	3.79
Fernando Valenzuela	5-8	1	142.1	76	64	4.24

Aerial shots of Dodger Stadium, featured in the opening credits of 'The Colbys' TV soap opera.

LOS ANGELES DODGERS 1988 SEASON

San Diego Padres

NATIONAL LEAGUE WEST DIVISION

Team Colours: Brown, orange and white
Postal Address: 9449 Friars Road, San Diego, California 92108, USA
Telephone: (619) 283 7294
History of Franchise: San Diego Padres 1969–
Honours: Won NL 1984. Yet to win World Series
Retired Uniform: 6–Steve Garvey

RECENT PADRES TOTALS
(NL Rankings out of 12):

	1988 (Rk)	1987 (Rk)	1986 (Rk)	1985 (Rk)
Games W/L Pct:	.516(5)	.401(12)	.457(8)	.512(6)
Pitching ERA:	3.28(4)	4.21(10)	3.99(11)	3.40(4)
Batting Ave:	.247(7)	.260(7)	.261(2)	.255(5)
Home Runs:	94(11)	113(11)	136(6)	109(10)
Fielding Pct:	.980(3)	.976(10)	.978(5)	.980(4)
Total Errors:	120(2)	147(10)	137(5)	.124(5)
Stolen Bases:	123(7)	198(2)	96(11)	60(12)

Pitcher Mark Davis gained twice as many saves in 1988 as in his previous seven seasons put together.

SEASON RECORDS SINCE 1969

Year	Position	W	L	Pct	GB/GA	Attendance
1969	Sixth	52	110	.321	−41	613,327
1970	Sixth	63	99	.389	−39	633,439
1971	Sixth	61	100	.379	−28½	549,085
1972	Sixth	58	95	.379	−36½	644,272
1973	Sixth	60	102	.370	−39	611,826
1974	Sixth	60	102	.370	−42	1,075,399
1975	Fourth	71	91	.438	−37	1,281,747
1976	Fifth	73	89	.451	−29	1,458,478
1977	Fifth	69	93	.426	−29	1,376,269
1978	Fourth	84	78	.519	−11	1,670,107
1979	Fifth	68	93	.422	−22	1,456,967
1980	Sixth	73	89	.451	−19½	1,139,026
1981	Sixth/sixth	41	69	.373		519,161
1982	Fourth	81	81	.500	−8	1,607,516
1983	Fourth	81	81	.500	−10	1,539,819
1984	First	92	70	.568	+12	1,983,904
1985	Third	83	79	.512	−12	2,210,352
1986	Fourth	74	88	.457	−22	1,805,776
1987	Sixth	65	97	.401	−25	1,454,061
1988	Third	83	78	.516	−11	1,506,896

San Diego – Jack Murphy Stadium and 17,000 parked cars in the former bed of the diverted San Diego River.

SAN DIEGO-JACK MURPHY STADIUM

Location: 9449 Friars Road
Cost: $28m
First NL game: 8 April 1969
Videoscreen: 100'×66' DiamondVision 1985
Record crowd: 58,359 (6 October 1984) NLCS v. Cubs
Record season attendance: 2,210,352 (1985)
Other stadium users: NFL Chargers, NCAA Aztecs
A pitchers park ranked: No. 9 for NL hitters
Ave total runs/game (NL Rk) 1986 & 1987:
At San Diego 8.35(9), Away 8.99(4)

Weather	Apr.	May	Jun.	Jul.	Aug.	Sept.	Oct.
Temp (deg. C):	16	17	19	21	22	21	19
Rainfall (cm):	2.0	0.5	0.2	–	0.2	0.2	0.7
Rainy days:	4	3	1	0	1	1	3

1988 tickets: $3.50 general, to $8.50 box
Newspapers: *San Diego Tribune, San Diego Union*
Radio: KFMB 760AM
TV: KUSI Ch51. Cable: CSN (Jerry Coleman, Dave Campbell, Ted Leitner, Bob Chandler)
San Diego hotels used by NL clubs: Sheraton (Chi, NY), Marriott (Mon, St L, SF), Omni (Pit), Town & Country (5 others)

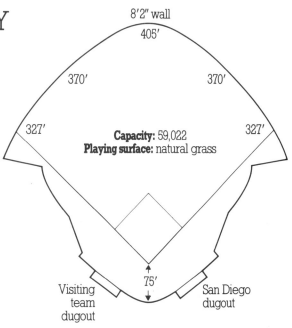

1988 SEASON

Chairwoman/Owner: Mrs Joan Kroc
President: Chub Feeney (to 25 September)
VP/Baseball Operations: Jack McKeon
Managers: Larry Bowa (to 28 May), Jack McKeon
1988 Padres Roster: 12% purchased/free agents, 44% acquired by trades, 44% drafted by Padres

1988 Spring Training Site: Desert Sun Stadium, Ray A. Kroc Baseball Complex, Yuma, Arizona
1988 Minor League farm club teams: AAA–Las Vegas Stars (Pac); AA–Wichita Pilots (T); A–Riverside Red Wave (Cal), Charleston Rainbows (SA); Rookie–Spokane Indians (NW)

1988 home games: 21 day, 60 night
1988 away games: 27 day, 54 night
1988 games: 42 on turf, 120 on grass
   147 outside, 15 indoors

LEADING PADRES (1988 REGULAR SEASON):

Batters	AtBats	Runs	Hits	HRs	RBIs	Ave
Tony Gwynn	521	64	163	7	70	.313
Roberto Alomar	545	84	145	9	41	.266
Randy Ready	331	43	88	7	39	.266
Marvell Wynne	333	37	88	11	42	.264
Dickie Thon	258	36	68	1	18	.264
Keith Moreland	511	40	131	5	64	.256
Garry Templeton	362	35	90	3	36	.249
Benito Santiago	492	49	122	10	46	.248
John Kruk	378	54	91	9	44	.241
Carmelo Martinez	365	48	86	18	65	.236
Chris Brown	247	14	58	2	19	.235

Pitchers	W-L	Saves	Inns	BBs	SOs	ERA
Mark Davis	5-10	28	98.1	42	102	2.01
Dave Leiper	3-0	1	54.0	14	33	2.17
Lance McCullers	3-6	10	97.2	55	81	2.49
Eric Show	16-11	0	243.2	53	144	3.26
Andy Hawkins	14-11	0	217.2	76	91	3.35
Greg Booker	2-2	0	63.2	19	43	3.39
Dennis Rasmussen	16-10	0	204.2	58	112	3.43
Mark Grant	2-8	0	97.2	36	61	3.69
Ed Whitson	13-11	0	205.1	45	118	3.77
Jimmy Jones	9-14	0	179.0	44	82	4.12

Outfielder Tony Gwynn, 1,151 hits in 902 games in seven years at San Diego.

San Francisco Giants

NATIONAL LEAGUE WEST DIVISION

Team Colours: Black, orange and white
Postal Address: Candlestick Park, San Francisco, California 94124, USA
Telephone: (415) 468 3700
History of Franchise: Troy Trojans 1879–82, New York Giants 1883–1957, San Francisco Giants 1958– (Known as Gothams 1883–85)
Honours (since 1958): Won NL 1962. Yet to win World Series in SF
Retired Uniforms: Christy Mathewson, John McGraw, 3–Bill Terry, 4–Mel Ott, 11–Carl Hubbell, 24–Willie Mays, 27–Juan Marichal, 44–Willie McCovey

RECENT GIANTS TOTALS
(NL Rankings out of 12):

	1988 (Rk)	1987 (Rk)	1986 (Rk)	1985 (Rk)
Games W/L Pct:	.512(6)	.556(4)	.512(5)	.383(11)
Pitching ERA:	3.39(6)	3.68(1)	3.33(3)	3.61(6)
Batting Ave:	.248(5)	.260(7)	.253(7)	.233(12)
Home Runs:	113(3)	205(2)	114(9)	115(8)
Fielding Pct:	.979(7)	.980(4)	.977(11)	.976(9)
Total Errors:	129(7)	129(6)	143(10)	148(9)
Stolen Bases:	121(8)	126(10)	148(8)	99(9)

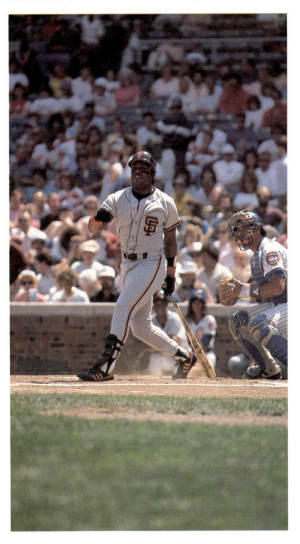

Kevin Mitchell, 394 games in four years for the Mets, Padres and Giants.

SEASON RECORDS SINCE 1969

Year	Position	W	L	Pct	GB/GA	Attendance
1969	Second	90	72	.556	−3	870,341
1970	Third	86	76	.531	−16	728,498
1971	First	90	72	.556	+1	1,088,083
1972	Fifth	69	86	.445	−26½	637,327
1973	Third	88	74	.543	−11	834,193
1974	Fifth	72	90	.444	−30	519,991
1975	Third	80	81	.497	−27½	522,925
1976	Fourth	74	88	.457	−28	626,868
1977	Fourth	75	87	.463	−23	700,056
1978	Third	89	73	.549	−6	1,740,480
1979	Fourth	71	91	.438	−19½	1,456,392
1980	Fifth	75	86	.466	−17	1,096,115
1981	Fifth/third	56	55	.505		632,276
1982	Third	87	75	.537	−2	1,200,948
1983	Fifth	79	83	.488	−12	1,251,530
1984	Sixth	66	96	.407	−26	1,001,545
1985	Sixth	62	100	.383	−33	818,697
1986	Third	83	79	.512	−13	1,528,748
1987	First	90	72	.556	+6	1,917,863
1988	Fourth	83	79	.512	−11½	1,786,482

Brett Butler laying down a bunt; 1,046 games in eight years for the Braves, Indians, and Giants.

CANDLESTICK PARK

Location: Candlestick Point, Bayshore Freeway
Cost: $24.6m
First NL game: 12 April 1960
The Giants played at Seals Stadium 1958–59. Despite its reputation for fog and swirling cold winds, there have been only 20 rainouts at Candlestick Park. The 1987 renovation ($30m) included a $4.5m Sony Jumbotron 24'×32' screen. AstroTurf used 1971–78; natural grass again from 1979.
Record crowd: 59,363 (11 October 1987) NLCS v. St Louis
Record season attendance: 1,917,863 (1987)
Other stadium user: NFL San Francisco 49ers
A pitchers park ranked: No. 12 for NL hitters
Ave total runs/game (NL Rk) 1986 & 1987:
At San Francisco 8.06(11), Away 9.03(3)

Weather	Apr.	May	Jun.	Jul.	Aug.	Sept.	Oct.
Temp (deg. C):	13	14	16	17	17	18	16
Rainfall (cm):	4.0	1.0	0.2	–	–	0.5	0.3
Rainy days:	6	4	2	0	0	2	4

1988 tickets: $2.50 general, to $10 box
Newspapers: *San Francisco Chronicle, Sacramento Bee* (see Oakland AL)
Radio: KNBR 680AM (11stns)
TV: KTVU Ch2 (5stns). Cable: GiantsVision (Ron Fairly, Wayne Hagin, Steve Physioc, Duane Kuiper, Joe Morgan, Carolyn Burns)
SF hotels used by NL clubs: Hyatt (Phi), Hilton (Chi, LA, Cin), Westin (NY, SD, St L, Hou), Renaissance (Pit, Mon, Atl) (see Oakland AL)

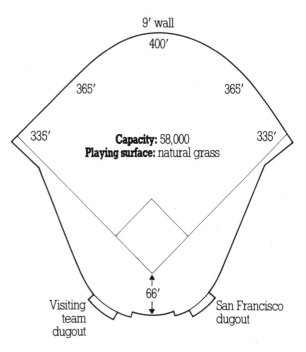

1988 SEASON

Chairman: Bob Lurie
President/General Manager: Al Rosen
Manager: Roger Craig
1988 Giants Roster: 27% purchased/free agents, 35% acquired by trades, 38% drafted by Giants

1988 Spring Training Site: Scottsdale Stadium, Sheraton Scottsdale Resort, Scottsdale, Arizona
1988 Minor League farm club teams: AAA–Phoenix Firebirds (Pac); AA–Shreveport Captains (T); A–San Jose (Cal), Clinton (MW); Rookie–Everett (NW), Pocatello (P)

1988 home games: 39 day, 42 night
1988 away games: 28 day, 53 night
1988 games: 42 on turf, 120 on grass
      147 outside, 15 indoors

LEADING GIANTS (1988 REGULAR SEASON):

Batters	AtBats	Runs	Hits	HRs	RBIs	Ave
Ernest Riles	187	26	55	3	28	.294
Brett Butler	568	109	163	6	43	.287
Will Clarke	575	102	162	29	109	.282
Mike Aldrete	389	44	104	3	50	.267
Robby Thompson	477	66	126	7	48	.264
Candy Maldonado	499	53	127	12	68	.255
Jose Uribe	493	47	124	3	35	.252
Kevin Mitchell	505	60	127	19	80	.251
Bob Melvin	273	23	64	8	27	.234
Matt Williams	156	17	32	8	19	.205
Bob Brenly	206	13	39	5	22	.189

Pitchers	W-L	Saves	Inns	BBs	SOs	ERA
Don Robinson	10-5	6	176.2	49	122	2.45
Craig Lefferts	3-8	11	92.1	23	58	2.92
Rick Reuschel	19-1	0	245.0	42	92	3.12
Dave Dravecky	2-2	0	37.0	8	19	3.16
Kelly Downs	13-9	0	168.0	47	118	3.32
Mike Krukow	7-4	0	124.2	31	75	3.54
Scott Garrelts	5-9	13	98.0	46	86	3.58
Mike LaCoss	7-7	0	114.1	47	70	3.62
Atlee Hammaker	9-9	5	144.2	41	65	3.73
Joe Price	1-6	4	61.2	27	49	3.94

Second baseman and shortstop Jose Uribe, 548 games in five years with St Louis and the Giants.

National League Statistics

NATIONAL LEAGUE PENNANT WINNERS

Year	Club	W	L	Pct	GA	NL Total Attendance
1876	Chicago	52	14	.788	6	
1877	Boston	31	17	.646	3	
1878	Boston	41	19	.683	4	
1879	Providence	55	23	.705	6	
1880	Chicago	67	17	.798	15	
1881	Chicago	56	27	.667	9	
1882	Chicago	55	29	.655	3	
1883	Boston	63	35	.643	4	
1884	Providence	84	28	.750	10½	
1885	Chicago	87	25	.777	2	
1886	Chicago	90	34	.726	2½	
1887	Detroit	79	45	.637	3½	
1888	New York	84	47	.641	9	
1889	New York	83	43	.659	1	
1890	Brooklyn	86	43	.667	6½	
1891	Boston	87	51	.630	3½	
1892	Boston	102	48	.680	8½	
1893	Boston	86	44	.662	4½	
1894	Baltimore	89	39	.695	3	
1895	Baltimore	87	43	.669	3	
1896	Baltimore	90	39	.698	9½	
1897	Boston	93	39	.705	2	
1898	Boston	102	47	.685	6	
1899	Brooklyn	88	42	.677	4	
1900	Brooklyn	82	54	.603	4½	
1901	Pittsburgh	90	49	.647	7½	1,920,031
1902	Pittsburgh	103	36	.741	27½	1,683,012
1903	Pittsburgh	91	49	.650	6½	2,390,362
1904	New York	106	47	.693	13	2,664,271
1905	New York	105	48	.686	9	2,734,310
1906	Chicago	116	36	.763	20	2,781,213
1907	Chicago	107	45	.704	17	2,640,220
1908	Chicago	99	55	.643	1	3,512,108
1909	Pittsburgh	110	42	.724	6½	3,496,420
1910	Chicago	104	50	.675	13	3,494,544
1911	New York	99	54	.647	7½	3,231,768
1912	New York	103	48	.682	10	2,735,759
1913	New York	101	51	.664	12½	2,831,531
1914	Boston	94	59	.614	10½	1,707,397
1915	Philadelphia	90	62	.592	7	2,430,142
1916	Brooklyn	94	60	.610	2½	3,051,634
1917	New York	98	56	.636	10	2,361,136
1918	Chicago	84	45	.651	10½	1,372,127
1919	Cincinnati	96	44	.686	9	2,878,203
1920	Brooklyn	93	61	.604	7	4,036,575
1921	New York	94	59	.614	4	3,986,984
1922	New York	93	61	.604	7	3,941,820
1923	New York	95	58	.621	4½	4,069,817
1924	New York	93	60	.608	1½	4,340,644
1925	Pittsburgh	95	58	.621	8½	4,353,704
1926	St Louis	89	65	.578	2	4,920,399
1927	Pittsburgh	94	60	.610	1½	5,309,917
1928	St Louis	95	59	.617	2	4,881,097
1929	Chicago	98	54	.645	10½	4,925,713
1930	St Louis	92	62	.597	2	5,446,532
1931	St Louis	101	53	.656	13	4,583,815
1932	Chicago	90	64	.584	4	3,841,334
1933	New York	91	61	.599	5	3,162,821
1934	St Louis	95	58	.621	2	3,200,105
1935	Chicago	100	54	.649	4	3,657,309
1936	New York	92	62	.597	5	3,903,691
1937	New York	95	57	.625	3	4,204,228
1938	Chicago	89	63	.586	2	4,560,837
1939	Cincinnati	97	57	.630	4½	4,707,177
1940	Cincinnati	100	53	.645	12	4,389,693
1941	Brooklyn	100	54	.649	2½	4,777,647
1942	St Louis	106	48	.688	2	4,353,353
1943	St Louis	105	49	.682	18	3,769,342
1944	St Louis	105	49	.682	14½	3,974,588
1945	Chicago	98	56	.636	3	5,260,703
1946	a) St Louis	98	58	.628	2	8,902,107
1947	Brooklyn	94	60	.610	5	10,388,470
1948	Boston	91	62	.595	6½	9,770,743
1949	Brooklyn	97	57	.630	1	9,484,718
1950	Philadelphia	91	63	.591	2	8,320,616
1951	b) New York	98	59	.624	1	7,244,002
1952	Brooklyn	96	57	.627	4½	6,339,148
1953	Brooklyn	105	49	.682	13	7,419,721
1954	New York	97	57	.630	5	8,013,519
1955	Brooklyn	98	55	.641	13½	7,674,412
1956	Brooklyn	93	61	.604	1	8,649,567
1957	Milwaukee	95	59	.617	9	8,819,601
1958	Milwaukee	92	62	.597	8	10,164,596
1959	c) Los Angeles	88	68	.564	2	9,994,525
1960	Pittsburgh	95	59	.617	7	10,684,963
1961	Cincinnati	93	61	.604	4	8,731,502
1962	d) San Francisco	103	62	.624	1	11,360,159
1963	Los Angeles	99	63	.611	6	11,382,227
1964	St Louis	93	69	.574	1	12,045,190
1965	Los Angeles	97	65	.599	2	13,581,136
1966	Los Angeles	95	67	.586	1½	15,015,471
1967	St Louis	101	60	.627	10½	12,971,430
1968	St Louis	97	65	.599	9	11,785,358
1969	New York (E)	100	62	.617	8	15,094,946
1970	Cincinnati (W)	102	60	.630	14½	16,662,198
1971	Pittsburgh (E)	97	65	.599	7	17,324,857
1972	Cincinnati (W)	95	59	.617	10½	15,529,730
1973	New York (E)	82	79	.509	1½	16,675,322
1974	Los Angeles (W)	102	60	.630	4	16,978,314
1975	Cincinnati (W)	108	54	.667	20	16,600,490
1976	Cincinnati (W)	102	60	.630	10	16,660,529
1977	Los Angeles (W)	98	64	.605	10	19,070,228
1978	Los Angeles (W)	95	67	.586	2½	20,106,921
1979	Pittsburgh (E)	98	64	.605	2	21,178,419
1980	Philadelphia (E)	91	71	.562	1	21,124,084
1981	e) Los Angeles (W)	63	47	.573	—	12,478,390
1982	St Louis (E)	92	70	.568	3	21,507,425
1983	Philadelphia (E)	90	72	.556	6	21,549,285
1984	San Diego (W)	92	70	.568	12	20,781,436
1985	St Louis (E)	101	61	.623	3	22,292,154
1986	New York (E)	108	54	.667	21½	22,333,471
1987	St Louis (E)	95	67	.586	3	24,734,155
1988	Los Angeles (W)	94	67	.584	7	24,460,442

GA: Games ahead of second-place club. a) Defeated Brooklyn, two games to none, in playoff. b) Defeated Brooklyn, two games to one, in playoff for pennant. c) Defeated Milwaukee, two games to none, in playoff.
d) Defeated Los Angeles, two games to one, in playoff. e) First half 36–21; second half 27–26 of strike-hit season.

NL REGULAR SEASON RECORDS SINCE 1900

TEAM RECORDS
Most wins: 116 Chicago 1906
Most defeats: 120 New York 1962
Earliest West Division win: 7 September 1975
Earliest East Division win: 17 September 1986
Highest winning percentage (since 1969): .667 Cincinnati 1975, New York 1986
Lowest winning percentage (since 1969): .509 New York 1973
Finished most games ahead: 27½ Pittsburgh 1902
Finished most games behind: 48 Montreal 1969
Most innings: 26 Brooklyn 1–1 Boston 1920
Longest time: 7hrs 23mins, SF 8–6 LA 1964
Shortest time: 51mins, NY 6–1 Philadelphia 1919
Most runs scored by one team: 28 St Louis v. Philadelphia 1929
Most runs scored by both teams: 49 Chicago 26–23 Phila 1922
Consecutive wins: 26 New York 1916 (1 tie)
Consecutive defeats: 23 Philadelphia 1961
Most players used in a season: 54 New York 1967
Fewest players used in a season: 20 Chicago 1905
Largest game attendance: 78,672 LA–SF 1958
Largest home attendance: 3,608,881 LA 1982
Largest NL attendance: 24,734,155 in 1987
First NL game: 22 April 1876 Boston–Philadelphia
First night game: 24 May 1935 Cincinnati–Philadelphia

PLAYER GAME RECORDS
Most at bats: 11 (by 6 players)
Runs: 6 Mel Ott, NY 1934 and 1944
6 Frank Torre, Milwaukee 1957
Hits: 7 Rennie Stennett, Pittsburgh 1975
RBIs: 12 James Bottomly, St Louis 1924
Home runs: 4 (by 6 players)
Stolen bases: 5 (by 5 players)
Innings pitched: 26 Leon Cadore, Brooklyn, and Joe Oeschger, Boston (Boston 1–1 Brooklyn), 1 May 1920
Strikeouts: 19 Steve Carlton, St Louis 1969 and Tom Seaver, New York 1970
Consecutive strikeouts: 10 Tom Seaver, NY 1970
Youngest player: 15yrs 10m 11d Joe Nuxhall, Cincinnati 1944
Oldest player: 52yrs 29d James O'Rourke, NY 1904

PLAYER SEASON RECORDS
Best batting average: .424 Rogers Hornsby, St Louis 1924
At Bats: 701 Juan Samuel, Philadelphia 1984
Runs: 158 Charlie Klein, Philadelphia 1930
Hits: 254 Frank O'Doul, Philadelphia 1929, Bill Terry, NY 1930
RBIs: 190 Lewis Wilson, Chicago 1930
Home runs: 56 Lewis Wilson, Chicago 1930
Grand Slam homers: 5 Ernie Banks, Chicago 1955
Consecutive games batted safely: 44 Pete Rose, Cincinnati 1978
Most recent .400 hitter: .401 Bill Terry, NY 1930
Hit by pitcher: 50 Ron Hunt, Montreal 1971
Stolen bases: 118 Lou Brock, St Louis 1974
Caught stealing: 36 Miller Huggins, St Louis 1914
Games pitched: 106 Mike Marshall, LA 1974
Innings pitched: 434 Joe McGinnity, NY 1903
Wins by RH pitcher: 37 Christy Mathewson, NY 1908
Wins by LH pitcher: 27 S. Koufax 1966, S. Carlton 1972
Most losses: 29 Vic Willis, Boston 1905

Manager Pete Rose, W–365, L–322 in five seasons, is under pressure to bring the Reds a pennant.

Most strikeouts: 382 Sandy Koufax, LA 1965
Lowest ERA (+300 Inns): 1.12 Bob Gibson, St Louis 1968
Most games saved: 45 Bruce Sutter, St Louis 1984
Consecutive games won: 24 Carl Hubbell, NY 1936–37
Consecutive games lost: 23 Clif Curtis, Boston 1910–11

PLAYER CAREER RECORDS
Seasons as player: 24 Pete Rose 1963–86
Years one club: 22 Mel Ott, NY, Stan Musial, St Louis
Games: 3,562 Pete Rose, Cinc/Phila/Mont.
Consecutive games: 1,207 Steve Garvey, 1975–83
Best batting average (+15yrs): .359 Rogers Hornsby 1915–33
At Bats: 14,053 Pete Rose, Cinc/Phila/Mont.
Runs: 2,165 Pete Rose 1963–86
Hits: 4,256 Pete Rose, Cinc/Phila/Mont.
RBIs: 2,202 Hank Aaron 1954–74
Home runs: 733 Hank Aaron (755 in all), Milwaukee/Atlanta
Grand Slam homers: 18 Willie McCovey, 1959–80
Hit by pitcher: 243 Ron Hunt 1963–74
Stolen bases: 938 Lou Brock, Chicago/St Louis
Caught stealing: 307 Lou Brock 1961–79
Most years pitched: 22 Steve Carlton 1965–86
Games pitched: 1,013 Kent Tekulve 1974–88
Innings pitched: 5,246 Warren Spahn 1942/1946–65
Wins by RH pitcher: 373 Christy Mathewson 1900–16
Wins by LH pitcher: 363 Warren Spahn, Bos/Mil/NY/SF
Most losses: 230 Phil Niekro 1964–83/1987
Most strikeouts: 4,000 Steve Carlton, St L/Phila/SF
Lowest ERA (+300 wins): 2.56 Grover Alexander 1911–30
Games saved: 300 Bruce Sutter 1976–86/88
Years a manager: 32 John McGraw 1899/1902–32
Most years an umpire: 37 Bill Klem 1905–41

NL MOST VALUABLE PLAYERS 1911–1988

1911	Frank Schulte, Chicago (OF)	**1946**	Stan Musial, St Louis (1B)	**1971**	Joe Torre, St Louis (3B)
1912	Larry Doyle, New York (2B)	**1947**	Bob Elliott, Boston (3B)	**1972**	Johnny Bench, Cincinnati (C)
1913	Jake Daubert, Brooklyn (1B)	**1948**	Stan Musial, St Louis (OF)	**1973**	Pete Rose, Cincinnati (OF)
1914	Johnny Evers, Boston (2B)	**1949**	Jackie Robinson, Brooklyn (2B)	**1974**	Steve Garvey, Los Angeles (1B)
1924	Dazzy Vance, Brooklyn (P)	**1950**	Jim Konstanty, Philadelphia (P)	**1975**	Joe Morgan, Cincinnati (2B)
1925	Rogers Hornsby, St Louis (2B)	**1951**	Roy Campanella, Brooklyn (C)	**1976**	Joe Morgan, Cincinnati (2B)
1926	Bob O'Farrell, St Louis (C)	**1952**	Hank Sauer, Chicago (OF)	**1977**	George Foster, Cincinnati (OF)
1927	Paul Waner, Pittsburgh (OF)	**1953**	Roy Campanella, Brooklyn (C)	**1978**	Dave Parker, Pittsburgh (OF)
1928	Jim Bottomley, St Louis (1B)	**1954**	Willie Mays, New York (OF)	**1979**	Keith Hernandez, St Louis (1B) / Willie Stargell, Pittsburgh (1B)
1929	Rogers Hornsby, Chicago (2B)	**1955**	Roy Campanella, Brooklyn (C)	**1980**	Mike Schmidt, Philadelphia (3B)
1931	Frankie Frisch, St Louis (2B)	**1956**	Don Newcombe, Brooklyn (P)	**1981**	Mike Schmidt, Philadelphia (3B)
1932	Chuck Klein, Philadelphia (OF)	**1957**	Henry Aaron, Milwaukee (OF)	**1982**	Dale Murphy, Atlanta (OF)
1933	Carl Hubbell, New York (P)	**1958**	Ernie Banks, Chicago (SS)	**1983**	Dale Murphy, Atlanta (OF)
1934	Dizzy Dean, St Louis (P)	**1959**	Ernie Banks, Chicago (SS)	**1984**	Ryne Sandberg, Chicago (2B)
1935	Gabby Hartnett, Chicago (C)	**1960**	Dick Groat, Pittsburgh (SS)	**1985**	Willie McGee, St Louis (OF)
1936	Carl Hubbell, New York (P)	**1961**	Frank Robinson, Cincinnati (OF)	**1986**	Mike Schmidt, Philadelphia (3B)
1937	Joe Medwick, St Louis (OF)	**1962**	Maury Wills, Los Angeles (SS)	**1987**	Andre Dawson, Chicago (OF)
1938	Ernie Lombardi, Cincinnati (C)	**1963**	Sandy Koufax, Los Angeles (P)	**1988**	Kirk Gibson, Los Angeles (OF)
1939	Bucky Walters, Cincinnati (P)	**1964**	Ken Boyer, St Louis (3B)		
1940	Frank McCormick, Cincinnati (1B)	**1965**	Willie Mays, San Francisco (OF)		
1941	Dolph Camilli, Brooklyn (1B)	**1966**	Roberto Clemente, Pittsburgh (OF)		
1942	Mort Cooper, St Louis (P)	**1967**	Orlando Cepeda, St Louis (1B)		
1943	Stan Musial, St Louis (OF)	**1968**	Bob Gibson, St Louis (P)		
1944	Marty Marion, St Louis (SS)	**1969**	Willie McCovey, San Francisco (1B)		
1945	Phil Cavarretta, Chicago (1B)	**1970**	Johnny Bench, Cincinnati (C)		

See page 120 for abbreviations of playing positions.

Kirk Gibson.

ROOKIE OF THE YEAR

1947	Jackie Robinson, Brooklyn (1B)	
1948	Alvin Dark, Boston (SS)	
1949	Don Newcombe, Brooklyn (P)	
1950	Sam Jethroe, Boston (OF)	
1951	Willie Mays, New York (OF)	
1952	Joe Black, Brooklyn (P)	
1953	Junior Gilliam, Brooklyn (2B)	
1954	Wally Moon, St Louis (OF)	
1955	Bill Virdon, St Louis (OF)	
1956	Frank Robinson, Cincinnati (OF)	
1957	Jack Sanford, Philadelphia (P)	
1958	Orlando Cepeda, San Francisco (1B)	
1959	Willie McCovey, San Francisco (1B)	
1960	Frank Howard, Los Angeles (OF)	
1961	Billy Williams, Chicago (OF)	
1962	Ken Hubbs, Chicago (2B)	
1963	Pete Rose, Cincinnati (2B)	
1964	Richie Allen, Philadelphia (3B)	
1965	Jim Lefebvre, Los Angeles (2B)	
1966	Tommy Helms, Cincinnati (2B)	
1967	Tom Seaver, New York (P)	
1968	Johnny Bench, Cincinnati (C)	
1969	Ted Sizemore, Los Angeles (2B)	
1970	Carl Morton, Montreal (P)	
1971	Earl Williams, Atlanta (C)	
1972	Jon Matlack, New York (P)	
1973	Gary Matthews, San Francisco (OF)	
1974	Bake McBride, St Louis (OF)	
1975	John Montefusco, San Francisco (P)	
1976	Pat Zachry, Cincinnati (P) / Butch Metzger, San Diego (P)	
1977	Andre Dawson, Montreal (OF)	
1978	Bob Horner, Atlanta (3B)	
1979	Rick Sutcliffe, Los Angeles (P)	
1980	Steve Howe, Los Angeles (P)	
1981	Fernando Valenzuela, Los Angeles (P)	
1982	Steve Sax, Los Angeles (2B)	
1983	Darryl Strawberry, New York (OF)	
1984	Dwight Gooden, New York (P)	
1985	Vince Coleman, St Louis (OF)	
1986	Todd Worrell, St Louis (P)	
1987	Benito Santiago, San Diego (C)	
1988	Chris Sabo, Cincinnati (3B)	

Chris Sabo.

Orel Leonard Hershiser IV.

CY YOUNG AWARD

1956	Don Newcombe, Brooklyn (RH)
1957	Warren Spahn, Milwaukee (LH)
1960	Vernon Law, Pittsburgh (RH)
1962	Don Drysdale, Los Angeles (RH)
1963	Sandy Koufax, Los Angeles (LH)
1965	Sandy Koufax, Los Angeles (LH)
1966	Sandy Koufax, Los Angeles (LH)
1967	Mike McCormick, San Francisco (LH)
1968	Bob Gibson, St Louis (RH)
1969	Tom Seaver, New York (RH)
1970	Bob Gibson, St Louis (RH)
1971	Ferguson Jenkins, Chicago (RH)
1972	Steve Carlton, Philadelphia (LH)
1973	Tom Seaver, New York (RH)
1974	Mike Marshall, Los Angeles (RH)
1975	Tom Seaver, New York (RH)
1976	Randy Jones, San Diego (LH)
1977	Steve Carlton, Philadelphia (LH)
1978	Gaylord Perry, San Diego (RH)
1979	Bruce Sutter, Chicago (RH)
1980	Steve Carlton, Philadelphia (LH)
1981	Fernando Valenzuela, Los Angeles (LH)
1982	Steve Carlton, Philadelphia (LH)
1983	John Denny, Philadelphia (RH)
1984	Rick Sutcliffe, Chicago (RH)
1985	Dwight Gooden, New York (RH)
1986	Mike Scott, Houston (RH)
1987	Steve Bedrosian, Philadelphia (RH)
1988	Orel Hershiser, Los Angeles (RH)

The American League

WEST DIVISION
California Angels
Chicago White Sox
Kansas City Royals
Minnesota Twins
Oakland Athletics
Seattle Mariners
Texas Rangers

EAST DIVISION
Baltimore Orioles
Boston Red Sox
Cleveland Indians
Detroit Tigers
Milwaukee Brewers
New York Yankees
Toronto Blue Jays

The American League was formed in 1900, when the Western Association (a minor league reorganised in 1894 by Charles Comiskey and Ban Johnson) changed its name, located clubs in eastern cities for 1901, and battled head-on with the older National League for fans, players and recognition.

The bickering continued until 1903 when the NL grudgingly conceded Major League status to the AL, and marked the agreement with the first World Series. Between 1901–71 only seven cities (Washington did so twice) lost their franchise and each time the club successfully relocated elsewhere. In 1969 the American League divided into an East and West Division, then in 1977 added two clubs to establish its 14 franchises.

As in the NL, each club plays a regular season of 162 games, but as there are two more teams to cater for, the AL fixture list is less unbalanced.

Each club plays the 7 teams in the other division 12 times (6 at home and 6 games away), but plays the 6 other teams in its own division 13 times. Three of the clubs are played 6 games at home and 7 away, while the other three are played 7 games at home and 6 away.

As each American League team plays 84 games against clubs in its own division and 78 games against the others, they cannot reach the play-offs by concentrating on beating teams from the same division.

In 1988, the 14 franchises played 1,134 games: 71 per cent at night, 28 per cent on artificial turf, and 28 per cent indoors. At the end of the regular season the winners of each division play off in the best of 7 games ALCS for the league pennant. The champion club then plays the NL champion in the best of 7 games, World Series.

Distances in miles		Tor	Tex	Sea	Oak	NY	Min	Mil	KC	Det	Cle	Chi	Cal	Bos	Bal
Baltimore	E	395	1350	2770	2880	195	1130	780	1660	520	360	695	2840	395	
Boston	E	565	1740	3100	3200	210	1405	1075	1429	735	650	980	3160		
California	W	2685	1505	1175	415	3025	2020	2185	1730	2445	2455	2175			
Chicago	W	510	1025	2075	2200	850	425	90	505	270	350				
Cleveland	E	290	1160	2610	2550	500	775	435	795	165					
Detroit	E	245	1290	2530	2470	635	695	360	765						
Kansas City	W	1005	545	2045	1915	1220	465	565							
Milwaukee	E	600	1125	2005	2225	940	335								
Minnesota	W	990	990	1640	2140	1285									
New York	E	485	1645	2925	3050										
Oakland	W	2705	1805	865											
Seattle	W	2505	2195												
Texas	W	1495													
Toronto	E														

AMERICAN LEAGUE PRESIDENTS

Byron Bancroft Johnson	1901 to 1927
Ernest S. Barnard	1927 to 1931
William Harridge	1931 to 1959
Joseph E. Cronin	1959 to 1973
Leland S. MacPhail, Jr.	1974 to 1983
Robert W. Brown	1984 to present

AMERICAN LEAGUE 1901–1988

Present Franchise		Games	Won	Lost	Tied	Pct
Baltimore	1954–88	5538	2962	2557	9	.536
Boston	1901–88	13638	6913	6641	84	.510
California*	1961–88	4474	2158	2313	3	.483
Chicago	1901–88	13647	6798	6748	101	.502
Cleveland	1901–88	13654	6910	6653	91	.509
Detroit	1901–88	13678	7074	6500	94	.520
Kansas City	1969–88	3173	1654	1517	2	.522
Milwaukee	1970–88	3015	1461	1552	2	.485
Minnesota	1961–88	4472	2254	2211	7	.505
New York	1903–88	13353	7567	5701	85	.570
Oakland	1968–88	3340	1712	1627	1	.512
Seattle	1977–88	1890	787	1101	2	.417
Texas	1972–88	2687	1251	1432	4	.466
Toronto	1977–88	1887	894	991	2	.474
Totals		**98446**	**50405**	**47554**	**487**	**.514**

* Known as Los Angeles 1961–65

Baltimore Orioles

AMERICAN LEAGUE EAST DIVISION

Team Colours: Black, orange and red
Postal Address: Memorial Stadium, Baltimore, Maryland 21218, USA
Telephone: (301) 243 9800
History of Franchise: Milwaukee Brewers 1901, St Louis Browns 1902–53, Baltimore Orioles 1954–
AL Honours (since 1954): 1966, 69, 70, 71, 79, 83
WS Honours (since 1954): 1966, 70, 83
Retired Uniforms: 4–Earl Weaver, 5–Brooks Robinson, 20–Frank Robinson, 22–Jim Palmer

RECENT ORIOLES TOTALS
(AL Rankings out of 14):

	1988 (Rk)	1987 (Rk)	1986 (Rk)	1985 (Rk)
Games W/L Pct:	.335(14)	.414(13)	.451(11)	.516(7)
Pitching ERA:	4.54(14)	5.01(13)	4.30(10)	4.38(8)
Batting Ave:	.238(14)	.258(11)	.258(8)	.263(7)
Home Runs:	137(7)	211(3)	169(6)	214(1)
Fielding Pct:	.980(6)	.982(3)	.978(10)	.979(8)
Total Errors:	119(6)	111(4)	135(10)	129(9)
Stolen Bases:	69(13)	69(14)	64(13)	51(12)

Catcher Terry Kennedy, 1,044 hits in 1,105 games with St Louis, San Diego and Baltimore.

SEASON RECORDS SINCE 1969

Year	Position	W	L	Pct	GB/GA	Attendance
1969	First	109	53	.673	+19	1,062,094
1970	First	108	54	.667	+15	1,057,069
1971	First	101	57	.639	+12	1,023,037
1972	Third	80	74	.519	−5	899,950
1973	First	97	65	.599	+8	960,303
1974	First	91	71	.562	+2	962,572
1975	Second	90	69	.566	−4½	1,002,157
1976	Second	88	74	.543	−10½	1,058,609
1977	Second	97	64	.602	−2½	1,195,769
1978	Fourth	90	71	.559	−9	1,051,724
1979	First	102	57	.642	+8	1,681,009
1980	Second	100	62	.617	−3	1,797,438
1981	Second/fourth	59	46	.562		1,024,247
1982	Second	94	68	.580	−1	1,613,031
1983	First	98	64	.605	+6	2,042,071
1984	Fifth	85	77	.525	−19	2,045,784
1985	Fourth	83	78	.516	−16	2,132,387
1986	Seventh	73	89	.451	−22½	1,973,178
1987	Sixth	67	95	.414	−31	1,835,692
1988	Seventh	54	107	.335	−34½	1,660,738

Frank Robinson hit 586 career home runs in 2,808 ML games.

MEMORIAL STADIUM

Location: 33rd Street, Ellerslie Avenue, 36th Street and Ednor Road
Cost: $6m
First AL game: 15 April 1954
Videoscreen: 25′ × 33′ DiamondVision
Record crowd: 54,458 (9 October 1966) WS v. LA
Record season attendance: 2,132,387 (1985)
A pitchers park ranked: No. 10 for AL hitters
Ave total runs/game (AL Rk) 1986 & 1987:
At Baltimore 9.36(9), Away 9.63(7)

Weather	Apr.	May	Jun.	Jul.	Aug.	Sept.	Oct.
Temp (deg. C):	12	17	22	25	24	20	14
Rainfall (cm):	8.0	9.0	9.6	10.3	10.5	7.9	7.1
Rainy days:	11	12	11	11	11	11	8

1988 tickets: $2.50 children/seniors, to $9.50 lower box
Newspapers: *Baltimore Sun, Washington Post*
Radio: WTOP 1500AM, WBAL 1090AM (40stns)
TV: WMAR Ch2 (10stns). Cable: Home Team Sports (Jon Miller, Joe Angel, Brooks Robinson, Jim Simpson, Mel Proctor, John Lowenstein)
Baltimore hotels used by AL clubs: Marriott (Mil, Tex, Cle, Min, NY), Stouffer (Det, KC), Sheraton (Tor, Chi, Cle 2), Cross Keys (KC 2, Mil 2, and other 4 clubs)

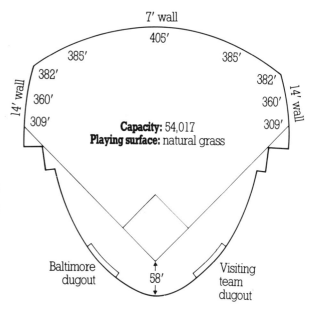

1988 SEASON

Chairman: Edward Bennett Wiliams (died 13 August), Larry Lucchino
Franchise sold for $70m to a four-man consortium in December
VP Baseball Operations: Roland Hemond
Manager: Cal Ripken Sr (to 12 April), Frank Robinson
1988 Orioles Roster: 21% purchased/free agents, 38% acquired by trades, 41% drafted by Orioles

1988 Spring Training Site: Bobby Maduro Miami Stadium, Miami, Florida (since 1958)
1988 Minor League farm club teams: AAA–Rochester Red Wings (Int) (since 1961); AA–Charlotte Knights (S); A–Hagerstown Suns (Car), Erie (NY-P); Rookie–Bluefield (Ap)

1988 home games: 15 day, 66 night
1988 away games: 24 day, 57 night
1988 games: 25 on turf, 137 on grass
150 outside, 12 indoors

First baseman Eddie Murray was traded to the Dodgers for 1989.

LEADING ORIOLES (1988 REGULAR SEASON):

Batters	AtBats	Runs	Hits	HRs	RBIs	Ave
Joe Orsulak	379	48	109	8	27	.288
Eddie Murray	603	75	171	28	84	.284
Cal Ripken	575	87	152	23	81	.264
Mickey Tettleton	283	31	74	11	37	.261
Rick Schu	270	22	69	4	20	.256
Larry Sheets	452	38	104	10	47	.230
Pete Stanicek	261	29	60	4	17	.230
Terry Kennedy	265	20	60	3	16	.226
Jim Traber	352	25	78	10	45	.222
Billy Ripken	512	52	106	2	34	.207
Ken Gerhart	262	27	51	9	23	.195

Pitchers	W-L	Saves	Inns	BBs	SOs	ERA
Dave Schmidt	8-5	2	129.2	38	67	3.40
Tom Niedenfuer	3-4	18	59.0	19	40	3.51
Doug Sisk	3-3	0	94.1	45	26	3.72
Jose Bautista	6-15	0	171.2	45	76	4.30
Jeff Ballard	8-12	0	153.1	42	41	4.40
Mark Thurmond	1-8	3	74.2	27	29	4.58
Mark Williamson	5-8	2	117.2	40	69	4.90
Jay Tibbs	4-15	0	158.2	63	82	5.39
Mike Morgan	1-6	1	71.1	23	29	5.43
Oswald Peraza	5-7	0	86.0	37	61	5.55

Boston Red Sox

AMERICAN LEAGUE EAST DIVISION

Team Colours: Red, white and blue
Postal Address: 4 Yawkey Way, Boston, Massachusetts 02215, USA
Telephone: (617) 267 9440
History of Franchise: Boston Red Sox 1901– (Known as Somersets 1901–04, Puritans 1905–06)
AL Honours: 1903, 04, 12, 15, 16, 18, 46, 67, 75, 86
WS Honours: 1903, 12, 15, 16, 18
Retired Uniforms: 1–Bobby Doerr, 4–Joe Cronin, 9–Ted Williams

RECENT RED SOX TOTALS
(AL Rankings out of 14):

	1988 (Rk)	1987 (Rk)	1986 (Rk)	1985 (Rk)
Games W/L Pct:	.549(3)	.481(8)	.590(1)	.500(8)
Pitching ERA:	3.97(7)	4.77(12)	3.93(3)	4.06(6)
Batting Ave:	.283(1)	.278(1)	.271(2)	.282(1)
Home Runs:	124(10)	174(9)	144(11)	162(5)
Fielding Pct:	.984(2)	.982(3)	.979(8)	.977(10)
Total Errors:	93(2)	110(3)	129(9)	145(14)
Stolen Bases:	65(14)	77(13)	41(14)	66(14)

Infielder Wade Boggs. In his seven years and 1,027 games for Boston he has six consecutive 200–hit seasons, and a .356 career batting average.

SEASON RECORDS SINCE 1969

Year	Position	W	L	Pct	GB/GA	Attendance
1969	Third	87	75	.537	−22	1,833,246
1970	Third	87	75	.537	−21	1,595,278
1971	Third	85	77	.525	−18	1,678,732
1972	Second	85	70	.548	−½	1,441,718
1973	Second	89	73	.549	−8	1,481,002
1974	Third	84	78	.519	−7	1,566,411
1975	First	95	65	.594	+4½	1,748,587
1976	Third	83	79	.512	−15½	1,895,846
1977	Second	97	64	.602	−2½	2,074,549
1978	Second	99	64	.607	−1	2,320,643
1979	Third	91	69	.569	−11½	2,353,114
1980	Fourth	83	77	.519	−19	1,956,092
1981	Fifth/second	59	49	.546		1,060,379
1982	Third	89	73	.549	−6	1,950,124
1983	Sixth	78	84	.481	−20	1,782,285
1984	Fourth	86	76	.531	−18	1,661,618
1985	Fifth	81	81	.500	−18½	1,786,633
1986	First	95	66	.590	+5½	2,147,641
1987	Fifth	78	84	.481	−20	2,231,551
1988	First	89	73	.549	+1	2,464,851

Pitcher Roger Clemens holds the ML record of 20 strikeouts in a game.

FENWAY PARK

Location: Yawkey Way, Lansdowne Street, Ipswich Street
First AL game: 20 April 1912
Formerly played at Huntingdon Avenue Grounds and then Braves Field on Sundays. Fenway Park was rebuilt 1934 (after fires in 1926, 1932)
Hand operated scoreboard, colour videoboard
Record crowd: 47,627 (22 September 1935) dh v. NYY (Post-War record: 38,843 (13 Sept 1988) v. Balt.
Record season attendance: 2,464,851 (1988)
A pitchers park ranked: No. 9 for AL hitters
Ave total runs/game (AL Rk) 1986 & 1987:
At Boston 9.62(6), Away 9.87(5)
(Fenway is by tradition a hitters park)

Weather	Apr.	May	Jun.	Jul.	Aug.	Sept.	Oct.
Temp (deg. C):	10	15	20	22	21	18	13
Rainfall (cm):	8.8	8.8	8.1	6.8	8.8	8.1	7.6
Rainy days:	11	11	10	10	10	9	9

1988 tickets: $5 bleachers, to $14 field box
Newspapers: *Boston Globe*, *Boston Herald-American*
Radio: WRKO 99.1 FM (79stns)
TV: WSBK Ch38. Cable: NESN (Ken Coleman, Joe Castiglione, Bob Montgomery, Sean McDonough)
Boston hotels used by AL clubs: Marriott (KC, Cal, Chi, Mil, Sea), Sheraton (other 8 clubs)

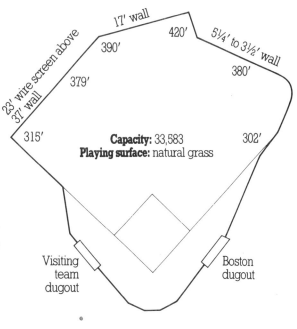

BOSTON RED SOX FENWAY PARK

1988 SEASON

President: Mrs Jean R. Yawkey
Chief Executive Officer: Haywood C. Sullivan
VP/General Manager: Lou Gorman
Managers: John McNamara (to 14 July), Joe Morgan
1988 Red Sox Roster: 20% purchased/free agents, 5% acquired by trades, 75% drafted by Red Sox

1988 Spring Training Site: Chain O'Lakes Park, Winter Haven, Florida
1988 Minor League farm club teams: AAA–Pawtuckett (Int); AA–New Britain (E); A–Lynchburg (Car), Winter Haven (FS), Elmira Pioneers (NY-P)

1988 home games: 35 day, 46 night
1988 away games: 24 day, 57 night
1988 games: 24 on turf, 138 on grass
150 outside, 12 indoors

LEADING RED SOX (1988 REGULAR SEASON):

Batters	AtBats	Runs	Hits	HRs	RBIs	Ave
Wade Boggs	584	128	214	5	58	.366
Mike Greenwell	590	86	192	22	119	.325
Ellis Burks	540	93	159	18	92	.294
Dwight Evans	559	96	164	21	111	.293
Jody Reed	338	60	99	1	28	.293
Marty Barrett	612	83	173	1	65	.283
Rick Cerone	264	31	71	3	27	.269
Jim Rice	485	57	128	15	72	.264
Todd Benzinger	405	47	103	13	70	.254
Spike Owen	257	40	64	5	18	.249
Rich Gedman	299	33	69	9	39	.231
Larry Parrish	406	32	88	14	52	.217

Pitchers	W-L	Saves	Inns	BBs	SOs	ERA
Lee Smith	4-5	29	83.2	37	96	2.80
Roger Clemens	18-12	0	264.0	62	291	2.93
Bob Stanley	6-4	5	101.2	29	57	3.19
Mike Boddicker	13-15	0	236.0	77	156	3.39
Dennis Lamp	7-6	0	82.2	19	49	3.48
Wes Gardner	8-6	2	149.0	64	106	3.50
Bruce Hurst	18-6	0	216.2	65	166	3.66
Jeff Sellers	1-7	0	85.2	56	70	4.83
Dennis Boyd	9-7	0	129.2	41	71	5.34
Mike Smithson	9-6	0	126.2	37	73	5.97

Would today's stadium architects looking for a Major League franchise dare to copy Fenway Park's left field 'Green Monster' in their plans?

Cleveland Indians

AMERICAN LEAGUE EAST DIVISION

Team Colours: Navy blue, red and white
Postal Address: Cleveland Stadium, Cleveland, Ohio 44114, USA
Telephone: (216) 861 1200
History of Franchise: Cleveland Indians 1901– (Known as Bronchos 1901, Blues/Bluebirds 1902–04, Naps 1905–11, Molly McGuires 1912–14)
AL Honours: 1920, 48, 54
WS Honours: 1920, 48
Retired Uniforms: 3–Earl Averill, 5–Lou Boudreau, 19–Bob Feller

RECENT INDIANS TOTALS
(AL Rankings out of 14):

	1988 (Rk)	1987 (Rk)	1986 (Rk)	1985 (Rk)
Games W/L Pct:	.481(9)	.377(14)	.519(7)	.370(14)
Pitching ERA:	4.16(11)	5.28(14)	4.58(12)	4.51(14)
Batting Ave:	.261(6)	.263(7)	.284(1)	.265(4)
Home Runs:	134(8)	187(8)	157(10)	116(13)
Fielding Pct:	.979(8)	.975(14)	.975(13)	.977(10)
Total Errors:	124(9)	153(14)	157(14)	141(11)
Stolen Bases:	97(9)	140(3)	141(1)	132(3)

Mel Hall has played 732 games in eight years with the Cubs and Indians.

SEASON RECORDS SINCE 1969

Year	Position	W	L	Pct	GB/GA	Attendance
1969	Sixth	62	99	.385	−46½	619,970
1970	Fifth	76	86	.469	−32	729,752
1971	Sixth	60	102	.370	−43	591,361
1972	Fifth	72	84	.462	−14	759,871
1973	Sixth	71	91	.438	−26	605,073
1974	Fourth	77	85	.475	−14	1,114,262
1975	Fourth	79	80	.497	−15½	977,039
1976	Fourth	81	78	.509	−16	948,776
1977	Fifth	71	90	.441	−28½	900,365
1978	Sixth	69	90	.434	−29	800,584
1979	Sixth	81	80	.503	−22	1,011,644
1980	Sixth	79	81	.494	−23	1,033,872
1981	Sixth/fifth	52	51	.504		661,395
1982	Sixth	78	84	.481	−17	1,044,021
1983	Seventh	70	92	.432	−28	768,941
1984	Sixth	75	87	.463	−29	734,269
1985	Seventh	60	102	.370	−39½	655,181
1986	Fifth	84	78	.519	−11½	1,471,977
1987	Seventh	61	101	.377	−37	1,077,898
1988	Sixth	78	84	.481	−11	1,411,610

Pitcher Doug Jones had just nine saves and seven wins in three seasons before establishing himself in 1988.

CLEVELAND STADIUM

Location: Boudreau Boulevard
Cost: $3m
First AL game: 31 July 1932
This is the Indians' third ballpark, and the team's permanent home since 1947
Scoreboard: $1.5m 136'×51'
Messages board: 86'×24'
Record crowd: 86,288 (10 October 1948) WS v. Bos
Record season attendance: 2,620,627 (1948)
Other stadium user: NFL Cleveland Browns
Stadium ranked: No. 5 for AL hitters
Ave total runs/game (AL Rk) 1986 & 1987:
At Cleveland 10.55(1), Away 10.25(1)

Weather	Apr.	May	Jun.	Jul.	Aug.	Sept.	Oct.
Temp (deg. C):	9	14	20	22	21	18	12
Rainfall (cm):	8.8	8.8	8.4	8.8	7.6	7.1	6.6
Rainy days:	15	13	11	10	9	9	10

1988 tickets: $3 children, to $9.50 box
Newspapers: *The Plain Dealer, Akron Beacon Journal*
Radio: WWWE 1100AM (29stns)
TV: WUAB Ch43 (3stns) (Herb Score, Paul Olden, Jack Corrigan)
Cleveland hotels used by AL clubs: Hollenden House (NY, Chi, Mil, Bos), Marriott (Tor), Stouffer (Min, Tex), Bond Court (other 6 clubs)

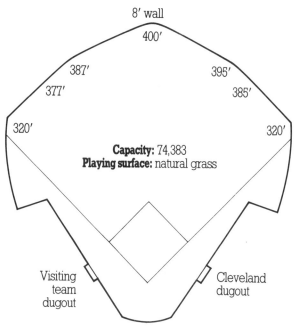

1988 SEASON

Chairman/V. Chairman: Richard & David Jacobs
President/CEO: Hank Peters
VP Baseball Admin/Player Relations: Dan O'Brien
Manager: Doc Edwards
1988 Indians Roster: 27% purchased/free agents, 29% acquired by trades, 44% drafted by Indians

1988 Spring Training Site: HiCorbett Field, Tucson, Arizona (since 1947)
(The AL Indians have played the NL Giants 513 times in Spring training since 1934)
1988 Minor League farm club teams: AAA–Colorado Springs Sky Socks (Pac); AA–Williamsport Bills (E); A–Kingston (Car), Waterloo (MW); Rookie–Burlington (Ap)

1988 home games: 25 day, 56 night
1988 away games: 20 day, 61 night
1988 games: 25 on turf, 137 on grass
150 outside, 12 indoors

LEADING INDIANS (1988 REGULAR SEASON):

Batters	AtBats	Runs	Hits	HRs	RBIs	Ave
Terry Francona	212	24	66	1	12	.311
Julio Franco	613	88	186	10	54	.303
Mel Hall	515	69	144	6	71	.280
Carmen Castillo	176	12	48	4	14	.273
Cory Snyder	511	71	139	26	75	.272
Joe Carter	621	85	168	27	98	.271
Andy Allanson	434	44	114	5	50	.263
Ron Kittle	225	31	58	18	43	.258
Randy Washington	223	30	57	2	21	.256
Willie Upshaw	493	58	121	11	50	.245
Brook Jacoby	552	59	133	9	49	.241

Pitchers	W-L	Saves	Inns	BBs	SOs	ERA
Doug Jones	3-4	37	83.1	16	72	2.27
Brad Havens	2-3	1	57.1	17	30	3.14
Greg Swindell	18-14	0	242.0	45	180	3.20
Tom Candiotti	14-8	0	216.2	53	137	3.28
John Farrell	14-10	0	210.1	67	92	4.24
Don Gordon	3-4	1	59.1	19	20	4.40
Rich Yett	9-6	0	134.1	55	71	4.62
Scott Bailes	9-14	0	145.0	46	53	4.90
Bud Black	4-4	1	81.0	34	63	5.00
Rod Nichols	1-7	0	69.1	23	31	5.06

Dominican infielder Julio Franco, seven years for the Phillies and Indians, was traded to Texas for 1989.

Detroit Tigers

AMERICAN LEAGUE EAST DIVISION

Team Colours: Orange, white and navy blue/black
Postal Address: Tiger Stadium, Detroit, Michigan 48216, USA
Telephone: (313) 962 4000
History of Franchise: Detroit Tigers 1901– (Detroit played in NL 1881–88) (Known as Creams in Western League, became Tigers 1895)
AL Honours: 1907, 08, 09, 34, 35, 40, 45, 68, 84
WS Honours: 1935, 45, 68, 84
Retired Uniforms: 2–Charles Gehringer, 5–Hank Greenberg, 6–Al Kaline

RECENT TIGERS TOTALS
(AL Rankings out of 14):

	1988 (Rk)	1987 (Rk)	1986 (Rk)	1985 (Rk)
Games W/L Pct:	.543(4)	.605(1)	.537(4)	.522(6)
Pitching ERA:	3.71(4)	4.02(3)	4.02(6)	3.78(4)
Batting Ave:	.250(12)	.272(4)	.263(6)	.253(10)
Home Runs:	143(6)	225(1)	198(1)	202(2)
Fielding Pct:	.982(4)	.980(8)	.982(3)	.977(10)
Total Errors:	109(4)	122(8)	108(3)	143(13)
Stolen Bases:	87(11)	106(11)	138(4)	75(10)

George 'Sparky' Anderson took the 1988 MLB All-Stars to Japan.

SEASON RECORDS SINCE 1969

Year	Position	W	L	Pct	GB/GA	Attendance
1969	Second	90	72	.556	−19	1,577,481
1970	Fourth	79	83	.488	−29	1,501,293
1971	Second	91	71	.562	−12	1,591,073
1972	First	86	70	.551	+½	1,892,386
1973	Third	85	77	.525	−12	1,724,146
1974	Sixth	72	90	.444	−19	1,243,080
1975	Sixth	57	102	.358	−37½	1,058,836
1976	Fifth	74	87	.460	−24	1,467,020
1977	Fourth	74	88	.457	−26	1,359,856
1978	Fifth	86	76	.531	−13½	1,714,893
1979	Fifth	85	76	.528	−18	1,630,929
1980	Fifth	84	78	.519	−19	1,785,293
1981	Fourth/second	60	49	.550		1,149,144
1982	Fourth	83	79	.512	−12	1,636,058
1983	Second	92	70	.568	−6	1,829,636
1984	First	104	58	.642	+15	2,704,794
1985	Third	84	77	.522	−15	2,286,609
1986	Third	87	75	.537	−8½	1,899,437
1987	First	98	64	.605	+2	2,061,829
1988	Second	88	74	.543	−1	2,081,162

Some of baseball's most demonstrative fans are found at historic Tiger Stadium.

TIGER STADIUM

Location: Michigan Avenue, Cochrane Avenue, Kaline Drive and Trumbull Avenue
First AL game: 20 April 1912
The second oldest ML ballpark, extensively renovated in 1977 after being sold to City of Detroit for $1 (one) and leased back for 30 years
Electronic scoreboard $2m replaced 1979
Record crowd: 58,369 (20 July 1947) dh v. NYY
Record season attendance: 2,704,794 (1984)
A pitchers park ranked: No. 13 for AL hitters
Ave total runs/game (AL Rk) 1986 & 1987:
At Detroit 9.22(10), Away 10.18(4)

Weather	Apr.	May	Jun.	Jul.	Aug.	Sept.	Oct.
Temp (deg. C):	9	14	20	23	22	18	12
Rainfall (cm):	7.9	8.6	7.6	7.6	7.6	5.8	6.3
Rainy days:	11	13	11	9	9	10	10

1988 tickets: $4 bleachers, to $10.50 box
Newspapers: *Detroit News*, *Detroit Free Press*
Radio: WJR 760AM
TV: WDIV Ch4. Cable: PASS (Ernie Harwell, Paul Carey, George Kell, Al Kaline, Jim Northrup, Larry Osterman)
Detroit hotels used by AL clubs: Hyatt (Tor, Cal), Pontchartrain (NY, Tex, Mil), Omni (other 8 clubs, and Tex 2)

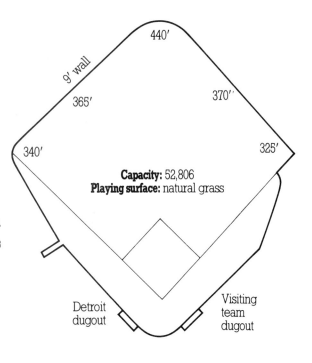

Capacity: 52,806
Playing surface: natural grass

1988 SEASON

Chairman: John Fetzer
Owner/V. Chairman: Tom Monaghan
President/CEO: Jim Campbell
General Manager: Bill Lajoie
Manager: George 'Sparky' Anderson
1988 Tigers Roster: 14% purchased/free agents, 47% acquired by trades, 39% drafted by Tigers

1988 Spring Training Site: Tigertown, Marchant Stadium, Lakeland, Florida (since 1946)
1988 Minor League farm club teams: AAA–Toledo Mud Hens (Int); AA–Glens Falls (E); A–Lakeland (FS), Fayetteville Generals (SA); Rookie–Bristol (Ap)

1988 home games: 27 day, 54 night
1988 away games: 27 day, 54 night
1988 games: 24 on turf, 138 on grass
150 outside, 12 indoors

LEADING TIGERS (1988 REGULAR SEASON):

Batters	AtBats	Runs	Hits	HRs	RBIs	Ave
Alan Trammell	466	73	145	15	69	.311
Dave Bergman	289	37	85	5	35	.294
Lou Whitaker	403	54	111	12	55	.275
Luis Salazar	452	61	122	12	62	.270
Chet Lemon	512	67	135	17	64	.264
Pat Sheridan	347	47	88	11	47	.254
Matt Nokes	382	53	96	16	53	.251
Fred Lynn	391	46	96	25	56	.246
Tom Brookens	441	62	107	5	38	.243
Ray Knight	299	34	65	3	33	.217
Gary Pettis	458	65	96	3	36	.210
Darrell Evans	437	48	91	22	64	.208

Pitchers	W-L	Saves	Inns	BBs	SOs	ERA
Mike Henneman	9-6	22	91.1	24	58	1.87
Paul Gibson	4-2	0	92.0	34	50	2.93
Jeff Robinson	13-6	0	172.0	72	114	2.98
Guillermo Hernandez	6-5	10	67.2	31	59	3.06
Eric King	4-1	3	68.2	34	45	3.41
Jack Morris	15-13	0	235.0	83	168	3.94
Walt Terrell	7-16	0	206.1	78	84	3.97
Frank Tanana	14-11	0	203.0	64	127	4.21
Doyle Alexander	14-11	0	229.0	46	126	4.32
Ted Power	6-7	0	99.0	38	57	5.91

Consistent shortstop Alan Trammell, 1,650 hits in 1,568 games in 12 years with Detroit.

Milwaukee Brewers

AMERICAN LEAGUE EAST DIVISION

Team Colours: Royal blue, gold and white
Postal Address: Milwaukee County Stadium, Milwaukee, Wisconsin 53214, USA
Telephone: (414) 933 4114
History of Franchise: Seattle Pilots 1969, Milwaukee Brewers 1970–
Honours (since 1970): Won AL 1982. Yet to win World Series

RECENT BREWERS TOTALS
(AL Rankings out of 14):

	1988 (Rk)	1987 (Rk)	1986 (Rk)	1985 (Rk)
Games W/L Pct:	.537(5)	.562(3)	.478(8)	.441(12)
Pitching ERA:	3.45(2)	4.62(9)	4.01(5)	4.39(9)
Batting Ave:	.257(9)	.276(2)	.255(9)	.263(7)
Home Runs:	113(13)	163(13)	127(13)	101(14)
Fielding Pct:	.980(6)	.976(12)	.976(12)	.977(10)
Total Errors:	120(7)	145(12)	146(12)	142(12)
Stolen Bases:	159(1)	176(1)	100(9)	69(11)

SEASON RECORDS SINCE 1969

Year	Position	W	L	Pct	GB/GA	Attendance
Seattle Pilots (West Division)
1969	Sixth	64	98	.395	−33	677,944
Milwaukee Brewers (West Division)
1970	Fourth	65	97	.401	−33	933,690
1971	Sixth	69	92	.429	−32	731,531
Milwaukee Brewers (East Division)
1972	Sixth	65	91	.417	−21	600,440
1973	Fifth	74	88	.457	−23	1,092,158
1974	Fifth	76	86	.469	−15	955,741
1975	Fifth	68	94	.420	−28	1,213,357
1976	Sixth	66	95	.410	−32	1,012,164
1977	Sixth	67	95	.414	−33	1,114,938
1978	Third	93	69	.574	−6½	1,601,406
1979	Second	95	66	.590	−8	1,918,343
1980	Third	86	76	.531	−17	1,857,408
1981	Third/first	62	47	.569		878,432
1982	First	95	67	.586	+1	1,978,896
1983	Fifth	87	75	.537	−11	2,397,131
1984	Seventh	67	94	.416	−36½	1,608,509
1985	Sixth	71	90	.441	−28	1,360,265
1986	Sixth	77	84	.478	−18	1,265,041
1987	Third	91	71	.562	−7	1,909,244
1988	Third	87	75	.537	−2	1,923,238

Outfielder Robin Yount, 2,407 hits in 2,131 games with Milwaukee.

Ted Higuera, W–69, L–38 in four years with Milwaukee, after pitching for six seasons in the Mexican League.

COUNTY STADIUM

Location: South 46th Street off Bluemound Road
Cost: $5m
First AL game: 15 May 1968
Stadium opened 1953 for old Milwaukee Braves
Record crowd: 56,562 (17 October 1982) WS v. St L
Record season attendance: 2,397,131 (1983)
Stadium ranked: No. 4 for AL hitters
Ave total runs/game (AL Rk) 1986 & 1987:
At Milwaukee 9.71(5), Away 9.30(11)

Weather	Apr.	May	Jun.	Jul.	Aug.	Sept.	Oct.
Temp (deg. C):	7	12	18	21	20	16	11
Rainfall (cm):	7.1	7.3	9.0	8.6	6.8	7.6	5.0
Rainy days:	11	12	11	9	9	8	8

1988 tickets: $4 bleachers, to $11 mezzanine
Newspapers: *Milwaukee Journal, Milwaukee Sentinel*
Radio: WTMJ 620AM (49stns)
TV: WVTV Ch18 (8stns) (Bob Uecker, Pat Hughes, Mike Hegan, Jim Paschke)
Milwaukee hotels used by AL clubs: Hyatt (Tor, Cle, Cal, Chi), Pfister (other 9 clubs)

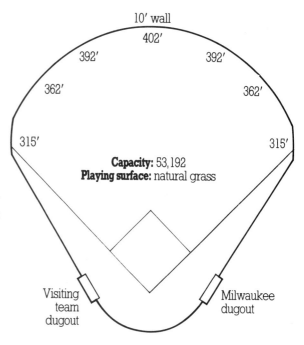

1988 SEASON

President/CEO: Bud Selig
VP/General Manager: Harry Dalton
Manager: Tom Trebelhorn
1988 Brewers Roster: 16% purchased/free agents, 32% acquired by trades, 52% drafted by Brewers

1988 Spring Training Site: Compadre Stadium, Chandler, Arizona (since 1986)
1988 Minor League farm club teams: AAA–Denver Zephers (AmA); AA–El Paso Diablos (T); A–Stockton Ports (Cal); Beloit (MW); Rookie–Helena (P)

1988 home games: 30 day, 51 night
1988 away games: 22 day, 59 night
1988 games: 24 on turf, 138 on grass
150 outside, 12 indoors

LEADING BREWERS (1988 REGULAR SEASON):

Batters	AtBats	Runs	Hits	HRs	RBIs	Ave
Paul Molitor	609	115	190	13	60	.312
Robin Yount	621	92	190	13	91	.306
Jim Gantner	539	67	149	0	47	.276
Joey Meyer	327	22	86	11	45	.263
Glenn Braggs	272	30	71	10	42	.261
Rob Deer	492	71	124	23	85	.252
B. J. Surhoff	493	47	121	5	38	.245
Dale Sveum	467	41	113	9	51	.242
Jeffrey Leonard	374	45	88	8	44	.235
Greg Brock	364	53	77	6	50	.212

Pitchers	W-L	Saves	Inns	BBs	SOs	ERA
Paul Mirabella	2-2	4	60.0	21	33	1.65
Dan Plesac	1-2	30	52.1	12	52	2.41
Ted Higuera	16-9	0	227.1	59	192	2.45
Chuck Crim	7-6	9	105.0	28	58	2.91
Don August	13-7	0	148.1	48	66	3.09
Chris Bosio	7-15	6	182.0	38	84	3.36
Juan Nieves	7-5	1	110.1	50	73	4.08
Bill Wegman	13-13	0	199.0	50	84	4.12
Odell Jones	5-0	1	80.2	29	48	4.35
Tom Filer	5-8	0	101.2	33	39	4.43
Mike Birkbeck	10-8	0	124.0	37	64	4.72

Plans are afoot to replace County Stadium Milwaukee.

New York Yankees

AMERICAN LEAGUE EAST DIVISION

Team Colours: Navy blue, red and white
Postal Address: Yankee Stadium, Bronx, New York 10451, USA
Telephone: (212) 293 4300
History of Franchise: Baltimore Orioles 1901–02, New York Yankees 1903–. (Known as Highlanders 1903–12, Yankees since 1913)
AL Honours (since 1903): 1921, 22, 23, 26, 27, 28, 32, 36, 37, 38, 39, 41, 42, 43, 47, 49, 50, 51, 52, 53, 55, 56, 57, 58, 60, 61, 62, 63, 64, 76, 77, 78, 81 (33 times)
WS Honours (since 1903): 1923, 27, 28, 32, 36, 37, 38, 39, 41, 43, 47, 49, 50, 51, 52, 53, 56, 58, 61, 62, 77, 78 (22 times)
Retired Uniforms: 1–Billy Martin, 3–Babe Ruth, 4–Lou Gehrig, 5–Joe DiMaggio, 7–Mickey Mantle, 8–Yogi Berra & Bill Dickey, 9–Roger Maris, 10–Phil Rizzuto, 15–Thurman Munson, 16–Whitey Ford, 32–Elston Howard, 37–Casey Stengel

SEASON RECORDS SINCE 1969

Year	Position	W	L	Pct	GB/GA	Attendance
1969	Fifth	80	81	.497	−28½	1,067,996
1970	Second	93	69	.574	−15	1,136,879
1971	Fourth	82	80	.506	−21	1,070,771
1972	Fourth	79	76	.510	−6½	966,328
1973	Fourth	80	82	.494	−17	1,262,077
1974	Second	89	73	.549	−2	1,273,075
1975	Third	83	77	.519	−12	1,288,048
1976	First	97	62	.610	+10½	2,012,434
1977	First	100	62	.617	+2½	2,103,092
1978	First	100	63	.613	+1	2,335,871
1979	Fourth	89	71	.556	−13½	2,537,765
1980	First	103	59	.636	+3	2,627,417
1981	First/sixth	59	48	.551		1,614,533
1982	Fifth	79	83	.488	−16	2,041,219
1983	Third	91	71	.562	−7	2,257,976
1984	Third	87	75	.537	−17	1,821,815
1985	Second	97	64	.602	−2	2,214,587
1986	Second	90	72	.556	−5½	2,268,116
1987	Fourth	89	73	.549	−9	2,427,672
1988	Fifth	85	76	.528	−3½	2,633,703

RECENT YANKEES TOTALS
(AL Rankings out of 14):

	1988 (Rk)	1987 (Rk)	1986 (Rk)	1985 (Rk)
Games W/L Pct:	.528(7)	.549(4)	.556(3)	.602(2)
Pitching ERA:	4.24(12)	4.36(6)	4.11(8)	3.69(3)
Batting Ave:	.263(5)	.262(9)	.271(2)	.267(3)
Home Runs:	148(4)	196(5)	188(3)	176(3)
Fielding Pct:	.978(11)	.983(2)	.979(8)	.979(8)
Total Errors:	134(12)	102(2)	127(8)	126(7)
Stolen Bases:	146(2)	105(12)	139(5)	155(1)

First baseman Don Mattingly did not see eye to eye with owner, George Steinbrenner in 1988.

Outfielder Dave Winfield, over 16 seasons for the Padres and Yankees.

YANKEE STADIUM

Location: East 161st Street, and River Avenue
First AL game: 18 April 1923
Highlanders/Yankees had previously played at Hilltop Park and Polo Grounds, Manhattan. Yankees shared Shea with the Mets 1974–75 during $60m remodelling.
Videoscreen: Mitsubishi DiamondVision
Record crowd ('old' YS): 81,841 (30 May 1938)
                    ('new' YS): 56,821 (14 October 1976)
Record season attendance: 2,633,703 (1988)
A pitchers park ranked: No. 8 for AL hitters
Ave total runs/game (AL Rk) 1986 & 1987:
At New York 9.42(8), Away 9.59(9)
For 1988 left field fences extended, but centre and right field fences brought in.

Weather	Apr.	May	Jun.	Jul.	Aug.	Sept.	Oct.
Temp (deg. C):	11	17	22	25	24	20	15
Rainfall (cm):	8.4	8.8	7.6	9.3	10.1	8.4	7.3
Rainy days:	11	11	10	12	10	9	9

1988 tickets: $1 seniors, to $11 box
Newspapers: *NY Times, NY Daily News, NY Post*
Radio: WABC 770AM
TV: WPIX Ch11. Cable: SportsChannel (Hank Greenwald, Tommy Hutton, Phil Rizzuto, Mickey Mantle, Bill White, Ken Harrelson)
New York hotel used by all AL clubs: Grand Hyatt (see NY Mets NL)

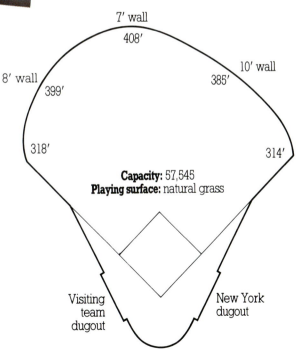

NEW YORK YANKEES YANKEE STADIUM 71

1988 SEASON

Principal Owner: George Steinbrenner
VP/Baseball Admin: Bob Quinn
VP/General Manager: Lou Piniella (to 9 June), Bob Quinn
Managers: Billy Martin (to 23 June), Lou Piniella (to 7 October), Dallas Green
1988 Yankees Roster: 38% purchased/free agents, 48% acquired by trades, 14% drafted by Yankees

1988 Spring Training Site: Fort Lauderdale Stadium, Fort Lauderdale, Florida (since 1962)
1988 Minor League farm club teams: AAA–Columbus Clippers (Int); AA–Albany-Colonie (E); A–Ft Lauderdale (FS), Prince William (Car), Oneonta (NY-P); Rookie–Sarasota (GC)

1988 home games: 20 day, 61 night
1988 away games: 27 day, 54 night
1988 games: 25 on turf, 137 on grass
150 outside, 12 indoors

LEADING YANKEES (1988 REGULAR SEASON):

Batters	AtBats	Runs	Hits	HRs	RBIs	Ave
Dave Winfield	559	96	180	25	107	.322
Don Mattingly	599	94	186	18	88	.311
Claudell Washington	455	62	140	11	64	.308
Rickey Henderson	554	118	169	6	50	.305
Don Slaught	322	33	91	9	43	.283
Ken Phelps	297	54	78	24	54	.263
Jack Clark	496	81	120	27	93	.242
Rafael Santana	480	50	115	4	38	.240
Willie Randolph	404	43	93	2	34	.230
Mike Pagliarulo	444	46	96	15	67	.216

Pitchers	W-L	Saves	Inns	BBs	SOs	ERA
John Candelaria	13-7	1	157.0	23	121	3.38
Dave Righetti	5-4	25	87.0	37	70	3.52
Neil Allen	5-3	0	117.1	37	61	3.84
Al Leiter	4-4	0	57.1	33	60	3.92
Ron Guidry	2-3	0	56.0	15	32	4.18
Rick Rhoden	12-12	0	197.0	56	94	4.20
Dale Mohorcic	4-8	6	74.2	29	44	4.22
Steve Shields	5-5	0	82.1	30	55	4.37
Charles Hudson	6-6	2	106.1	36	58	4.49
Tommy John	9-8	0	176.1	46	81	4.49
Rich Dotson	12-9	0	171.0	72	77	5.00

Brooklyn-born pitcher John Candelaria, W–164, L–102 in 14 years with the Pirates, Angels, Mets and Yankees.

Toronto Blue Jays

AMERICAN LEAGUE EAST DIVISION

Team Colours: Blue, red and white
Postal Address: Box 7777, Adelaide St PO, Toronto, Ontario M5C 2K7, Canada
Telephone: (416) 595 0077
History of Franchise: Toronto Blue Jays 1977–
Honours: Yet to win AL or World Series

First baseman Fred McGriff had a great year in 1988.

SEASON RECORDS SINCE 1977

Year	Position	W	L	Pct	GB/GA	Attendance
1977	Seventh	54	107	.335	−45½	1,701,052
1978	Seventh	59	102	.366	−40	1,562,585
1979	Seventh	53	109	.327	−50½	1,431,651
1980	Seventh	67	95	.414	−36	1,400,327
1981	Seventh/seventh	37	69	.349		755,083
1982	Sixth	78	84	.481	−17	1,275,978
1983	Fourth	89	73	.549	−9	1,930,415
1984	Second	89	73	.549	−15	2,110,009
1985	First	99	62	.615	+2	2,468,925
1986	Fourth	86	76	.531	−9½	2,455,477
1987	Second	96	66	.593	−2	2,778,429
1988	Third	87	75	.537	−2	2,595,175

RECENT BLUE JAYS TOTALS
(AL Rankings out of 14):

	1988 (Rk)	1987 (Rk)	1986 (Rk)	1985 (Rk)
Games W/L Pct:	.537(5)	.593(2)	.531(6)	.615(1)
Pitching ERA:	3.80(5)	3.74(1)	4.08(7)	3.29(1)
Batting Ave:	.268(3)	.269(5)	.269(4)	.269(2)
Home Runs:	158(1)	215(2)	181(5)	158(6)
Fielding Pct:	.982(4)	.982(3)	.984(1)	.980(3)
Total Errors:	110(5)	111(4)	100(1)	125(6)
Stolen Bases:	107(6)	106(11)	110(6)	144(2)

EXHIBITION STADIUM

Location: Exhibition Place via Lakeshore Boulevard
Cost: $18m
First AL game: 7 April 1977
Videoscreen: Large SkyVision 35' × 115'
Record crowd: 47,828 (1 July 1987) v. NY
Record season attendance: 2,778,429 (1987)
Other stadium user: CFL Toronto Argonauts
Blue Jays will move to the SkyDome during 1989
A pitchers park ranked: No. 12 for AL hitters
Ave total runs/game (AL Rk) 1986 & 1987:
At Toronto 9.55(7), Away 10.25(1)
1988 tickets: $4 general, to $15 field
Newspapers: *Toronto Star, Toronto Sun, Toronto Globe & Mail*
Radio: CJCL 1430AM (59stns)
TV: CFTO Ch9. Cable: The Sports Network (Jerry Howarth, Tom Cheek, Don Chevrier, Tony Kubek)
Toronto hotels used by AL clubs: Sheraton (Chi, Cal, Mil), Hilton (KC, Oak, Tex), Westin (7 others), Inn on the Park (Bal 2)

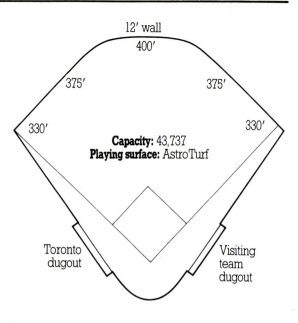

Jesse Barfield, Toronto, hit 40 of his 174 home runs in 1986.

THE SKYDOME (from 1989):
277 Front Street West, Toronto, Ontario M5V 2X4, Canada
Tel: (416) 963 3513
Location: At foot of massive CN Tower in central Toronto. 17,000 parking spots and ideal for public transport.
Cost: More than (Canadian) $380m
Capacity: 53,000 for baseball
The playing surface will be AstroTurf-8. There will be a Sony Jumbotron scoreboard. The 282ft high retractable roof will be able to open and close in about 20 minutes, uncovering the whole field and 90 per cent of seats. Designed to cater for a wide range of sports, shows, exhibitions, there will be a 364 suite hotel, with rooms overlooking the playing field.
Weather from April–October outside the SkyDome:
8–22 degrees C; 6.1–8.1 cm rainfall

1988 SEASON

Chairman: R. Howard Webster
CEO: N. E. Hardy
VP/Baseball General Manager: Pat Gillick
Manager: Jimy Williams
1988 Blue Jays Roster: 18% purchased/free agents, 32% acquired by trades, 50% drafted by Blue Jays

1988 Spring Training Site: Grant Field, Cecil P. Englebert Recreational Complex, Dunedin, Florida.
1988 Minor League farm club teams: AAA–Syracuse Chiefs (Int); AA–Knoxville (S); A–Dunedin (FS), Myrtle Beach (SA), St Catharines (NY-P); Rookie–Medicine Hat (P)

1988 home games: 32 day, 49 night
1988 away games: 18 day, 63 night
1988 games: 99 on turf, 63 on grass
150 outside, 12 indoors

LEADING BLUE JAYS (1988 REGULAR SEASON):

Batters	AtBats	Runs	Hits	HRs	RBIs	Ave
Rance Mulliniks	337	49	101	12	48	.300
Manny Lee	381	38	111	2	38	.291
Tony Fernandez	648	76	186	5	70	.287
Fred McGriff	536	100	151	34	82	.282
Kelly Gruber	569	75	158	16	81	.278
George Bell	614	78	165	24	97	.269
Nelson Liriano	276	36	73	3	23	.264
Ernie Whitt	398	63	100	16	70	.251
Jesse Barfield	468	62	114	18	56	.244
Lloyd Moseby	472	77	113	10	42	.239

Pitchers	W-L	Saves	Inns	BBs	SOs	ERA
Tom Henke	4-4	25	68.0	24	66	2.91
Dave Stieb	16-8	0	207.1	79	147	3.04
John Cerutti	6-7	1	123.2	42	65	3.13
Jeff Musselman	8-5	0	85.0	30	39	3.18
Jimmy Key	12-5	0	131.1	30	65	3.29
Duane Ward	9-3	15	111.2	60	91	3.30
Mike Flanagan	13-13	0	211.0	80	99	4.18
Jim Clancy	11-13	1	196.1	47	118	4.49
David Wells	3-5	4	64.1	31	56	4.62
Todd Stottlemyre	4-8	0	98.0	46	67	5.69

Toronto's SkyDome beside the CN Tower. The first indoor stadium in the AL East, and the 5th in the majors.

California Angels

AMERICAN LEAGUE WEST DIVISION

Team Colours: Scarlet, navy blue and white
Postal Address: PO Box 2000, Anaheim, California 92803, USA
Telephone: (714) 937 6700
History of Franchise: Los Angeles Angels 1961–65, renamed California Angels 1966–
Honours: Yet to win AL or World Series
Retired Uniforms: 26–Gene Autry, 29–Rod Carew

RECENT ANGELS TOTALS
(AL Rankings out of 14):

	1988 (Rk)	1987 (Rk)	1986 (Rk)	1985 (Rk)
Games W/L Pct:	.463(9)	.463(11)	.568(2)	.556(4)
Pitching ERA:	4.32(13)	4.38(7)	3.84(2)	3.91(5)
Batting Ave:	.261(6)	.252(14)	.255(9)	.251(14)
Home Runs:	124(10)	172(11)	167(7)	153(9)
Fielding Pct:	.978(11)	.981(6)	.983(2)	.982(1)
Total Errors:	135(13)	117(7)	107(2)	112(2)
Stolen Bases:	86(12)	125(7)	109(7)	106(8)

First baseman Wally Joyner, 509 hits, 69 homers in 461 games for the disappointing Angels.

SEASON RECORDS SINCE 1969

Year	Position	W	L	Pct	GB/GA	Attendance
1969	Third	71	91	.438	−26	758,388
1970	Third	86	76	.531	−12	1,077,741
1971	Fourth	76	86	.469	−25½	926,373
1972	Fifth	75	80	.484	−18	744,190
1973	Fourth	79	83	.488	−15	1,058,206
1974	Sixth	68	94	.420	−22	917,269
1975	Sixth	72	89	.447	−25½	1,058,163
1976	Fourth	76	86	.469	−14	1,006,774
1977	Fifth	74	88	.457	−28	1,432,633
1978	Second	87	75	.537	−5	1,755,366
1979	First	88	74	.543	+3	2,523,575
1980	Sixth	65	95	.406	−31	2,297,327
1981	Fourth/seventh	51	59	.464		1,441,545
1982	First	93	69	.574	+3	2,807,360
1983	Fifth	70	92	.432	−29	2,555,016
1984	Second	81	81	.500	−3	2,402,997
1985	Second	90	72	.556	−1	2,567,427
1986	First	92	70	.568	+5	2,655,892
1987	Sixth	75	87	.463	−10	2,696,299
1988	Fourth	75	87	463	−29	2,340,865

Outfielder Chili Davis in was traded from the Giants in 1988.

ANAHEIM STADIUM

Location: 2000 State College Boulevard
Cost: $24m
First AL game: 19 April 1966
LA Angels played at Wrigley Field (LA) 1961, and Dodger Stadium 1962–65. There have only been 8 games rained out at Anaheim.
Videoscreen: Sony CRT 26'×35', two black and white 20'×48'
Record crowd: 64,406 (5 October 1982) ALCS v. Mil.
Record season attendance: 2,807,360 (1982)
Other stadium user: NFL Los Angeles Rams
A pitchers park ranked: No. 11 for AL hitters
Ave total runs/game (AL Rk) 1986 & 1987:
At Anaheim 9.18(11), Away 9.60(8)

Weather	Apr.	May	Jun.	Jul.	Aug.	Sept.	Oct.
Temp (deg. C):	17	18	20	22	23	22	20
Rainfall (cm):	3.2	0.2	–	–	–	0.5	0.7
Rainy days:	4	2	1	0	0	1	2

1988 tickets: $3 general, to $8 box
Newspapers: *Long Beach Press Telegram, The Register* (see LA Dodgers NL)
Radio: KMPC 710AM (22stns)
TV: KTLA Ch5 (11stns) (Allan Conin, Ken Brett, Bob Starr, Joe Torre)
LA hotels used by AL clubs: Hyatt (Min), Marriott (NY, Bos), Doubletree (other 10 clubs) (see LA Dodgers NL)

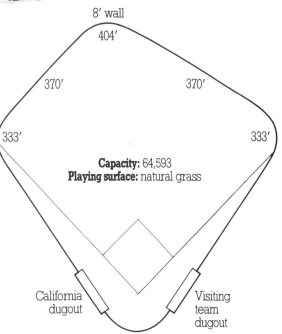

1988 SEASON

Chairman/President: Gene Autry
VP/General Manager/COO: Mike Port
Manager: Cookie Rojas (to 23 September), Doug Rader
1988 Angels Roster: 51% purchased/free agents, 17% acquired by trades, 32% drafted by Angels

1988 Spring Training Sites: Gene Autry Park, Mesa, Arizona, and Angels Stadium, Palm Springs, California (since 1961)
1988 Minor League farm club teams: AAA–Edmonton Trappers (Pac); AA–Midland (T); A–Palm Springs (Cal), Quad City (MW), Bend Bucks (NW)

1988 home games: 21 day, 60 night
1988 away games: 24 day, 57 night
1988 games: 24 on turf, 138 on grass
150 outside, 12 indoors

LEADING ANGELS (1988 REGULAR SEASON):

Batters	AtBats	Runs	Hits	HRs	RBIs	Ave
Johnny Ray	602	75	184	6	83	.306
Bob Boone	352	38	104	5	39	.295
Wally Joyner	597	81	176	13	85	.295
Tony Armas	368	42	100	13	49	.272
Chili Davis	600	81	161	21	93	.268
Devon White	455	76	118	11	51	.259
Jack Howell	500	59	127	16	63	.254
Brian Downing	484	80	117	25	64	.242
Mark McLemore	233	38	56	2	16	.240
Dick Schofield	527	61	126	6	34	.239

Pitchers	W-L	Saves	Inns	BBs	SOs	ERA
Bryan Harvey	7-5	17	76.0	20	67	2.13
Greg Minton	4-5	7	79.0	34	46	2.85
Stewart Cliburn	4-2	0	84.0	32	42	4.07
Doug Corbett	2-1	1	45.2	23	28	4.14
Mike Witt	13-16	0	249.2	87	133	4.15
Chuck Finley	9-15	0	194.1	82	111	4.17
Kirk McCaskill	8-6	0	146.1	61	98	4.31
Dan Petry	3-9	0	139.2	59	64	4.38
Terry Clark	6-6	0	94.0	31	39	5.07
Willie Fraser	12-13	0	194.2	80	86	5.41

Move some stands, replace some turf and Anaheim Stadium becomes home for the NFL Los Angeles Rams.

CALIFORNIA ANGELS 1988 SEASON

Chicago White Sox

AMERICAN LEAGUE WEST DIVISION

Team Colours: Navy blue, red and white
Postal Address: 324 West 35th Street, Chicago, Illinois 60616, USA
Telephone: (312) 924 1000
History of Franchise: Chicago White Sox 1901–
AL Honours: 1901, 06, 17, 19, 59
WS Honours: 1906, 17
Retired Uniforms: 2–Nellie Fox, 4–Luke Appling, 9–Minnie Minoso, 11–Luis Aparicio, 16–Ted Lyons, 19–Billy Pearce

RECENT WHITE SOX TOTALS
(AL Rankings out of 14):

	1988 (Rk)	1987 (Rk)	1986 (Rk)	1985 (Rk)
Games W/L Pct:	.441(11)	.475(10)	.444(12)	.525(5)
Pitching ERA:	4.12(9)	4.30(4)	3.93(3)	4.07(7)
Batting Ave:	.244(13)	.258(13)	.247(14)	.253(10)
Home Runs:	132(9)	173(10)	121(14)	146(10)
Fielding Pct:	.975(14)	.981(6)	.981(4)	.982(1)
Total Errors:	154(14)	116(6)	117(4)	111(1)
Stolen Bases:	98(8)	138(5)	115(5)	108(7)

Relief pitcher Bobby Thigpen, 57 saves in 139 games in three years for the White Sox.

SEASON RECORDS SINCE 1969

Year	Position	W	L	Pct	GB/GA	Attendance
1969	Fifth	68	94	.420	−29	589,546
1970	Sixth	56	106	.346	−42	495,355
1971	Third	79	83	.488	−22½	833,891
1972	Second	87	67	.565	−5½	1,186,018
1973	Fifth	77	85	.475	−17	1,316,527
1974	Fourth	80	80	.500	−9	1,163,596
1975	Fifth	75	86	.466	−22½	770,800
1976	Sixth	64	97	.398	−25½	914,945
1977	Third	90	72	.556	−12	1,657,135
1978	Fifth	71	90	.441	−20½	1,491,100
1979	Fifth	73	87	.456	−14	1,280,702
1980	Fifth	70	90	.438	−26	1,200,365
1981	Third/sixth	54	52	.509		946,651
1982	Third	87	75	.537	−6	1,567,787
1983	First	99	63	.611	+20	2,132,821
1984	Fifth	74	88	.457	−10	2,136,988
1985	Third	85	77	.525	−6	1,669,888
1986	Fifth	72	90	.444	−20	1,424,313
1987	Sixth	75	87	.463	−10	1,208,060
1988	Fifth	71	90	.441	−32½	1,115,525

COMISKEY PARK

Location: 324 West 35th Street
First AL game: 1 July 1910
White Sox played at 39th St Grounds 1900–09, before moving into White Sox Park, now the oldest in the majors. Some 1968–9 home games played at Milwaukee. A $150m stadium will be built to replace Comiskey Park by 1991
Videoscreen: Mitsubishi DiamondVision 1982
Record crowd: 55,555 (20 May 1973) dh v. Minn
Record season attendance: 2,136,988 (1984)
Stadium ranked: No. 2 for AL hitters
Ave total runs/game (AL Rk) 1986 & 1987:
At Chicago 9.16(12), Away 8.35(13)
By tradition Comiskey Park favours pitchers

Weather	Apr.	May	Jun.	Jul.	Aug.	Sept.	Oct.
Temp (deg. C):	10	15	21	24	23	19	13
Rainfall (cm):	9.6	8.6	10.1	10.3	7.9	7.6	6.6
Rainy days:	11	12	11	9	9	9	9

1988 tickets: $4 bleachers, to $10.50 golden box
Newspapers: *Chicago Sun-Times, Daily Herald* (see Cubs, NL)
Radio: WMAQ 670AM (11stns)
TV: WFLD Ch32 (4stns). Cable: SportsVision (Lorn Brown, Del Crandall, John Rooney, Tom Paciorek)
Chicago hotels used by AL clubs: (see Cubs, NL) Hyatt (Cle, Cal, Mil), Palmer House (NY), Westin (other 9 clubs)

First baseman Greg Walker, Chicago, tags out Rickey Henderson in a run-down.

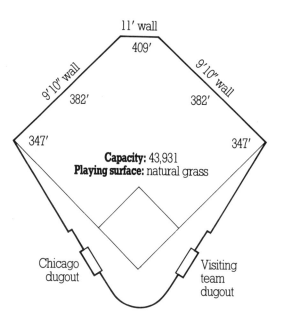

Capacity: 43,931
Playing surface: natural grass

CHICAGO WHITE SOX Comiskey Park

1988 SEASON

Chairman: Jerry Reinsdorf
President: Eddie Einhorn
VP/General Manager: Larry Himes
Manager: Jim Fregosi (to 7 October), Jeff Torborg
1988 White Sox Roster: 16% purchased/free agents, 50% acquired by trades, 34% drafted by White Sox

1988 Spring Training Site: Payne Park, Sarasota, Florida (since 1960) (new Sarasota facility 1989)
1988 Minor League farm club teams: AAA–Vancouver Canadians (Pac); AA–Birmingham Barons (S); A–Tampa Tarpons (FS), South Bend (MW), Utica Blue Sox (NY-P); Rookie–Sarasota (GC)

1988 home games: 19 day, 62 night
1988 away games: 23 day, 58 night
1988 games: 26 on turf, 136 on grass
148 outside, 14 indoors

LEADING WHITE SOX (1988 REGULAR SEASON):

Batters	AtBats	Runs	Hits	HRs	RBIs	Ave
Dave Gallagher	347	59	105	5	31	.303
Harold Baines	599	55	166	13	81	.277
Carlton Fisk	253	37	70	19	50	.277
Steve Lyons	472	59	127	5	45	.269
Ozzie Guillen	566	58	148	0	39	.261
Mark Salas	196	17	49	3	9	.250
Greg Walker	377	45	93	8	42	.247
Fred Manrique	345	43	81	5	37	.235
Dan Pasqua	422	48	96	20	50	.227
Daryl Boston	281	37	61	15	31	.217
Ivan Calderon	264	40	56	14	35	.212

Pitchers	W-L	Saves	Inns	BBs	SOs	ERA
Barry Jones	2-2	1	26.0	17	17	2.42
Shawn Hillegas	3-2	0	40.0	18	26	3.15
Bobby Thigpen	5-8	34	90.0	33	62	3.30
Jerry Reuss	13-9	0	183.0	43	73	3.44
Donn Pall	0-2	0	28.2	8	16	3.45
Melindo Perez	12-10	0	197.0	72	138	3.79
Jack McDowell	5-10	0	158.2	68	84	3.97
Bill Long	8-11	2	174.0	43	77	4.03
Jeff Bittiger	2-4	0	61.2	29	33	4.23
John Davis	2-5	1	63.2	50	37	6.64

Outfielder Harold Baines, nine years with the White Sox.

Kansas City Royals

AMERICAN LEAGUE WEST DIVISION

Team Colours: Royal blue, gold and white
Postal Address: PO Box 419969, Kansas City, Missouri 64141, USA
Telephone: (816) 921 2200
History of Franchise: Kansas City Royals 1969–
AL Honours: 1980, 85
WS Honours: 1985
Retired Uniform: 10–Dick Howser

RECENT ROYALS TOTALS
(AL Rankings out of 14):

	1988 (Rk)	1987 (Rk)	1986 (Rk)	1985 (Rk)
Games W/L Pct:	.522(8)	.512(6)	.469(9)	.562(3)
Pitching ERA:	3.65(3)	3.86(2)	3.82(1)	3.49(2)
Batting Ave:	.259(8)	.262(8)	.252(12)	.252(13)
Home Runs:	121(12)	168(12)	137(12)	154(8)
Fielding Pct:	.979(8)	.979(10)	.980(5)	.980(3)
Total Errors:	124(9)	131(10)	123(7)	127(8)
Stolen Bases:	137(3)	125(7)	97(10)	128(5)

SEASON RECORDS SINCE 1969

Year	Position	W	L	Pct	GB/GA	Attendance
1969	Fourth	69	93	.426	−28	902,183
1970	Fourth	65	97	.401	−33	693,047
1971	Second	85	76	.528	−16	910,784
1972	Fourth	76	78	.494	−16½	707,656
1973	Second	88	74	.543	−6	1,345,341
1974	Fifth	77	85	.475	−13	1,173,292
1975	Second	91	71	.562	−7	1,151,836
1976	First	90	72	.556	+2½	1,680,265
1977	First	102	60	.630	+8	1,852,603
1978	First	92	70	.568	+5	2,255,493
1979	Second	85	77	.525	−3	2,261,845
1980	First	97	65	.599	+14	2,288,714
1981	Fifth/first	50	53	.485		1,279,403
1982	Second	90	72	.556	−3	2,284,464
1983	Second	79	83	.488	−20	1,963,875
1984	First	84	78	.519	+3	1,810,018
1985	First	91	71	.562	+1	2,162,717
1986	Third	76	86	.469	−16	2,320,764
1987	Second	83	79	.512	−2	2,392,471
1988	Third	84	77	.522	−19½	2,350,181

Mark Gubicza was KC's best pitcher in 1988.

Veteran infielder George Brett, 2,399 hits in 2,013 games in 16 years with the Royals.

ROYALS STADIUM

Location: Harry S Truman Sports Complex, Intersection I–70 and Blue Ridge Cutoff
Cost: $70m
First AL game: 10 April 1973
The first AL park to have AstroTurf. Scoreboard screen 40′×60′. Royals previously played at Municipal Stadium. Jackson County has plans to rename the ballpark Kauffman Stadium.
Record crowd: 42,633 (9 October 1980) ALCS v. NYY
Record season attendance: 2,392,471 (1987)
Stadium ranked: No. 6 for AL hitters
Ave total runs/game (AL Rk) 1986 & 1987:
At Kansas City 8.54(14), Away 8.33(14)

Weather	Apr.	May	Jun.	Jul.	Aug.	Sept.	Oct.
Temp (deg. C):	12	18	22	26	25	20	14
Rainfall (cm):	8.8	10.8	14.0	11.1	9.6	10.5	8.1
Rainy days:	11	12	11	9	9	10	7

1988 tickets: $3 general, to $10 box
Newspapers: *KC Star-Times, KC Kansan*
Radio: WMBZ 980AM (110stns)
TV: WDAF Ch4 (Denny Matthews, Fred White, Denny Trease, Paul Splittorff)
KC hotels used by AL clubs: Alameda Plaza (Bos), Westin (Det, NY, Cal, Tex), Adam's Rib (8 others)

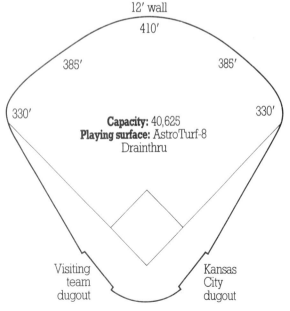

Capacity: 40,625
Playing surface: AstroTurf-8 Drainthru

1988 SEASON

Co-owners: Ewing Kauffman, Avron Fogelman
President: Joe Burke
VP/General Manager: John Schuerholz
Manager: John Watham
1988 Royals Roster: 28% purchased/free agents, 33% acquired by trades, 39% drafted by Royals

1988 Spring Training Site: Boardwalk & Baseball Amusement Park, Baseball City, Orlando, Florida (1988)
1988 Minor League farm club teams: AAA–Omaha (AmA); AA–Memphis Chicks (S); A–Virginia Generals (Car); Baseball City (FS), Appleton Foxes (MW); Rookie–Eugene Emeralds (NW), Boardwalk (GC)

1988 home games: 16 day, 65 night
1988 away games: 26 day, 55 night
1988 games: 99 on turf, 63 on grass
150 outside, 12 indoors

LEADING ROYALS (1988 REGULAR SEASON):

Batters	AtBats	Runs	Hits	HRs	RBIs	Ave
George Brett	589	90	180	24	103	.306
Kevin Seitzer	559	90	170	5	60	.304
Pat Tabler	444	53	125	2	66	.282
Danny Tartabull	507	80	139	26	102	.274
Willie Wilson	591	81	155	1	37	.262
Kurt Stillwell	459	63	115	10	53	.251
Bill Buckner	285	19	71	3	43	.249
Bo Jackson	439	63	108	25	68	.246
Jamie Quirk	196	22	47	8	25	.240
Frank White	537	48	126	8	58	.235

Pitchers	W-L	Saves	Inns	BBs	SOs	ERA
Steve Farr	5-4	20	82.2	30	72	2.50
Mark Gubicza	20-8	0	269.2	83	183	2.70
Charlie Leibrandt	13-12	0	243.0	62	125	3.19
Jeff Montgomery	7-2	1	62.2	30	47	3.45
Jerry Don Gleaton	0-4	3	38.0	17	29	3.55
Bret Saberhagen	14-16	0	260.2	59	171	3.80
Rick Anderson	2-1	0	34.0	9	9	4.24
Floyd Bannister	12-13	0	189.1	68	113	4.33
Israel Sanchez	3-2	1	35.2	18	14	4.54

Outfielder Danny Tartabull, 483 hits in 470 games for Seattle and KC.

84 KANSAS CITY ROYALS 1988 SEASON

Minnesota Twins

AMERICAN LEAGUE WEST DIVISION

Team Colours: Navy blue, scarlet and white
Postal Address: Hubert H. Humphrey Metrodome, 501 Chicago Avenue South, Minneapolis, Minnesota 55415, USA
Telephone: (612) 375 1366
History of Franchise: (First) Washington Senators 1901–60, Minnesota Twins 1961–
AL Honours (since 1961): 1965, 87
WS Honours (since 1961): 1987
Retired Uniforms: 3–Harmon Killebrew, 29–Rod Carew

RECENT TWINS TOTALS
(AL Rankings out of 14):

	1988 (Rk)	1987 (Rk)	1986 (Rk)	1985 (Rk)
Games W/L Pct:	.562(2)	.525(5)	.438(13)	.475(9)
Pitching ERA:	3.93(6)	4.63(10)	4.77(14)	4.48(11)
Batting Ave:	.274(2)	.261(10)	.261(7)	.264(5)
Home Runs:	151(3)	196(5)	196(2)	141(11)
Fielding Pct:	.985(1)	.984(1)	.980(5)	.980(3)
Total Errors:	84(1)	98)1)	118(5)	120(3)
Stolen Bases:	107(6)	113(10)	81(12)	68(13)

Dutch-born Bert Blyleven, 19 years with the Twins, Rangers, Pirates and Indians, was traded to California for 1989.

SEASON RECORDS SINCE 1969

Year	Position	W	L	Pct	GB/GA	Attendance
1969	First	97	65	.599	+9	1,349,328
1970	First	98	64	.605	+9	1,261,887
1971	Fifth	74	86	.463	−26½	940,858
1972	Third	77	77	.500	−15½	797,901
1973	Third	81	81	.500	−13	907,499
1974	Third	82	80	.506	−8	662,401
1975	Fourth	76	83	.478	−20½	737,156
1976	Third	85	77	.525	−5	715,394
1977	Fourth	84	77	.522	−17½	1,162,727
1978	Fourth	73	89	.451	−19	787,878
1979	Fourth	82	80	.506	−6	1,070,521
1980	Third	77	84	.478	−19½	769,206
1981	Seventh/fourth	41	68	.376		469,090
1982	Seventh	60	102	.370	−33	921,186
1983	Fifth	70	92	.432	−29	858,939
1984	Second	81	81	.500	−3	1,598,692
1985	Fourth	77	85	.475	−14	1,651,814
1986	Sixth	71	91	.438	−21	1,255,453
1987	First	85	77	.525	+2	2,081,976
1988	Second	91	71	.562	−13	3,030,672

Jeff Reardon, 235 saves in 10 years with the Mets, Expos and Twins.

HUBERT H. HUMPHREY METRODOME

Location: 501 Chicago Avenue, near junction of Interstate highways 94 and 35 West
Cost: $55m
First AL game: 6 April 1982
The roof is two layers of teflon-coated fibreglass, 186ft above the AstroTurf.
The Twins previously played at Metropolitan Stadium, Bloomington.
Record crowd: 55,376 (25 October 1987) WS v. St L.
Record season attendance: 3,030,672 (1988)
Other stadium users: NFL Minnesota Vikings, NCAA Minnesota Golden Gophers
Stadium ranked: No. 3 AL hitters park
Ave total runs/game (AL Rk) 1986 & 1987:
At Metrodome 10.02(3), Away 9.55(10)
Weather April–October outside Metrodome
7–22 degrees C; 4.5–9.8cm rainfall
1988 tickets: $3 general, to $10 reserve
Newspapers: *Minnesota Star-Tribune, St Paul Pioneer Press-Dispatch*
Radio: WCCO 830AM
TV: KMSP Ch9 (Jim Kaat, Herb Carneal, John Gordon, Ted Robinson)
Minneapolis hotels used by AL clubs: Hyatt (Det, Bos, Cal, Tor, KC, Oak), Marriott (Cle, Chi, Mil, Bal, Sea, Tex), Crowne Plaza (NY)

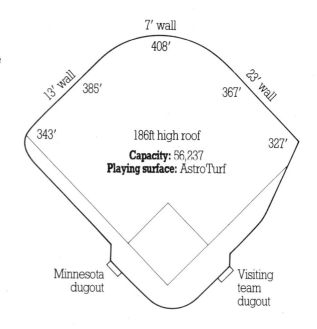

1988 SEASON

Owner: Carl Pohlad
President: Jerry Bell
VP Baseball Operations: Andy MacPhail
Manager: Tom Kelly
1988 Twins Roster: 41% purchased/free agents, 41% acquired by trades, 18% drafted by Twins

1988 Spring Training Site: Tinker Field, Orlando, Florida (since 1936)
1988 Minor League farm club teams: AAA–Portland Beavers (Pac); AA–Orlando (S); A–Vistula Oaks (Cal), Kenosha (MW); Rookie–Elizabethton (Ap)

1988 home games: 25 day, 56 night
1988 away games: 26 day, 55 night
1988 games: 99 on turf, 63 on grass
74 outside, 88 indoors

LEADING TWINS (1988 REGULAR SEASON):

Batters	AtBats	Runs	Hits	HRs	RBIs	Ave
Kirby Puckett	657	109	234	24	121	.356
John Moses	206	33	65	2	12	.316
Kent Hrbek	510	75	159	25	76	.312
Gary Gaetti	468	66	141	28	88	.301
Dan Gladden	576	91	155	11	62	.269
Gene Larkin	505	56	135	8	70	.267
Tommy Herr	304	42	80	1	21	.263
Randy Bush	394	51	103	14	51	.263
Tim Laudner	375	38	94	13	54	.251
Greg Gagne	461	70	109	14	48	.236
Steve Lombardozzi	287	34	60	3	27	.209

Pitchers	W-L	Saves	Inns	BBs	SOs	ERA
Alan Anderson	16-9	0	202.1	37	83	2.45
Jeff Reardon	2-4	42	73.0	15	56	2.47
Frank Viola	24-7	0	255.1	54	193	2.64
Keith Atherton	7-5	3	74.0	22	43	3.41
Les Straker	2-5	1	82.2	25	23	3.92
Juan Berenguer	8-4	2	100.0	61	99	3.96
Fred Toliver	7-6	0	114.2	52	69	4.24
Mark Portugal	3-3	3	57.2	17	31	4.53
Charlie Lea	7-7	0	130.0	50	72	4.85
Bert Blyleven	10-17	0	207.1	51	145	5.43

The noisy HHH Metrodome during the 1987 World Series.

Oakland Athletics

AMERICAN LEAGUE WEST DIVISION

Team Colours: Green, gold and white
Postal Address: Oakland-Alameda County Coliseum, PO Box 2220, Oakland, California 94621, USA
Telephone: (415) 638 4900
History of Franchise: Philadelphia Athletics 1901–54, Kansas City Athletics 1955–67, Oakland A's/Athletics 1968–
AL Honours (since 1968): 1972, 73, 74, 88
WS Honours (since 1968): 1972, 73, 74

RECENT ATHLETICS TOTALS
(AL Rankings out of 14):

	1988 (Rk)	1987 (Rk)	1986 (Rk)	1985 (Rk)
Games W/L Pct:	.642(1)	.500(7)	.469(9)	.475(9)
Pitching ERA:	3.44(1)	4.32(5)	4.31(11)	4.39(9)
Batting Ave:	.263(4)	.260(11)	.252(12)	.264(5)
Home Runs:	156(2)	199(4)	163(8)	155(7)
Fielding Pct:	.983(3)	.977(10)	.978(10)	.977(10)
Total Errors:	105(3)	142(11)	135(10)	140(10)
Stolen Bases:	129(5)	140(3)	139(2)	117(6)

In 10 years as a manager Tony LaRussa's hard hitting White Sox and Oakland teams have won 752 and lost 683.

SEASON RECORDS SINCE 1969

Year	Position	W	L	Pct	GB/GA	Attendance
1969	Second	88	74	.543	−9	778,232
1970	Second	89	73	.549	−9	778,355
1971	First	101	60	.627	+16	914,993
1972	First	93	62	.600	+5½	921,323
1973	First	94	68	.580	+6	1,000,763
1974	First	90	72	.556	+5	845,693
1975	First	98	64	.605	+7	1,075,518
1976	Second	87	74	.540	−2½	780,593
1977	Seventh	63	98	.391	−38½	495,412
1978	Sixth	69	93	.426	−23	526,999
1979	Seventh	54	108	.333	−34	306,763
1980	Second	83	79	.512	−14	842,259
1981	First/second	64	45	.587		1,311,761
1982	Fifth	68	94	.420	−25	1,735,489
1983	Fourth	74	88	.457	−25	1,294,941
1984	Fourth	77	85	.475	−7	1,353,231
1985	Fourth	77	85	.475	−14	1,334,609
1986	Third	76	86	.469	−16	1,314,646
1987	Third	81	81	.500	−4	1,678,921
1988	First	104	58	.642	+13	2,287,335

Second baseman Glenn Hubbard, 11 years at Atlanta and Oakland.

OAKLAND-ALAMEDA COUNTY COLISEUM

Location: Nimitz Freeway and Hegenberger Road
First AL game: 17 April 1968
The free hitting Athletics play in a stadium notorious for its poor sight lines and strong outfield winds.
Videoscreen: Mitsubishi DiamondVision
Record crowd: 49,437 (17 October 1974) WS v. LA
Record season attendance: 2,287,335 (1988)
A pitchers park ranked: No. 14 for AL hitters
Ave total runs/game (AL Rk) 1986 & 1987:
At Oakland 8.80(13), Away 10.25(1)

Weather	Apr.	May	Jun.	Jul.	Aug.	Sept.	Oct.
Temp (deg. C):	13	14	16	17	17	18	16
Rainfall (cm):	4.0	1.0	0.2	–	–	0.5	0.2
Rainy days:	6	4	2	0	0	2	4

1988 tickets: $3 bleachers, to $9 box
Newspapers: *San Francisco Examiner, San Jose Mercury-News* (see SF Giants, NL)
Radio: KSFO 560AM
TV: XPIX Ch5 (8stns) (Bill King, Lou Simmons, Ray Fosse, Monte Moore, Sylvester Jackson)
Oakland hotels used by AL clubs: Hilton (Tor, NY), Hyatt (11 others) (see Giants)

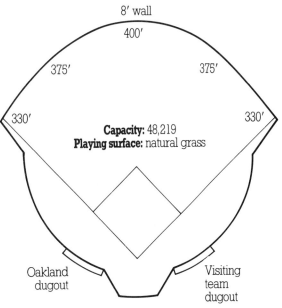

Capacity: 48,219
Playing surface: natural grass

1988 SEASON

Chairman/Owner/General Partner: Walter A. Haas Jr
Executive VP: Roy Eisenhardt
VP Baseball Operations: Sandy Alderson
Manager: Tony LaRussa
1988 Athletics Roster: 27% purchased/free agents, 34% acquired by trades, 39% drafted by Athletics

1988 Spring Training Site: Phoenix Stadium, Phoenix, Arizona
1988 Minor League farm club teams: AAA–Tacoma Tigers (Pac); AA–Huntsville Stars (S); A–Modesta (Cal), Madison Muskies (MW), Medford (NW)

1988 home games: 40 day, 41 night
1988 away games: 25 day, 56 night
1988 games: 25 on turf, 137 on grass
150 outside, 12 indoors

LEADING ATHLETICS (1988 REGULAR SEASON):

Batters	AtBats	Runs	Hits	HRs	RBIs	Ave
Jose Canseco	610	120	187	42	124	.307
Dave Henderson	507	100	154	24	94	.304
Luis Polonia	288	51	84	2	27	.292
Carney Lansford	556	80	155	7	57	.279
Terry Steinbach	351	42	93	9	51	.265
Mark McGwire	550	87	143	32	99	.260
Dave Parker	377	43	97	12	55	.257
Ron Hassey	323	32	83	7	45	.257
Stan Javier	397	49	102	2	35	.257
Glenn Hubbard	294	35	75	3	33	.255
Walt Weiss	452	44	113	3	39	.250
Don Baylor	264	28	58	7	34	.220

Pitchers	W-L	Saves	Inns	BBs	SOs	ERA
Dennis Eckersley	4-2	45	72.2	11	70	2.35
Greg Cadaret	5-2	3	71.2	36	65	2.89
Eric Plunk	7-2	5	78.0	39	79	3.00
Gene Nelson	9-6	3	111.2	38	67	3.06
Todd Burns	8-2	1	102.2	34	57	3.16
Dave Stewart	21-12	0	275.2	110	192	3.23
Rick Honeycutt	3-2	7	79.2	25	47	3.50
Bob Welch	17-9	0	244.2	81	158	3.64
Storm Davis	16-7	0	201.2	91	127	3.70
Curt Young	11-8	0	156.1	50	69	4.14

Pitcher Bob Welch was traded from the Dodgers in 1988.

Seattle Mariners

AMERICAN LEAGUE WEST DIVISION

Team Colours: Mariner blue, gold and white
Postal Address: PO Box 4100, 411 First Avenue South, Seattle, Washington 98104, USA
Telephone: (206) 628 3555
History of Franchise: Seattle Mariners 1977–
Honours: Yet to win AL or World Series

Outfielder Mickey Brantley, 258 hits in 268 games for Seattle.

SEASON RECORDS SINCE 1977

Year	Position	W	L	Pct	GB/GA	Attendance
1977	Sixth	64	98	.395	−38	1,338,511
1978	Seventh	56	104	.350	−35	877,440
1979	Sixth	67	95	.414	−21	844,455
1980	Seventh	59	103	.364	−38	836,204
1981	Sixth/fifth	44	65	.404		636,276
1982	Fourth	76	86	.469	−17	1,070,404
1983	Seventh	60	102	.370	−39	813,537
1984	Fifth	74	88	.457	−10	870,372
1985	Sixth	74	88	.457	−17	1,128,696
1986	Seventh	67	95	.414	−25	1,029,045
1987	Fourth	78	84	.481	−7	1,134,255
1988	Seventh	68	93	.422	−35½	1,020,354

RECENT MARINERS TOTALS
(AL Rankings out of 14):

	1988 (Rk)	1987 (Rk)	1986 (Rk)	1985 (Rk)
Games W/L Pct:	.422(13)	.481(8)	.414(14)	.457(11)
Pitching ERA:	4.15(10)	4.49(8)	4.65(13)	4.68(13)
Batting Ave:	.257(9)	.272(3)	.253(11)	.255(9)
Home Runs:	148(4)	161(14)	158(9)	171(4)
Fielding Pct:	.979(8)	.980(8)	.975(13)	.980(3)
Total Errors:	123(8)	122(8)	156(13)	122(5)
Stolen Bases:	95(10)	174(2)	93(11)	94(9)

THE KINGDOME

Location: 201 King Street
Cost: $67m
First AL game: 6 April 1977
The King County Domed Stadium has a 133½ft high roof. The original AstroTurf was replaced in 1983.
Videoscreen: $3.2m 24′×36′ DiamondVision 1981
Record crowd: 57,762 (6 April 1977) v. Cal. 58,905 for 1979 All-Star Game
Record season attendance: 1,338,511 (1977)
Other stadium user: NFL Seattle Seahawks
Stadium ranked: No. 1 AL hitters park
Ave total runs/game (AL Rk) 1986 & 1987: At Kingdome 10.12(2), Away 9.10(12)
Weather April–October outside Kingdome 9–19 degrees C; 1.8–9.8cm rainfall
1988 tickets: $3.50 admission, to $9.50 box
Newspapers: *Seattle Times*, *Seattle Post*
Radio: KIRO 710AM (23stns)
TV: KIRO Ch7, KTZZ Ch22 (Dave Niehaus, Rick Rizzs, Joe Simpson)
Seattle hotels used by AL clubs: Sheraton (Bos), Crowne Plaza (Det, Cle, Cal, Chi, Oak, Tex, Mil), Warwick (Tor), Westin (Bal, NY, Min, KC)

Pitcher Mark Langston would be a Cy Young Award contender with a better team around him.

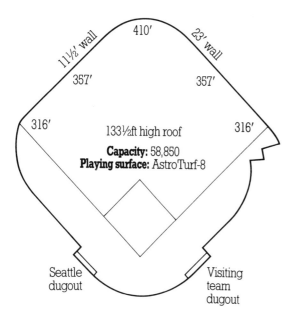

92 SEATTLE MARINERS THE KINGDOME

1988 SEASON

Owner: George Argyros
President: Chuck Armstrong
VP Baseball Operations: Dick Balderston (to July), Woody Woodward
Manager: Dick Williams (to 6 June), Jim Snyder (to 6 October), Jim Lefebre
1988 Mariners Roster: 18% purchased/free agents, 37% acquired by trades, 45% drafted by Mariners

1988 Spring Training Site: Diablo Stadium, Tempe, Arizona (since 1977)
1988 Minor League farm club teams: AAA–Calgary Cannons (Pac); AA–Burlington (E); A–San Bernardino Spirit (Cal), Wausau Timbers (MW); Rookie–Bellingham (NW)

1988 home games: 20 day, 61 night
1988 away games: 21 day, 60 night
1988 games: 99 on turf, 63 on grass
75 outside, 87 indoors

LEADING MARINERS (1988 REGULAR SEASON):

Batters	AtBats	Runs	Hits	HRs	RBIs	Ave
Mario Davis	478	67	141	18	69	.295
Darnell Coles	195	32	57	10	34	.292
Harold Reynolds	598	61	169	4	41	.283
Mickey Brantley	577	76	152	15	56	.263
Henry Cotto	386	50	100	8	33	.259
Scott Bradley	335	45	86	4	33	.257
Rey Quinones	499	63	124	12	52	.248
Steve Balboni	413	46	97	23	66	.235
David Valle	290	29	67	10	50	.231
Jim Presley	544	50	125	14	62	.230
Jay Buhner	261	36	56	13	38	.215

Pitchers	W-L	Saves	Inns	BBs	SOs	ERA
Mike Jackson	6-5	4	99.1	43	76	2.63
Scott Bankhead	7-9	0	135.0	38	102	3.07
Mark Langston	15-11	0	261.1	110	235	3.34
Bill Wilkinson	2-2	2	31.0	15	25	3.48
Mike Schooler	5-8	15	48.1	24	54	3.54
Mike Moore	9-15	1	228.2	63	182	3.78
Jerry Reed	1-1	1	86.1	33	48	3.96
Bill Swift	8-12	0	174.2	65	47	4.59
Mike Campbell	6-10	0	114.2	43	63	5.89
Steve Trout	4-7	0	56.1	31	14	7.83

Infielder Jim Presley, 103 home runs in 682 games in five years with the Mariners.

Texas Rangers

AMERICAN LEAGUE WEST DIVISION

Team Colours: Blue, red and white
Postal Address: PO Box 1111, Arlington, Texas 76010, USA
Telephone: (817) 273 5222
History of Franchise: (Second) Washington Senators 1961–71, Texas Rangers 1972–
Honours (since 1972): Yet to win AL or World Series

RECENT RANGERS TOTALS
(AL Rankings out of 14):

	1988 (Rk)	1987 (Rk)	1986 (Rk)	1985 (Rk)
Games W/L Pct:	.435(12)	.463(11)	.537(4)	.385(13)
Pitching ERA:	4.05(8)	4.63(10)	4.11(8)	4.56(12)
Batting Ave:	.252(11)	.266(6)	.267(5)	.253(10)
Home Runs:	112(14)	194(7)	184(4)	129(12)
Fielding Pct:	.978(11)	.976(12)	.980(5)	.980(3)
Total Errors:	131(11)	151(13)	122(6)	120(3)
Stolen Bases:	130(4)	120(9)	103(8)	130(4)

Outfielder Ruben Sierra, 426 hits in 427 games with Texas.

SEASON RECORDS SINCE 1969

Year	Position	W	L	Pct	GB/GA	Attendance
Washington (East Division)						
1969	Fourth	86	76	.531	−23	918,106
1970	Sixth	70	92	.432	−38	824,789
1971	Fifth	63	96	.396	−38½	655,156
Texas (West Division)						
1972	Sixth	54	100	.351	−38½	662,974
1973	Sixth	57	105	.352	−37	686,085
1974	Second	84	76	.525	−5	1,193,902
1975	Third	79	83	.488	−19	1,127,924
1976	Fourth	76	86	.469	−14	1,164,982
1977	Second	94	68	.580	−8	1,250,721
1978	Second	87	75	.537	−5	1,447,963
1979	Third	83	79	.512	−5	1,519,654
1980	Fourth	76	85	.472	−20½	1,198,175
1981	Second/third	57	48	.543		850,076
1982	Sixth	64	98	.395	−29	1,154,432
1983	Third	77	85	.475	−22	1,363,469
1984	Seventh	69	92	.429	−14½	1,102,471
1985	Seventh	62	99	.385	−28½	1,112,497
1986	Second	87	75	.537	−5	1,692,021
1987	Sixth	75	87	.463	−10	1,763,053
1988	Sixth	70	91	.435	−33½	1,581,901

Outfielder Pete Incaviglia, 79 home runs in 408 games with the Rangers.

ARLINGTON STADIUM

Location: 1500 Copeland Road
First AL game: 21 April 1972
Built 1964 for (AA) Dallas-Fort Worth Spurs. The expansions and renovations carried out in 1972, 1978, 1984 have reduced the effects of the strong, hot Texas winds.
Videoscreen: Mitsubishi DiamondVision
Record crowd: 43,705 (23 July 1983) v. Tor.
Record season attendance: 1,763,053 (1987)
Stadium ranked neutral: No. 7 AL hitters park
Ave total runs/game (AL Rk) 1986 & 1987:
At Texas 9.81(4), Away 9.85(6)

Weather	Apr.	May	Jun.	Jul.	Aug.	Sept.	Oct.
Temp (deg. C):	18	23	27	29	29	26	20
Rainfall (cm):	10.8	11.3	7.9	4.5	5.8	8.1	6.8
Rainy days:	9	9	7	5	6	6	7

1988 tickets: $2 general, to $10 box
Newspapers: *Fort Worth Star-Telegram, Dallas Morning News, Dallas Times Herald*
Radio: WBAP 820AM (14stns)
TV: KTVT Ch11. Cable: HSE (Mark Holtz, Eric Nadel, Bob Carpenter, Steve Busby)
Texas hotels used by AL clubs: Arlington Hilton (NY, Mil), Sheraton (11 others)

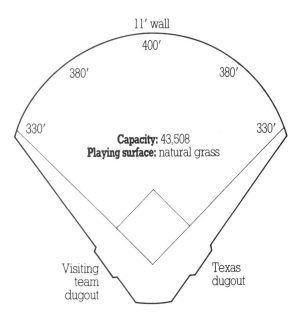

1988 SEASON

Chairman: Eddie Chiles (to September), Edward Gaylord
President/COO: Mike Stone
General Manager: Tom Grieve
Manager: Bobby Valentine
1988 Rangers Roster: 26% purchased/free agents, 26% acquired by trades, 48% drafted by Rangers

1988 Spring Training Site: Rangers Complex, Charlotte Co. Stadium, Port Charlotte, Florida (1987)
1988 Minor League farm club teams: AAA–Oklahoma City 89ers (AmA); AA–Tulsa Drillers (T); A–Charlotte (FS), Gastonia (SA); Rookie–Gulf Coast (GC), Butte Copper Kings (P)

1988 home games: 8 day, 73 night
1988 away games: 28 day, 53 night
1988 games: 26 on turf, 136 on grass
148 outside, 14 indoors

LEADING RANGERS (1988 REGULAR SEASON):

Batters	AtBats	Runs	Hits	HRs	RBIs	Ave
Curtis Wilkerson	338	41	99	0	28	.293
Geno Petralli	351	35	99	7	36	.282
Scott Fletcher	515	59	142	0	47	.276
Pete O'Brien	547	57	149	16	71	.272
Ruben Sierra	615	77	156	23	91	.254
Steve Buechele	503	68	126	16	58	.250
Pete Incaviglia	418	59	104	22	54	.249
Cecil Espy	347	46	86	2	39	.248
Oddibe McDowell	437	55	108	6	37	.247
Mike Stanley	249	21	57	3	27	.229

Pitchers	W-L	Saves	Inns	BBs	SOs	ERA
Craig McMurtry	3-3	3	60.0	24	35	2.25
Cecilio Guante	5-6	12	79.2	26	65	2.82
Charlie Hough	15-16	0	252.0	126	174	3.32
Jose Guzman	11-13	0	206.2	82	157	3.70
Jeff Russell	10-9	0	188.2	66	88	3.82
Bobby Witt	8-10	0	174.1	101	148	3.92
Ed Vande Berg	2-2	2	37.0	11	18	4.14
Paul Kilgus	12-15	0	203.1	71	88	4.16
Mitch Williams	2-7	18	68.0	47	61	4.63
Ray Hayward	4-6	0	62.2	35	37	5.46

There were only eight day games under the grilling Texas sun at Arlington Stadium in 1988.

American League Statistics

AMERICAN LEAGUE PENNANT WINNERS

Year	Club	W	L	Pct	GA	AL Total Attendance
1901	Chicago	83	53	.610	4	1,683,584
1902	Philadelphia	83	53	.610	5	2,206,454
1903	Boston	91	47	.659	14½	2,344,888
1904	Boston	95	59	.617	1½	3,024,028
1905	Philadelphia	92	56	.622	2	3,120,752
1906	Chicago	93	58	.616	3	2,938,076
1907	Detroit	92	58	.613	1½	3,398,764
1908	Detroit	90	63	.588	½	3,611,366
1909	Detroit	98	54	.645	3½	3,739,570
1910	Philadelphia	102	48	.680	14½	3,270,689
1911	Philadelphia	101	50	.669	13½	3,339,514
1912	Boston	105	47	.691	14	3,263,631
1913	Philadelphia	96	57	.627	6½	3,526,805
1914	Philadelphia	99	53	.651	8½	2,747,591
1915	Boston	101	50	.669	2½	2,434,684
1916	Boston	91	63	.591	2	3,451,885
1917	Chicago	100	54	.649	9	2,858,858
1918	Boston	75	51	.595	2½	1,707,999
1919	Chicago	88	52	.629	3½	3,654,236
1920	Cleveland	98	56	.636	2	5,084,300
1921	New York	98	55	.641	4½	4,620,328
1922	New York	94	60	.610	1	4,874,355
1923	New York	98	54	.645	16	4,602,589
1924	Washington	92	62	.597	2	5,255,439
1925	Washington	96	55	.636	8½	5,186,851
1926	New York	91	63	.591	3	4,912,583
1927	New York	110	44	.714	19	4,612,951
1928	New York	101	53	.656	2½	4,221,188
1929	Philadelphia	104	46	.693	18	4,662,470
1930	Philadelphia	102	52	.662	8	4,685,730
1931	Philadelphia	107	45	.704	13½	3,883,292
1932	New York	107	47	.695	13	3,133,232
1933	Washington	99	53	.651	7	2,926,210
1934	Detroit	101	53	.656	7	2,763,606
1935	Detroit	93	58	.616	3	3,688,007
1936	New York	102	51	.667	19½	4,178,922
1937	New York	102	52	.662	13	4,735,835
1938	New York	99	53	.651	9½	4,445,684
1939	New York	106	45	.702	17	4,270,602
1940	Detroit	90	64	.584	1	5,433,791
1941	New York	101	53	.656	17	4,911,956
1942	New York	103	51	.669	9	4,200,216
1943	New York	98	56	.636	13½	3,696,559
1944	St Louis	89	65	.578	1	4,798,158
1945	Detroit	88	65	.575	1½	5,580,420
1946	Boston	104	50	.675	12	9,621,182
1947	New York	97	57	.630	12	9,486,069
1948	a) Cleveland	97	58	.626	1	11,150,099
1949	New York	97	57	.630	1	10,730,647
1950	New York	98	56	.636	3	9,142,361
1951	New York	98	56	.636	5	8,882,674
1952	New York	95	59	.617	2	8,293,896
1953	New York	99	52	.656	8½	6,964,076
1954	Cleveland	111	43	.721	8	7,922,364
1955	New York	96	58	.623	3	8,942,971
1956	New York	97	57	.630	9	7,893,683
1957	New York	98	56	.636	8	8,196,218
1958	New York	92	62	.597	10	7,296,034
1959	Chicago	94	60	.610	5	9,149,454
1960	New York	97	57	.630	8	9,226,526
1961	New York	109	53	.673	8	10,163,016
1962	New York	96	66	.593	5	10,015,056
1963	New York	104	57	.646	10½	9,094,487
1964	New York	99	63	.611	1	9,235,151
1965	Minnesota	102	60	.630	7	8,860,764
1966	Baltimore	97	63	.606	9	10,166,738
1967	Boston	92	70	.568	1	11,336,923
1968	Detroit	103	59	.636	12	11,317,387
1969	Baltimore (E)	109	53	.673	19	12,134,745
1970	Baltimore (E)	108	54	.667	15	12,085,135
1971	Baltimore (E)	101	57	.639	12	11,868,560
1972	Oakland (W)	93	62	.600	5½	11,438,538
1973	Oakland (W)	94	68	.580	6	13,433,604
1974	Oakland (W)	90	72	.556	5	13,047,294
1975	Boston (E)	95	65	.594	4½	13,189,423
1976	New York (E)	97	62	.610	10½	14,657,802
1977	New York (E)	100	62	.617	2½	19,639,551
1978	b) New York (E)	100	63	.613	1	20,529,965
1979	Baltimore (E)	102	57	.642	8	22,371,979
1980	Kansas City (W)	97	65	.599	14	21,890,052
1981	c) New York (E)	59	48	.551	—	14,065,986
1982	Milwaukee (E)	95	67	.586	1	23,080,449
1983	Baltimore (E)	98	64	.605	6	23,991,053
1984	Detroit (E)	104	58	.642	15	23,961,427
1985	Kansas City (W)	91	71	.562	1	24,532,225
1986	Boston (E)	95	66	.590	5½	25,172,732
1987	Minnesota (W)	85	77	.525	2	27,277,351
1988	Oakland (W)	104	58	.642	13	28,497,310

GA: Games ahead of second-place club. a) Defeated Boston in one-game playoff. b) Defeated Boston in one-game playoff to win division. c) First half 34–22; second 25–26 of strike-hit season.

Shortstop Cal Ripken Jr., 1,236 hits, 183 homers with the Orioles. He has a streak of 1,088 consecutive games.

AL REGULAR SEASON RECORDS SINCE 1900

TEAM RECORDS
Most wins: 111 Cleveland 1954
Most defeats: 117 Philadelphia 1916
Earliest West Division win: 15 September 1971
Earliest East Division win: 13 September 1969
Highest winning percentage (since 1969): .673 Baltimore 1969
Lowest winning percentage (since 1969): .525 Minnesota 1987
Finished most games ahead: 20 Chicago 1983
Finished most games behind: 50½ Toronto 1979
Most innings: 25 Chicago 7–6 Milwaukee 1984
Longest time: 8hrs 6mins, Chicago-Milwaukee 1984
Shortest time: 55mins, St Louis 6–2 NY 1926
Most runs scored by one team: 29 Boston v. St Louis 1950
Most runs scored by both teams: 36 Boston 22–14 Philadelphia 1950
Consecutive wins: 19 Chicago 1906 (1 tie), and New York 1947
Consecutive defeats: 21 Baltimore 1988
Most players used in a season: 56 Philadelphia 1915
Fewest players used in a season: 18 Boston 1905
Largest attendance: 84,587 Cleveland–New York 1954
Largest home season attendance: 3,030,672 Minnesota 1988
Best AL attendance: 28,497,310 in 1988
First AL game: 24 April 1901 Chicago-Cleveland
First night game: 16 May 1939 Cleveland-Philadelphia

PLAYER GAME RECORDS
Most at bats: 11 (by 8 players)
Runs: 6 John Pesky, Boston 1946, Spike Owen, Boston 1986
Hits: 9 John Burnett, Cleveland 1932
RBIs: 11 Tony Lazzeri, NY 1936
Home runs: 4 Lou Gehrig, NY 1932, Pat Seerey, Chicago 1948, Rocco Colavito, Cleveland 1959
Stolen bases: 6 Eddie Collins, Philadelphia 1912 (twice)
Innings pitched: 24 Joe Harris, Boston, and John Coombs, Philadelphia (Philadelphia 4–1 Boston), 15 September 1906
Strikeouts: 20 Roger Clemens, Boston 1986
Consecutive strikeouts: 8 Nolan Ryan, California 1972 and 1973, Ron Davis, NY 1981, Roger Clemens, Boston 1986
Youngest player: 16yrs 8m 5d Carl Scheib, Philadelphia 1943
Oldest player: 59yrs 2m 18d LeRoy Paige, KC 1965

PLAYER SEASON RECORDS
Best batting average: .422 Napoleon Lajoie, Philadelphia 1901
At Bats: 705 Willie Wilson, KC 1980
Runs: 177 Babe Ruth, NY 1921
Hits: 257 George Sisler, St Louis 1920
RBIs: 184 Lou Gehrig, NY 1931
Home runs: 61 Roger Maris, NY 1961
Grand Slam homers: 6 Don Mattingly, NY 1987
Consecutive games batted safely: 56 Joe DiMaggio, NY 15 May–16 July 1941
Most recent .400 hitter: .406 Ted Williams, Boston 1941
Hit by pitcher: 35 Don Baylor, Boston 1986
Stolen bases: 130 Rickey Henderson, Oakland 1982
Caught stealing: 42 Rickey Henderson, Oakland 1982
Games pitched: 90 Mike Marshall, Minnesota 1979
Innings pitched: 464 Ed Walsh, Chicago 1908
Wins by RH pitcher: 41 John Chesbro, NY 1904
Wins by LH pitcher: 31 Bob Grove, Philadelphia 1931
Most losses: 26 John Townsend, Washington 1904, Robert Groom, Washington 1909
Most strikeouts: 383 Nolan Ryan, California 1973
Lowest ERA (+300 Inns): 1.14 Walter Johnson, Washington 1913
Most games saved: 46 Dave Righetti, NY 1986

Consecutive games won: 17 John Allen, Cleveland 1936, Dave McNally, Baltimore 1968
Consecutive games lost: 19 Robert Groom, Washington 1909, John Nabors, Philadelphia 1916

PLAYER CAREER RECORDS
Seasons as player: 25 Eddie Collins 1906–30
Most years with one club: 23 Brooks Robinson, Baltimore, Carl Yastrzemski, Boston
Games: 3,308 Carl Yastrzemski, Boston 1961–83
Consecutive games: 2,130 Lou Gehrig, NY 1925–39
Best batting average (+15yrs): .367 Ty Cobb 1905–28
At Bats: 11,988 Carl Yastrzemski, Boston
Runs: 2,245 Ty Cobb, Detroit/Philadelphia
Hits: 4,191 Ty Cobb, Detroit/Philadelphia
RBIs: 2,192 Babe Ruth, Boston/New York
Home runs: 708 Babe Ruth (Boston 49, NY 659)
Grand Slam homers: 23 Lou Gehrig, NY
Hit by pitcher: 267 Don Baylor 1970–88
Stolen bases: 892 Ty Cobb 1905–28
Caught stealing: 199 Bert Campaneris 1964–81/83
Most years pitched: 23 Early Wynn 1939/41–63
Games pitched: 807 Sparky Lyle 1967–80/82
Innings pitched: 5,924 Walter Johnson 1907–27
Wins by RH pitcher: 416 Walter Johnson
Wins by LH pitcher: 305 Ed Plank 1901–14/16–17
Most losses: 279 Walter Johnson
Most strikeouts: 3,508 Walter Johnson
Lowest ERA (+300 wins): 2.47 Walter Johnson
Games saved: 237 Dan Quisenberry 1979–88
Years a manager: 50 Connie Mack 1901–50
Years an umpire: 31 Tom Connolly 1901–31 (he also umpired in NL 1898–1900)

Bob Boone holds the Major League and American League records for most games as a catcher.

AL MOST VALUABLE PLAYERS 1911–1988

1911 Ty Cobb, Detroit (OF)	**1945** Hal Newhouser, Detroit (P)	**1970** Boog Powell, Baltimore (1B)
1912 Tris Speaker, Boston (OF)	**1946** Ted Williams, Boston (OF)	**1971** Vida Blue, Oakland (P)
1913 Walter Johnson, Washington (P)	**1947** Joe DiMaggio, New York (OF)	**1972** Richie Allen, Chicago (1B)
1914 Eddie Collins, Philadelphia (2B)	**1948** Lou Boudreau, Cleveland (SS)	**1973** Reggie Jackson, Oakland (OF)
1922 George Sisler, St Louis (1B)	**1949** Ted Williams, Boston (OF)	**1974** Jeff Burroughs, Texas (OF)
1923 Babe Ruth, New York (OF)	**1950** Phil Rizzuto, New York (SS)	**1975** Fred Lynn, Boston (OF)
1924 Walter Johnson, Washington (P)	**1951** Yogi Berra, New York (C)	**1976** Thurman Munson, New York (C)
1925 Roger Peckinpaugh, Washington (SS)	**1952** Bobby Shantz, Philadelphia (P)	**1977** Rod Carew, Minnesota (1B)
1926 George Burns, Cleveland (1B)	**1953** Al Rosen, Cleveland (3B)	**1978** Jim Rice, Boston (OF)
1927 Lou Gehrig, New York (1B)	**1954** Yogi Berra, New York (C)	**1979** Don Baylor, California (DH)
1928 Mickey Cochrane, Philadelphia (C)	**1955** Yogi Berra, New York (C)	**1980** George Brett, Kansas City (3B)
1931 Lefty Grove, Philadelphia (P)	**1956** Mickey Mantle, New York (OF)	**1981** Rollie Fingers, Milwaukee (P)
1932 Jimmie Foxx, Philadelphia (1B)	**1957** Mickey Mantle, New York (OF)	**1982** Robin Yount, Milwaukee (SS)
1933 Jimmie Foxx, Philadelphia (1B)	**1958** Jackie Jensen, Boston (OF)	**1983** Cal Ripken, Baltimore (SS)
1934 Mickey Cochrane, Detroit (C)	**1959** Nellie Fox, Chicago (2B)	**1984** Willie Hernandez, Detroit (P)
1935 Hank Greenberg, Detroit (1B)	**1960** Roger Maris, New York (OF)	**1985** Don Mattingly, New York (1B)
1936 Lou Gehrig, New York (1B)	**1961** Roger Maris, New York (OF)	**1986** Roger Clemens, Boston (P)
1937 Charlie Gehringer, Detroit (2B)	**1962** Mickey Mantle, New York (OF)	**1987** George Bell, Toronto (OF)
1938 Jimmie Foxx, Boston (1B)	**1963** Elston Howard, New York (C)	**1988** Jose Canseco, Oakland (OF)
1939 Joe DiMaggio, New York (OF)	**1964** Brooks Robinson, Baltimore (3B)	
1940 Hank Greenberg, Detroit (1B)	**1965** Zoilo Versalles, Minnesota (SS)	See page 120 for abbreviations of playing positions.
1941 Joe DiMaggio, New York (OF)	**1966** Frank Robinson, Baltimore (OF)	
1942 Joe Gordon, New York (2B)	**1967** Carl Yastrzemski, Boston (OF)	
1943 Spud Chandler, New York (P)	**1968** Denny McLain, Detroit (P)	
1944 Hal Newhouser, Detroit (P)	**1969** Harmon Killebrew, Minnesota (3B)	

Outfielder, Jose Canseco became the first ML player to hit 40 home runs and steal 40 bases in a season.

AMERICAN LEAGUE STATISTICS MOST VALUABLE PLAYERS

ROOKIE OF THE YEAR

1949	Roy Sievers, St Louis (OF)
1950	Walt Dropo, Boston (1B)
1951	Gil McDougald, New York (3B)
1952	Harry Byrd, Philadelphia (P)
1953	Harvey Kuenn, Detroit (SS)
1954	Bob Grim, New York (P)
1955	Herb Score, Cleveland (P)
1956	Luis Aparicio, Chicago (SS)
1957	Tony Kubek, New York (SS)
1958	Albie Pearson, Washington (OF)
1959	Bob Allison, Washington (OF)
1960	Ron Hansen, Baltimore (SS)
1961	Don Schwall, Boston (P)
1962	Tom Tresh, New York (SS)
1963	Gary Peters, Chicago (P)
1964	Tony Oliva, Minnesota (OF)
1965	Curt Blefary, Baltimore (OF)
1966	Tommie Agee, Chicago (OF)
1967	Rod Carew, Minnesota (2B)
1968	Stan Bahnsen, New York (P)
1969	Lou Piniella, Kansas City (OF)
1970	Thurman Munson, New York (C)
1971	Chris Chambliss, Cleveland (1B)
1972	Carlton Fisk, Boston (C)
1973	Al Bumbry, Baltimore (OF)
1974	Mike Hargrove, Texas (1B)
1975	Fred Lynn, Boston (OF)
1976	Mark Fidrych, Detroit (P)
1977	Eddie Murray, Baltimore (DH)
1978	Lou Whitaker, Detroit (2B)
1979	Alfredo Griffin, Toronto (SS) / John Castino, Minnesota (3B)
1980	Joe Charboneau, Cleveland (OF)
1981	Dave Righetti, New York (P)
1982	Cal Ripken, Baltimore (SS)
1983	Ron Kittle, Chicago (OF)
1984	Alvin Davis, Seattle (1B)
1985	Ozzie Guillen, Chicago (SS)
1986	Jose Canseco, Oakland (OF)
1987	Mark McGwire, Oakland (1B)
1988	Walt Weiss, Oakland (SS)

Walt Weiss.

CY YOUNG AWARD

1958	Bob Turley, New York (RH)
1959	Early Wynn, Chicago (RH)
1961	Whitey Ford, New York (LH)
1964	Dean Chance, Los Angeles (RH)
1967	Jim Lonborg, Boston (RH)
1968	Denny McLain, Detroit (RH)
1969	Mike Cuellar, Baltimore (tie) (LH)
1969	Denny McLain, Detroit (tie) (RH)
1970	Jim Perry, Minnesota (RH)
1971	Vida Blue, Oakland (LH)
1972	Gaylord Perry, Cleveland (RH)
1973	Jim Palmer, Baltimore (RH)
1974	Jim (Catfish) Hunter, Oakland (RH)
1975	Jim Palmer, Baltimore (RH)
1976	Jim Palmer, Baltimore (RH)
1977	Sparky Lyle, New York (LH)
1978	Ron Guidry, New York (LH)
1979	Mike Flanagan, Baltimore (LH)
1980	Steve Stone, Baltimore (RH)
1981	Rollie Fingers, Milwaukee (RH)
1982	Pete Vuckovich, Milwaukee (RH)
1983	LaMarr Hoyt, Chicago (RH)
1984	Willie Hernandez, Detroit (LH)
1985	Bret Saberhagen, Kansas City (RH)
1986	Roger Clemens, Boston (RH)
1987	Roger Clemens, Boston (RH)
1988	Frank Viola, Minnesota (LH)

Frank Viola, W-104, L-81 in seven years with the Twins.

The All-Star Game

THE MAJOR LEAGUE ALL-STAR GAME

Each May, official All-Star voting ballot papers are distributed at all Major League ballparks for the fans to choose their teams. In 1988 there were a couple of surprises as Oakland fans, with the Athletics enjoying a great first half of the season, swamped the ballot so that Jose Canseco, Mark McGwire and underrated catcher Terry Steinbach were starters for the AL, with Hubbard, Lansford, Parker, and rookie Walt Weiss polling heavily. Cards shortstop, Ozzie Smith, gained most votes overall – 2,106,757 – with Jose Canseco getting 1,765,499 for the AL.

The ballot paper had Brewers' DH, Paul Molitor, playing out of position at second base, but it didn't seem to handicap the AL, as the game followed the recent pattern (the visitors win) and the junior circuit triumphed.

After US Vice President, George Bush, threw out the first pitch with two local young ballplayers, the starting pitchers, Doc Gooden and Frank Viola, kept the batters subdued until Terry Steinbach, a controversial choice with the media, belted a lead-off home run off Gooden in the top of the 3rd inning which was tipped over the right field wall by Darryl Strawberry's glove (AL 1–0). (Steinbach had also hit a home run in his first ML at bat.) In the top of the 4th, Dave Winfield doubled to left field, Cal Ripken walked, Mark McGwire hit a single to left field (moving Winfield to third base and Ripken to second). The game's MVP, Terry Steinbach, then hit a sacrifice fly to left field, which allowed Winfield to score (AL 2–0).

In the bottom of the 4th inning, Vince Coleman singled to left field off pitcher Mark Gubicza, then stole second base. Coleman advanced to third base on Steinbach's throwing error, then scored on Gubicza's wild pitch (NL 1–2). However, that was the end of the senior circuit's rally as Dave Steib, Jeff Russell, and AL relievers, Doug Jones, Dan Plesac and Dennis Eckersley, tied up the game.

59 All-Star games have been played since 1933, with the NL winning 37, the AL 21, and one tied. The venues for future All-Star games will be:

1989 Anaheim Stadium, California (AL)
1990 Wrigley Field, Chicago (NL)
1991 The SkyDome, Toronto (AL)

In 1992, it will be the turn of a National League franchise, perhaps the Mets or Cardinals, or even a new expansion team. Then, in 1993, the Texas Rangers at Arlington, or new stadiums proposed for Baltimore and the Chicago White Sox will vie for the honour in the American League.

ALL-STAR GAME RESULTS

Year	Venue	Score
1933	Comiskey Park, Chicago	AL 4, NL 2
1934	Polo Grounds, New York	AL 9, NL 7
1935	Municipal Stadium, Cleveland	AL 4, NL 1
1936	Braves Field, Boston	NL 4, AL 3
1937	Griffith Stadium, Washington	AL 8, NL 3
1938	Crosley Field, Cincinnati	NL 4, AL 1
1939	Yankee Stadium, New York	AL 3, NL 1
1940	Sportsman's Park, St Louis	NL 4, AL 0
1941	Briggs Stadium, Detroit	AL 7, NL 5
1942	Polo Grounds, New York	AL 3, NL 1
1943	Shibe Park, Philadelphia	AL 5, NL 3
1944	Forbes Field, Pittsburgh	NL 7, AL 1
1946	Fenway Park, Boston	AL 12, NL 0
1947	Wrigley Field, Chicago	AL 2, NL 1
1948	Sportsman's Park, St Louis	AL 5, NL 2
1949	Ebbets Field, Brooklyn	AL 11, NL 7
1950	Comiskey Park, Chicago	NL 4, AL 3
1951	Briggs Stadium, Detroit	NL 8, AL 3
1952	Shibe Park, Philadelphia	NL 3, AL 2
1953	Crosley Field, Cincinnati	NL 5, AL 1
1954	Municipal Stadium, Cleveland	AL 11, NL 9
1955	County Stadium, Milwaukee	NL 6, AL 5
1956	Griffith Stadium, Washington	NL 7, AL 3
1957	Busch Stadium, St Louis	AL 6, NL 5
1958	Memorial Stadium, Baltimore	AL 4, NL 3
1959 1st	Forbes Field, Pittsburgh	NL 5, AL 4
2nd	Memorial Coliseum, Los Angeles	AL 5, NL 3
1960 1st	Municipal Stadium, Kansas City	NL 5, AL 3
2nd	Yankee Stadium, New York	NL 6, AL 0
1961 1st	Candlestick Park, San Francisco	NL 5, AL 4
2nd	Fenway Park, Boston	NL 1, AL 1
1962 1st	D.C. Stadium, Washington	NL 3, AL 1
2nd	Wrigley Field, Chicago	AL 9, NL 4
1963	Municipal Stadium, Cleveland	NL 5, AL 3
1964	Shea Stadium, New York	NL 7, AL 4
1965	Metropolitan Stadium, Minnesota	NL 6, AL 5
1966	Busch Memorial Stadium, St Louis	NL 2, AL 1
1967	Anaheim Stadium, California	NL 2, AL 1
1968	Astrodome, Houston	NL 1, AL 0
1969	RFK Memorial Stadium, Washington	NL 9, AL 3
1970	Riverfront Stadium, Cincinnati	NL 5, AL 4
1971	Tiger Stadium, Detroit	AL 6, NL 4
1972	Atlanta Stadium, Atlanta	NL 4, AL 3
1973	Royals Stadium, Kansas City	NL 7, AL 1
1974	Three Rivers Stadium, Pittsburgh	NL 7, AL 2
1975	County Stadium, Milwaukee	NL 6, AL 3
1976	Veterans Stadium, Philadelphia	NL 7, AL 1
1977	Yankee Stadium, New York	NL 7, AL 5
1978	San Diego Stadium, San Diego	NL 7, AL 3
1979	Kingdome, Seattle	NL 7, AL 6
1980	Dodger Stadium, Los Angeles	NL 4, AL 2
1981	Municipal Stadium, Cleveland	NL 5, AL 4
1982	Olympic Stadium, Montreal	NL 4, AL 1
1983	Comiskey Park, Chicago	AL 13, NL 3
1984	Candlestick Park, San Francisco	NL 3, AL 1
1985	Metrodome, Minnesota	NL 6, AL 1
1986	Astrodome, Houston	AL 3, NL 2
1987	Oakland Coliseum, Oakland	NL 2, AL 0
1988	Riverfront Stadium, Cincinnati	AL 2, NL 1

THE ALL-STAR GAME

National Hall of Fame

Jim 'Catfish' Hunter (left) inducted into the Hall of Fame in 1987.

NATIONAL BASEBALL HALL OF FAME AND MUSEUM

Cooperstown, a small town of fewer than 2,500 inhabitants in east central New York State, 200 miles north of New York City, has been the site of baseball's Hall of Fame since 1939. The Hall of Fame had started electing members back in January 1936, but the buildings at Cooperstown were not dedicated until June 1939, when all 11 surviving electees (Eddie Collins, Babe Ruth, Connie Mack, Cy Young, Honus Wagner, Grover Alexander, Tris Speaker, Nap Lajoie, George Sisler, Walter Johnson and Ty Cobb) attended ceremonies which also commemorated what some believed at the time to mark the centenary of baseball in the area.

Over the past 50 years, the Hall of Fame and Museum have expanded with new displays and galleries (the National Baseball Library was ready in 1968, a $3m expansion and renovation programme completed in 1980), to cater for over 200,000 visitors a year.

Postal Address: National Baseball Hall of Fame and Museum, PO Box 590, COOPERSTOWN, New York 13326, USA
Telephone: (607) 547 9988

The biggest annual occasion is Hall of Fame Day, in late July or early August, when the newly elected members (Willie Stargell in 1988) are inducted at emotional ceremonies held on the library steps.

MERITORIOUS SERVICE

Edward Barrow	(Manager-Executive)
Morgan G. Bulkeley	(Executive)
Alexander J. Cartwright	(Executive)
Henry Chadwick	(Writer-Statistician)
Happy Chandler	(Commissioner-Executive)
John 'Jocko' Conlan	(Umpire)
Thomas Connolly	(Umpire)
William G. Evans	(Umpire-Executive)
Andrew 'Rube' Foster	(Player-Executive)
Ford C. Frick	(Commissioner-Executive)
Warren Giles	(Executive)
William Harridge	(Executive)
Cal Hubbard	(Umpire)
B. Bancroft Johnson	(Executive)
William Klem	(Umpire)
Kenesaw M. Landis	(Commissioner)
Larry S. MacPhail	(Executive)
W. Branch Rickey	(Manager-Executive)
George M. Weiss	(Executive)
Tom Yawkey	(Executive)

BASEBALL HALL OF FAME

Player	Position	Career Dates
Henry Aaron	OF	1954–76
Grover Alexander	P	1911–30
Cap Anson	1B	1876–97
Luis Aparicio	SS	1956–73
Luke Appling	SS	1930–50
Earl Averill	OF	1929–41
J. Frank Baker	3B	1908–22
Dave Bancroft	SS	1915–30
Ernie Banks	SS-1B	1953–71
Jake Beckley	1B	1888–1907
James 'Cool Papa' Bell*	OF	
Chief Bender	P	1903–25
Yogi Berra	C	1946–65
Jim Bottomley	1B	1922–37
Lou Boudreau	SS	1938–52
Roger Bresnahan	C	1897–1915
Lou Brock	OF	1961–79
Dan Brouthers	1B	1879–1904
Mordecai Brown	P	1903–16
Jesse Burkett	OF	1890–1905
Roy Campanella	C	1948–57
Max Carey	OF	1910–29
Frank Chance	1B	1898–1914
Oscar Charleston*	OF	
Jack Chesbro	P	1899–1909
Fred Clarke	OF	1894–1915
John Clarkson	P	1882–94
Roberto Clemente	OF	1955–72
Ty Cobb	OF	1905–28
Mickey Cochrane	C	1925–37
Eddie Collins	2B	1906–30
Jimmy Collins	3B	1895–1908
Earle Combs	OF	1924–35
Roger Connor	1B	1880–97
Stan Coveleski	P	1912–28
Sam Crawford	OF	1899–1917
Joe Cronin	SS	1926–45
Candy Cummings	P	1872–77
Kiki Cuyler	OF	1921–38
Ray Dandridge*	3B	
Dizzy Dean	P	1930–47
Ed Delahanty	OF	1888–1903
Bill Dickey	C	1928–46
Martin DiHigo*	P	
Joe DiMaggio	OF	1936–51
Bobby Doerr	2B	1937–51
Don Drysdale	P	1956–69
Hugh Duffy	OF	1888–1906
Johnny Evers	2B	1902–29
Buck Ewing	C	1880–97
Red Faber	P	1914–33
Bob Feller	P	1936–56
Rick Ferrell	C	1929–47
Elmer Flick	OF	1898–1910
Whitey Ford	P	1950–67
Jimmie Foxx	1B	1925–45
Frankie Frisch	2B	1919–37
Pud Galvin	P	1879–92
Lou Gehrig	1B	1923–39
Charlie Gehringer	2B	1924–42
Bob Gibson	P	1959–75
Josh Gibson*	C	
Lefty Gomez	P	1930–43
Goose Goslin	OF	1921–38
Hank Greenberg	1B	1930–47
Burleigh Grimes	P	1916–34
Lefty Grove	P	1925–41
Chick Hafey	OF	1924–37
Jesse Haines	P	1918–37
Billy Hamilton	OF	1888–1901
Gabby Hartnett	C	1922–41
Harry Heilmann	OF	1914–32
Billy Herman	2B	1931–47
Harry Hooper	OF	1909–25
Rogers Hornsby	2B	1915–37
Waite Hoyt	P	1918–38
Carl Hubbell	P	1928–43
Catfish Hunter	P	1965–79
Monte Irvin*	OF	1949–56
Travis Jackson	SS	1922–36
Hugh Jennings	SS	1891–1918
Judy Johnson*	3B	
Walter Johnson	P	1907–27
Addie Joss	P	1902–10
Al Kaline	OF	1953–74
Tim Keefe	P	1880–93
Willie Keeler	OF	1892–1910
George Kell	3B	1943–57
Joe Kelley	OF	1891–1908
George Kelly	1B	1915–32
King Kelly	C	1878–93
Harmon Killebrew	1B-3B	1954–75
Ralph Kiner	OF	1946–55
Chuck Klein	OF	1928–44
Sandy Koufax	P	1955–66
Nap Lajoie	2B	1896–1916
Bob Lemon	P	1941–58
Buck Leonard*	1B	
Fred Lindstrom	3B	1924–36
John Henry Lloyd	SS-1B	
Ernie Lombardi	C	1931–47
Ted Lyons	P	1923–46
Mickey Mantle	OF	1951–68
Heinie Manush	OF	1923–39
Rabbit Maranville	SS-2B	1912–35
Juan Marichal	P	1960–75
Rube Marquard	P	1908–25
Eddie Mathews	3B	1952–68
Christy Mathewson	P	1900–16
Willie Mays	OF	1951–73
Tommy McCarthy	OF	1884–96
Willie McCovey	1B	1959–80
Joe McGinnity	P	1899–1908
Joe Medwick	OF	1932–48
Johnny Mize	1B	1936–53
Stan Musial	OF-1B	1941–63
Kid Nichols	P	1890–1906
Jim O'Rourke	OF	1876–1904
Mel Ott	OF	1926–47
Satchel Paige*	P	1948–65
Herb Pennock	P	1912–34
Eddie Plank	P	1901–17
Hoss Radbourn	P	1880–91
Pee Wee Reese	SS	1940–58
Sam Rice	OF	1915–35
Eppa Rixey	P	1912–33
Robin Roberts	P	1948–66
Brooks Robinson	3B	1955–77
Frank Robinson	OF	1956–76
Jackie Robinson	2B	1947–56
Edd Roush	OF	1913–31
Red Ruffing	P	1924–47
Amos Rusie	P	1889–1901
Babe Ruth	OF	1914–35
Ray Schalk	C	1912–29
Joe Sewell	SS	1920–33
Al Simmons	OF	1924–44
George Sisler	1B	1915–30
Enos Slaughter	OF	1938–59
Duke Snider	OF	1947–64
Warren Spahn	P	1942–65
Al Spalding	P	1871–78
Tris Speaker	OF	1907–28
Willie Stargell	OF-1B	1962–82
Bill Terry	1B	1923–36
Sam Thompson	OF	1885–1906
Joe Tinker	SS	1902–16
Pie Traynor	3B	1920–37
Dazzy Vance	P	1915–35
Arky Vaughan	SS	1932–48
Rube Waddell	P	1897–1910
Honus Wagner	SS	1897–1917
Bobby Wallace	SS	1894–1918
Ed Walsh	P	1904–17
Lloyd Waner	OF	1927–45
Paul Waner	OF	1926–45
Monte Ward	2B-P	1878–94
Mickey Welch	P	1880–92
Zach Wheat	OF	1909–27
Hoyt Wilhelm	P	1952–72
Billy Williams	OF	1959–76
Ted Williams	OF	1939–60
Hack Wilson	OF	1923–34
Early Wynn	P	1939–63
Cy Young	P	1890–1911
Ross Youngs	OF	1917–26

* No dates for parts of career in the Negro Leagues.

See page 120 for abbreviations of players' positions.

MANAGERS

Walt Alston
Charles Comiskey
Clark Griffith
Bucky Harris
Miller Huggins
Al Lopez
Connie Mack
Joe McCarthy
John McGraw
Bill McKechnie
Wilbert Robinson
Casey Stengel
Harry Wright
George Wright

Seven modern stars likely to gain election to the Hall of Fame are featured on the following pages.

NATIONAL HALL OF FAME 103

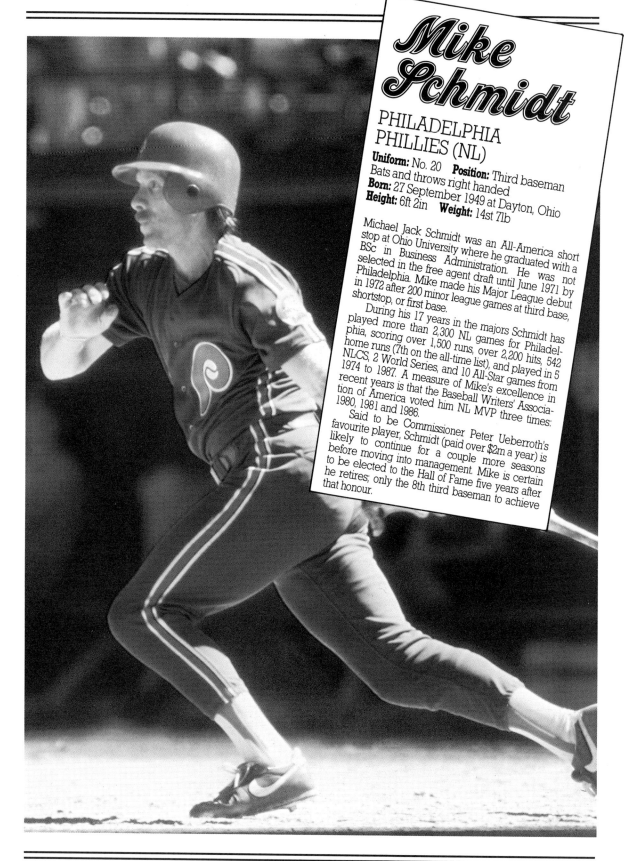

Mike Schmidt

PHILADELPHIA PHILLIES (NL)

Uniform: No. 20 **Position:** Third baseman
Bats and throws right handed
Born: 27 September 1949 at Dayton, Ohio
Height: 6ft 2in **Weight:** 14st 7lb

Michael Jack Schmidt was an All-America short stop at Ohio University where he graduated with a BSc in Business Administration. He was not selected in the free agent draft until June 1971 by Philadelphia. Mike made his Major League debut in 1972 after 200 minor league games at third base, shortstop, or first base.

During his 17 years in the majors Schmidt has played more than 2,300 NL games for Philadelphia, scoring over 1,500 runs, over 2,200 hits, 542 home runs (7th on the all-time list), and played in 5 NLCS, 2 World Series, and 10 All-Star games from 1974 to 1987. A measure of Mike's excellence in recent years is that the Baseball Writers' Association of America voted him NL MVP three times: 1980, 1981 and 1986.

Said to be Commissioner Peter Ueberroth's favourite player, Schmidt (paid over $2m a year) is likely to continue for a couple more seasons before moving into management. Mike is certain to be elected to the Hall of Fame five years after he retires; only the 8th third baseman to achieve that honour.

104 FUTURE HALL OF FAMERS

Dave Parker
OAKLAND ATHLETICS (AL)

Uniform: No. 39 **Position:** Outfielder or designated hitter
Throws right handed and bats left handed
Born: 9 June 1951 at Jackson, Mississippi
Height: 6ft 5in **Weight:** 16st 6lb

David Gene Parker was selected by Pittsburgh Pirates in the 14th round of the June 1970 free agent draft. He made his Major League debut in 1973 after 381 minor league games. Dave became a free agent in 1983 and signed for Cincinnati, then was traded to Oakland of the American League (in exchange for two pitchers) in 1987.

During his 16 years in the majors, Parker has played in more than 2,000 games, scored over 1,100 runs, 2,200 hits, 280 home runs and played in 3 NLCS and 1 World Series for Pittsburgh, and 6 All-Star games for the NL. He was voted NL MVP in 1978 but probably had his best season in 1985.

Dave played his first AL season and second World Series in 1988, for the hard-hitting Oakland Athletics.

FUTURE HALL OF FAMERS 105

Jim Rice
BOSTON RED SOX (AL)

Uniform: No. 14 **Position:** Leftfielder or designated hitter
Bats and throws right handed
Born: 8 March 1953 at Anderson, South Carolina
Height: 6ft 2in **Weight:** 15st 7lb

James Edward Rice was selected by Boston in the first round (15th player chosen) of the June 1971 free agent draft, and received a $45,000 signing bonus.

He made his Major League debut in 1974 after 430 minor league games. During his 15 years in the majors, Rice has played more than 2,000 games, scored over 1,200 runs, 2,400 hits, 370 home runs, played in 1 ALCS and World Series (in 1986), and 7 All-Star games for the AL between 1977 and 1986.

The Baseball Writers' Association of America voted Big Jim the AL MVP back in 1978 when he got 213 hits, 139 RBIs and 46 home runs. He is one of the few ML players to be paid more than $2m a year.

'Jim Ed's' main leisure interest is golf.

106 FUTURE HALL OF FAMERS

Don Sutton
LOS ANGELES DODGERS (NL)

Uniform: No. 20 **Position:** Pitcher
Bats and pitches right handed
Born: 2 April 1945 at Clio, Alabama
Height: 6ft 1in **Weight:** 13st 8lb

Donald Howard Sutton was signed as a free agent by the LA Dodgers in 1964 and made his Major League debut in 1966, after winning 23 of the minor league games he started.

Sutton became a free agent in 1980 and was signed by Houston, then traded to Milwaukee in the AL in 1982 for three players, to Oakland in 1984, California Angels in 1984, re-signed by the Dodgers in January 1988 but released in mid-season.

During his 23 years in the majors Don has pitched more than 5,200 innings in 760 games, winning over 320 of them for a career ERA of 3.25. Sutton played in 3 NLCS, 2 ALCS, 4 World Series, and 4 All-Star games for the NL between 1972 and 1977.

Don is involved in a number of national and local charities, and keen to stay in baseball in broadcasting or management.

FUTURE HALL OF FAMERS 107

Dale Murphy

ATLANTA BRAVES (NL)

Uniform: No. 3　**Position:** Outfielder
Bats and throws right handed
Born: 12 March 1956 at Portland, Oregon
Height: 6ft 4in　**Weight:** 15st 5lb

Dale Bryan Murphy was selected by Atlanta in the first round (5th player chosen) of the June 1974 free agent draft. He made his Major League debut for Atlanta in 1976 after 307 minor league games, many as a catcher or first baseman. During his 13 years in the majors, Dale has been on the disabled list for only seven weeks.

He has played in more than 1,600 games, scored over 1,000 runs, 1,600 hits, 340 home runs and played in 1 NLCS in 1982 for Atlanta, and 7 All-Star games for the NL between 1980 and 1987. Murphy is one of the few players who has twice been voted NL MVP, in 1982 and 1983.

In 1987, *Sports Illustrated* magazine recognised Dale as one of the eight top athletes in the world, 'Who cares most'. Murphy is closely involved in more than a dozen national and local charities.

In 1988 his salary was more than $2m.

108　FUTURE HALL OF FAMERS

Rickey Henderson

NEW YORK YANKEES (AL)

Uniform: No. 24 **Position:** Outfielder
Bats right handed and throws left handed
Born: 25 December 1958 at Chicago, Illinois
Height: 5ft 10in **Weight:** 14st

Rickey Henley Henderson was selected by the team he had supported as a youngster, the Oakland A's, in the 4th round of the June 1976 free agent draft.

Rickey made his Major League debut after playing 384 minor league games in which he gained his fearsome reputation for stealing bases. Rickey rates his minor league skipper, Tom Trebelhorn (now manager at Milwaukee), the greatest influence on his career.

In December 1984, Henderson was traded to the New York Yankees.

During his 10 years in the majors, Rickey has played more than 1,300 games, scored over 1,000 runs, 1,400 hits, and has about 800 stolen bases (an average of 80 per season), has played in 1 ALCS and 8 All-Star games between 1980 and 1988.

Henderson holds the ML record of 130 stolen bases in a season, became the youngest player (28) to get 700 stolen bases, and will soon overtake Lou Brock's ML base-stealing career record of 938.

His leisure interests away from the ballpark are swimming and fishing.

FUTURE HALL OF FAMERS 109

Ozzie Smith
ST LOUIS CARDINALS (NL)

Uniform: No. 1 **Position:** Shortstop
Bats right or left handed, throws right handed
Born: 26 December 1954 at Mobile, Alabama
Height: 5ft 10in **Weight:** 10st 10lb

Osborne Earl Smith was selected by Detroit in the 1976 free agent draft, and then in 1977 by San Diego.

He made his Major League debut for the Padres in 1978 after only 68 minor league games. In a sensational pre-season swap with fellow shortstop, Garry Templeton, Smith was traded to St Louis in February 1982.

'Ozzie the Wizard' seems certain to be elected to the Hall of Fame, but one might not guess it by looking at his career statistics. During 11 years in the majors, Smith has played more than 1,600 games, scored over 700 runs, 1,500 hits, collected 350 stolen bases, but hit fewer than 20 home runs.

What figures cannot show are Ozzie's qualities as a leader, role model for the young and his fellow ballplayers, nor his skill as a fielder. Smith is arguably the best fielder of his era and perhaps the greatest in Major League history. Ozzie has played in 3 NLCS and World Series for St Louis, all 8 All-Star games from 1981 to 1988 (leading vote getter in 1987 and 1988), and was the highest paid player of last season, with $2,340,000. He has been the subject of a book, and a film, *Ozzie – The Movie*.

In his spare time he likes jazz and works tirelessly for several major charities.

110 FUTURE HALL OF FAMERS

AMERICAN LEAGUE CHAMPIONSHIP SERIES 1988

Game 1: Wednesday 5 October 1988 at Fenway Park, Boston. Start: 1.20pm EDT
The two division champions were dominated by fine pitching until the top of the fourth inning, when Oakland's speedy, muscular, 6ft 3in slugger, Jose Canseco silenced the crowd's taunting chant of, 'Steroids, steroids' (Canadian Ben Johnson had been stripped of his Olympic 100m gold medal only days before), by hitting a 400ft homer over left field.

Boston tied the game in the bottom of the seventh, when pinch runner Kevin Romine scored on Wade Boggs' sacrifice fly into left field.

Oakland retook the lead in their next inning, as Carney Lansford scored on Dave Henderson's single into right field, then their ace reliever, Dennis Eckersley pitched two shutout innings, striking out Boston's Wade Boggs (who stranded seven runners), with the bases loaded in the ninth, to end the game.

*Oakland Athetics	000 100 010	–	2	6	0
Boston Red Sox	000 000 100	–	1	6	0

Stewart(6⅓), Honeycutt(⅔), Eckersley(2), and Steinbach/Hassey, Oak.; Hurst(9), and Gedman, Bos.
W– Honeycutt(1–0), L– Hurst(0–1), Sv– Eckersley(1).
HR– Canseco(1), Oak. LOB– Oak 6, Bos 9.
GWRBI– Henderson, Oak., 2h 44m. Att: 34,104.

Game 2: Thursday 6 October 1988 (Oakland lead series 1–0) at Fenway Park, Boston. Start: 8.22pm EDT
Starting pitchers, Roger Clemens and Storm Davis were effective until the bottom of the sixth innings, when Davis walked Dwight Evans and Mike Greenwell. Both Red Sox runners scored on hits by Jim Rice and Ellis Burks.

In the top of the seventh, Oakland got to Roger Clemens. First, Dave Henderson singled to centre, then Jose Canseco thumped a home run over the left field fence. Later in the inning, Carney Lansford scored the go-ahead run on an RBI single into left field by Mark McGwire. Red Sox catcher, Rich Gedman got the last of Boston's four hits when he homered off Oakland reliever Greg Caderet to tie the game.

Oakland hit two singles off Boston closer Lee Smith in the top of the ninth, then rookie shortstop Walt Weiss clipped an 0–2 fastball into centre field to score Ron Hassey. Boston flew west after the game in low spirits. They had lost all six regular season meetings at Oakland.

*Oakland Athletics	000 000 301	–	4	10	1
Boston Red Sox	000 002 100	–	3	4	1

Davis(6⅓), Cadaret(⅓), Nelson(1⅓), Eckersley(1), and Hassey, Oak.; Clemens(7), Stanley(⅓), Smith(1⅔) and Gedman, Bos.
W– Nelson(1–0); L– Smith(0–1), Sv– Eckersley(2).
HR– Canseco(2), Oak. Gedman(1), Bos. LOB– Oak 6, Bos 6.
GWRBI– Weiss, Oak., 3h 14m. Att: 34,605.

Game 3: Saturday 8 October 1988 (Oakland lead series 2–0) at Oakland Coliseum, Oakland. Start: 8.22pm EDT
Boston manager, Joe Morgan, switched his batting order around and it worked. His batters finally got the better of four Oakland pitchers, and Jose Canseco remained hitless for the game. Unfortunately for the Red Sox, Tony LaRussa's other sluggers were in form.

The Red Sox hit Bob Welch (usually unbeatable at the Coliseum) for six hits and led 5–0 after 1½ innings, but Boston's Mike Boddicker was unable to hold Oakland, who were ahead 6–5 after three. Boston threatened to rally in the top of the fifth but fell into a double play when catcher Rich Gedman was called out by umpire Ken Kaiser for elbowing Oakland second baseman Mike Gallego. Dennis Eckersley then pitched two perfect innings for his third save of the ALCS.

*Boston Red Sox	320 000 100	–	6	12	0
Oakland Athletics	042 010 12x	–	10	15	1

Boddicker(2⅔), Gardner(4⅔), Stanley(⅔) and Gedman, Bos.; Welch(1⅔), Nelson(3⅓), Young(1⅓), Plunk(⅓), Honeycutt(⅓), Eckersley(2), and Hassey, Oak.
W– Nelson(2–0), L– Boddicker(0–1), Sv– Eckersley(3).
HR– Greenwell(1), Bos.; McGwire(1), Lansford(1), Hassey(1), Henderson(1), Oak. LOB– Bos 8, Oak 6.
GWRBI– Hassey, Bos., 3h 05m. Att: 49,261.

Game 4: Sunday 9 October 1988 (Oakland lead series 3–0) at Oakland Coliseum, Oakland. Start: 3.00pm EDT
The word in Oakland was 'sweep'. The Athletics were seeking revenge for their 3–0 drubbing by the BoSox in 1975, and their 15th win in 16 games over Boston at home.

Oakland got the start they needed when Jose Canseco hit his third home run of the series to tie the ALCS record. In the third inning, Walt Weiss scored on Dave Henderson's double into left field for a 2–0 lead. Meanwhile, Oakland starter Dave Stewart was pitching seven solid innings, giving up just four hits (Boston's Marty Barrett scored when Jim Rice ground out in the top of the fifth), before relievers Rick Honeycutt, then ALCS MVP Dennis Eckersley closed the game with a record 4th save. Jose Canseco got his fifth hit of the series in the eighth, stole second base, and scored on Mark McGwire's single into centre field. Later in the inning, McGwire also scored, on Don Baylor's sacrifice fly to centre field. For Baylor the win meant his third consecutive World Series with different teams (Boston'86, Minnesota'87, Oakland'88).

*Boston Red Sox	000 001 000	–	1	4	0
Oakland Athletics	101 000 02x	–	4	10	1

Hurst(4), Smithson(2⅓), Smith(1⅔), and Gedman, Bos.; Stewart(7), Honeycutt(1), Eckersley(1), and Steinbach/Hassey, Oak. W– Stewart(1–0), L– Hurst(0–2), Sv– Eckersley(4). HR– Canseco(3). LOB– Bos 7, Oak 8.
GWRBI– Canseco, Oak., Time: 2h 55m. Att: 49,406.

* For explanation of these line scores see page 120

CHAMPIONSHIP SERIES RECORDS 1969–88

AMERICAN LEAGUE

Earliest date CS started: 2 October 1984
Latest date CS finished: 16 October 1985
Longest game: 12 innings 1969
  3hrs 54mins 1986
Shortest game: 1hr 51mins 1974
Largest game attendance: 64,406 in 1982
Largest CS attendance: 324,430 in 1986
Most CS as manager: 6 Earl Weaver
Most CS as umpire: 5 Larry Barnett (26)
Most CS as a player: 11 Reggie Jackson
Youngest: 19yrs 5m 29d Bert Blyleven 1970
Oldest: 41yrs 6m 13d Don Sutton 1986

BATTING
Games: 45 Reggie Jackson
At Bats: 163 Reggie Jackson
Hits: 37 Reggie Jackson
Runs: 22 George Brett
RBIs: 20 Reggie Jackson
Best batting average: .386 Mickey Rivers (57 ABs)
Home runs: 9 George Brett
Grand Slam homers: Mike Cuellar 1970, Don Baylor 1982
Stolen bases: 8 Amos Otis

PITCHING
CS as a pitcher: 6 (by 5 players)
Games: 11 Rollie Fingers
Games started: 10 Jim Hunter
Games won: 4 (by 6 players)
Games lost: 4 Doyle Alexander
Games saved: 4 by Dennis Eckersley
Inns pitched: 69 Jim Hunter
Strikeouts: 46 Nolan Ryan (AL & NL), 46 Jim Palmer
Strikeouts a game: 14 Joe Coleman 1972, Mike Boddicker 1983

NATIONAL LEAGUE

Earliest date CS started: 2 October 1984
Latest date CS finished: 19 October 1981
Longest game: 16 innings 1986
  4hrs 42mins 1986
Shortest game: 1hr 57mins 1972
Largest game attendance: 64,924 in 1977
Largest CS attendance: 395,597 in 1987
Most CS as manager: 7 Sparky Anderson (5 NL/2AL) and 6 Tom Lasorda
Most CS an umpire: 7 Harvey Douglas (26 games)
Most CS as a player: 8 Ritchie Hebner
Youngest: 19yrs 8m 28d Don Gullett 1970
Oldest: 43yrs 6m 8d Phil Niekro 1982

BATTING
Games: 28 Pete Rose
At Bats: 118 Pete Rose
Hits: 45 Pete Rose
Runs: 17 Pete Rose
RBIs: 21 Steve Garvey
Best batting average: .381 Pete Rose (118 ABs)
Home runs: 8 Steve Garvey
Grand Slam homers: Ron Cey 1977, Johnnie Baker 1977
Stolen bases: 9 Davey Lopes

PITCHING
CS as a pitcher: 6 (by 5 players)
Games: 15 Tug McGraw
Games started: 8 Steve Carlton
Games won: 4 (by 6 players)
Games lost: 7 Jerry Reuss
Games saved: 5 Tug McGraw
Inns pitched: 53 Steve Carlton
Strikeouts: 46 Nolan Ryan (AL & NL), 39 Steve Carlton
Strikeouts a game: 14 John Candelaria 1975, Mike Scott 1986

ALCS RESULTS

Year	Winner	Games		Total
1969	Baltimore (East)	3–0	Minnesota (West)	113,763
1970	Baltimore (East)	3–0	Minnesota (West)	81,945
1971	Baltimore (East)	3–0	Oakland (West)	110,800
1972	Oakland (West)	3–2	Detroit (East)	189,671
1973	Oakland (West)	3–2	Baltimore (East)	175,833
1974	Oakland (West)	3–1	Baltimore (East)	144,615
1975	Boston (East)	3–0	Oakland (West)	120,514
1976	New York (East)	3–2	Kansas City (West)	252,152
1977	New York (East)	3–2	Kansas City (West)	234,713
1978	New York (East)	3–1	Kansas City (West)	194,192
1979	Baltimore (East)	3–1	California (West)	191,293
1980	Kansas City (West)	3–0	New York (East)	141,819
1981	New York (East)	3–0	Oakland (West)	151,539
1982	Milwaukee (East)	3–2	California (West)	284,691
1983	Baltimore (East)	3–1	Chicago (West)	195,748
1984	Detroit (East)	3–0	Kansas City (West)	136,160
1985	Kansas City (West)	4–3	Toronto (East)	264,167
1986	Boston (East)	4–3	California (West)	324,430
1987	Minnesota (West)	4–1	Detroit (East)	257,631
1988	Oakland (West)	4–0	Boston (East)	167,376

NLCS RESULTS

Year	Winner	Games		Total
1969	New York (East)	3–0	Atlanta (West)	153,587
1970	Cincinnati (West)	3–0	Pittsburgh (East)	112,943
1971	Pittsburgh (East)	3–1	San Francisco (West)	157,348
1972	Cincinnati (West)	3–2	Pittsburgh (East)	234,814
1973	New York (East)	3–2	Cincinnati (West)	262,548
1974	Los Angeles (West)	3–1	Pittsburgh (East)	200,262
1975	Cincinnati (West)	3–0	Pittsburgh East)	155,740
1976	Cincinnati (West)	3–0	Philadelphia (East)	180,338
1977	Los Angeles (West)	3–1	Philadelphia (East)	240,584
1978	Los Angeles (West)	3–1	Philadelphia (East)	234,269
1979	Pittsburgh (East)	3–0	Cincinnati (West)	152,246
1980	Philadelphia (East)	3–2	Houston (West)	264,950
1981	Los Angeles (West)	3–2	Montreal (East)	250,098
1982	St Louis (East)	3–0	Atlanta (West)	158,589
1983	Philadelphia (East)	3–1	Los Angeles (West)	223,914
1984	San Diego (West)	3–2	Chicago (East)	247,623
1985	St Louis (East)	4–2	Los Angeles (West)	326,824
1986	New York (East)	4–2	Houston (West)	299,316
1987	St Louis (East)	4–3	San Francisco (West)	396,597
1988	Los Angeles (West)	4–3	New York (East)	373,695

NATIONAL LEAGUE CHAMPIONSHIP SERIES 1988

Game 1: Tuesday 4 October 1988
at Dodger Stadium, Los Angeles. Start: 10.08pm EDT
New York trailed 2-0 in the top of the ninth inning, then Darryl Strawberry's double to right field scored rookie Gregg Jefferies and Gary Carter's double to centre field scored Strawberry and Kevin McReynolds.
   *New York Mets   000 000 003 – 3 8 1
    Los Angeles Dodgers 100 000 100 – 2 4 0
Gooden(7), Myers(2), and Carter, NY; Hershiser(8⅓), J. Howell(⅔), and Scioscia, LA. W– Myers(1–0), NY. L– J. Howell(0–1), LA. LOB– New York 5, Los Angeles 4. GWRBI– Carter(1), NY. Time: 2h 45m. Att: 55,582.

Game 2: Wednesday 5 October 1988 (NY lead series 1–0)
at Dodger Stadium, Los Angeles. Start: 10.08pm EDT
An unfortunate NY newspaper article by Mets starter David Cone helped turn the Dodgers around, after losing 11 of their last 12 games with New York.
RBI singles off Cone by Mike Marshall, Steve Sax, a double by Mickey Hatcher, and another single by Marshall brought LA a 5-0 lead after two innings.
Keith Hernandez thumped a two-run homer in the fourth and an RBI single in the ninth, but by then Cone had egg on his face, and the Dodgers were home and dry.
   *New York Mets   000 200 001 – 3 6 0
    Los Angeles Dodgers 140 010 00x – 6 7 0
Cone(2), Aguilera(3), Leach(2), McDowell(1), and Carter, NY; Belcher(8⅓), Orosco(0), Pena(⅔), and Scioscia, LA. W– Belcher(1–0) LA, L– Cone(0–1) NY. LOB– NY 4, LA 7. GWRBI– Marshall(1) LA. Time: 3h 10m. Att: 55,780.

Game 3: Saturday 8 October 1988 (Series tied 1–1)
at Shea Stadium, New York. Start: 12.20pm EDT
Starting pitchers, Orel Hershiser and Ron Darling gave up ten hits between them in six innings before the cold and damp got to them. Proceedings warmed up in the eighth, when Dodgers reliever, Jay Howell, was ejected (and suspended for two games) after the umpires found pine tar in his glove.
   *Los Angeles Dodgers 021 000 010 – 4 7 2
    New York Mets   001 002 05x – 8 9 2
Hershiser(7), Howell(0), Pena(⅔), Orosco(0), Horton(⅓), and Scioscia/Dempsey, LA; Darling(6), McDowell(1⅔), Myers(⅓), Cone(1), and Carter, NY. W– Myers(2–0) NY, L– Pena(0–1) LA. LOB– LA 9, NY 9. GWRBI– Wilson, NY. Time: 3h 44m. Att: 44,672.

Game 4: Sunday 9 October 1988 (NY lead series 2–1)
at Shea Stadium, New York. Start: 8.22pm EDT
The aggressive Dodgers jumped to another quick lead on a two-run single by John Shelby. Then Darryl Strawberry's two-run homer, Kevin McReynolds' home run and Gary Carter's RBI triple put New York in charge after six.

However, LA sent the game into extra innings with an unlikely two-run homer by Mike Scioscia off Dwight Gooden in the ninth. Scores remained tied until the top of the twelfth, when Kirk Gibson homered to centre field.
   *Los Angeles Dodgers 200 000 002 001 – 5 7 1
    New York Mets   000 301 000 000 – 4 10 2
Tudor(5), Holton(1), Horton(2), Pena(3), Leary(⅓), Orosco(⅓), Hershiser(⅓), and Scioscia, LA; Gooden(8⅓), Myers(2), McDowell(1⅔), and Carter/Sasser, NY. W– Pena(1–1) LA, L– McDowell(0–1) NY, Sv– Hershiser(1) LA. LOB– LA 8, NY 10. GWRBI– Gibson, LA. Time: 4h 29m, Att: 54,014.

Game 5: Monday 10 October 1988 (Series tied 2–2)
at Shea Stadium, New York. Start: 12.20pm EDT
Less than 12 hours after game 4, everyone was back for more of this NLCS classic. Mets starter, burly Sid Fernandez gave up seven hits and six earned runs on RBI doubles by Rick Dempsey, Alfredo Griffin, and a three-run homer from Kirk Gibson. Lenny Dykstra belted a three-run homer over right field, and Gregg Jefferies collected another RBI single, but held on for the win.
   *Los Angeles Dodgers 000 330 001 – 7 12 0
    New York Mets   000 030 010 – 4 9 1
Belcher(7), Horton(⅓), Holton(1⅔), and Dempsey/Scioscia, LA; Fernandez(4), Leach(1), Aguilera(2), McDowell(2), and Carter, NY. W– Belcher(2–0) LA, L– Fernandez(0–1), NY. Sv– Holton(1) LA. LOB– LA 8, NY 5. GWRBI– Dempsey, LA. Time: 3h 07m. Att: 52,069.

Game 6: Tuesday 11 October 1988 (LA lead series 3–2)
at Dodger Stadium, Los Angeles. Start: 8.22pm EDT
Retired journalist, David Cone, pitched nine confident innings for the Mets yielding only five hits and one run, an RBI single to Mickey Hatcher in the fifth. New York's star hitter was Kevin McReynolds who went four-for-four with a homer and 3-RBIs to square the series.
   *New York Mets   101 021 000 – 5 11 0
    Los Angeles Dodgers 000 010 000 – 1 5 2
Cone(9), and Carter, NY; Leary(4), Holton(1⅓), Horton(1⅔), Orosco(2), and Scioscia, LA. W– Cone(1–1) NY, L– Leary(0–1) LA. LOB– NY 13, LA 7. GWRBI– McReynolds, NY. Time: 3h 16m. Att: 55,885.

Game 7: Wednesday 12 October 1988 (Series tied 3–3)
at Dodger Stadium, Los Angeles. Start: 8.22pm EDT
The Dodgers were 6–0 ahead in no time, thanks to indifferent pitching by Ron Darling, and three poor fielding plays from Gregg Jefferies, Wally Backman and Keith Hernandez. With NLCS MVP Orel Hershiser continuing his golden pitching streak the Dodgers had defied the odds, and Tom Lasorda had made amends to the 'Dodger in the Sky' for the 1983 NLCS upset.
   *New York Mets   000 000 000 – 0 5 2
    Los Angeles Dodgers 150 000 000 – 6 10 0
Darling(1), Gooden(3), Leach(2), Aguilera(2), and Carter and Sasser, NY; Hershiser(9), and Scioscia, LA. W– Hershiser(1–0), LA. L– Darling(0–1), NY. LOB– NY 8, LA 7. GWRBI– Gibson(2), LA. Time: 2h 51m. Att: 55,693.
* For explanation of these line scores see page 120

World Series 1988

The first All-California World Series since the Oakland As beat the Los Angeles Dodgers 4–1 in 1974, was thought likely to be the most one-sided for years. Tony LaRussa's burly bullies were expected to overpower the scrappy, injury hit Dodgers. However, there was the added spice of a west coast battle; north v. south, fog v. smog, bustle v. laid back, Bay Area v. Tinseltown, underdog v. favourite.

After a season in which they had won over 100 games, then swept Boston aside in the ALCS, the Athletics were rested, and confident of beating whichever team won the NLCS dog-fight. New York and LA had knocked lumps off each other during the regular season, then battled through a gruelling, see-saw coast-to-coast, seven-game playoff. Some Oakland players were even rash enough to declare they'd prefer to meet the Dodgers, only an hour to the south in steamy LA, rather than take an irksome five-hour plane ride to cold, damp New York. They did not seem to care which team they faced, the Athletics were more concerned about where they won.

Los Angeles were the underdogs and their trump cards did not seem the basis for a series victory. The charisma and aggression of Kirk Gibson, the brilliant pitching of Orel Hershiser, the club's team spirit in adversity, the lack of pressure that being the underdog brings, and then Tommy Lasorda, 61, a roly-poly, yappy, failed-pitcher of a manager regarded by some as a better cheerleader than strategist.

In the event, the Athletics and pundits got one thing right. The Series was played in a heatwave.

Game 1: Saturday 15 October 1988 at Dodger Stadium, Los Angeles. Start: 8.30pm EDT
As pop star Debbie Gibson sang the US National Anthem before Game 1 of the World Series, few could have guessed the Hollywood style drama her namesake and Dodgers catalyst, Kirk Gibson, had in store.

Gibson took pre-game batting practice, but was not in the starting line-up, because of injuries to his left hamstring and right knee. The lefthanded slugger remained, in uniform, in the locker room, where he swatted a few balls off a batting tee.

In a nervous, aggressive opening, LA starter Tim Belcher hit Jose Canseco on the right arm. Then, with his first pitch of the game, Oakland's Dave Stewart flattened Steve Sax. With Sax at first base, Mickey Hatcher belted the first home run of the 1988 series over left centrefield to give the Dodgers an improbable 2–0 lead.

A quick start made all the difference to LA in the NLCS, but AL champions Oakland had big bats who could reply with interest. On the top of the second inning, Belcher loaded the bases, after nearly beaning Carney Lansford with a pitch that went behind his head. Belcher struck out Dave Henderson but Jose Canseco hit his first ever grand slam home run (and the 15th in World Series history), over the centrefield fence. Oakland held their two run lead until the bottom of the sixth, when LA catcher Mike Scioscia smacked a base hit into left field to score Mike Marshall.

Los Angeles silenced Oakland's bats through the next three innings, so went into the bottom of the ninth, trailing 4–3. Two men were out, when the Athletics ace relief pitcher Dennis Eckersley walked ex-Oakland teammate, Mike Davis, to first base.

With the game down to its final out, Tommy Lasorda sent in Kirk Gibson to pinch hit for the Dodgers. Most of the 56,000 crowd were on their feet, cheering as Gibson fouled Eckersley's first pitch back to the screen (0 balls, 1 strike). He did the same to an identical fastball on the outside of the plate (0–2). On his third pitch, Gibson chopped the ball into the ground and it rolled foul along the right field line. (With two strikes against him he could not be out on a foul ball.)

Eckersley then worked the plate, throwing ball-one to the outside (1–2); the next pitch was fouled back into the catcher's mitt; and then, on another ball to the outside (2–2), Mike Davis easily stole his way onto second base. This changed things in LA's favour. With the tying run on second, Gibson needed only a base hit for Davis to score.

Eckersley's next pitch was a ball to the outside (3–2), meaning a full count, with two men out, the tying run at second, the winning run (Gibson) at the plate.

Eckersley pitched. It went down the middle of the strike zone, but Gibson hit the ball 370ft over the right field fence to give the Dodgers victory. After hitting only the 7th home run to win a World Series game (the first since Carlton Fisk for Boston in 1975), the hobbling Gibson, trying to favour each of his injured legs in turn, took 25 seconds to round the bases, before being mobbed by his teammates. Oakland, cruising since the second inning, could not believe it either.

```
 *Oakland Athletics    040 000 000  -  4 7 0
  Los Angeles Dodgers  200 001 002  -  5 7 0
```
Stewart(8), Eckersley(⅔), and Steinbach/Hassey, Oak; Belcher(2), Leary(3), Holton(2), Pena(2) and Scioscia, LA. W– Pena(1–0) LA. L– Eckersley(0–1) Oak. HR– Hatcher, Gibson, LA. Canseco, Oak. LOB– Oak 10, LA 5. GWRBI– Gibson, LA. Time: 3h 4m. Att: 55,983.

Game 2: Sunday 16 October 1988 (LA lead series 1–0) at Dodger Stadium, Los Angeles. Start: 8.25pm EDT
Orel Hershiser, 30, had baffled NL batters since mid-August with his sinking fastball, curveball, and occasional split-fingered fastball. In Game 2 of the World Series he did the same to the cream of the AL. Only Dave Parker (who had played in the NL until 1987), with three hits, was

able to lay a bat on him.

Unfortunately for shell-shocked Oakland, the Dodgers had no problems getting to Storm Davis. With five early runs on RBI singles by Franklin Stubbs, Mickey Hatcher, and a three-run home run over left field by Mike Marshall, LA had no need to call on their injured hero of Game 1, Kirk Gibson. No designated hitter is allowed in the NL ballpark, but all-rounder, Hershiser (a star with an ice hockey stick or a golf club), was more than ready with his baseball bat. He clipped a single in the 3rd, an RBI double in the fourth for a 6–0 lead, and another double in the sixth. (No pitcher had made three hits in a WS game since 1924.)

Straight after the game, Orel Leonard Hershiser IV, wearing a 'Louisville Slugger' T-shirt, had rapid confirmation that he was a winner, making the traditional TV commercial expected of modern US sporting heroes, 'I'm going to Disneyland'.

```
*Oakland Athletics      000 000 000  –  0  3 0
 Los Angeles Dodgers    005 100 00x  –  6 10 1
```
S. Davis(3⅓), Nelson(1⅔), C. Young(1), Plunk(1), Honeycutt(1) and Hassey, Oak.; Hershiser(9) and Scioscia, LA. W– Hershiser(1–0), L– S. Davis(0–1). HR– Marshall, LA. LOB– Oak 4, LA 5. GWRBI– Stubbs, LA. Time: 2h 30m. Att: 56,051.

Game 3: Tuesday 18 October (LA lead series 2–0) at Oakland Coliseum, Oakland. Start: 8.30pm EDT
The Athletics were glad to get back home, up to the adrenaline pumping atmosphere of the Coliseum where rock music blasts out between innings. With Bob Welch, the ex-Dodgers pitcher on the mound, the home team was confident of holding LA (without Kirk Gibson or Mike Marshall) through the early innings, until their fine bull-pen relief pitchers could take over. So it proved. With the bonus that Dodgers starter John Tudor left the game with an injured elbow in the second inning.

Oakland scored first, on an RBI single to left field by Ron Hassey in the third, but Los Angeles tied the game in the fifth, with an RBI double by Franklin Stubbs which fell into right field.

Oakland had a scare in the top of the sixth when Welch loaded the bases with nobody out. However, the Athletics got out of the jam when lefthanded reliever Greg Cadaret made Mike Scioscia foul out to third. Right hander Gene Nelson came into the game and got Jeff Hamilton to hit a grounder to Carney Lansford who forced out Danny Heep running from third base to home plate. Then Nelson got Alfredo Griffin to ground out to first baseman Mark McGwire.

It took Oakland until the bottom of the ninth inning to win the game. Jay Howell replaced Alejandro Pena for Los Angeles, but after getting Jose Canseco to pop out to second base, Mark McGwire hit a 2–2 pitch just over the left field fence. As the flame-haired slugger returned to home plate and bashed forearms in celebration with his teammates, Oakland's relief was plain to see. McGwire's game ending home run was the second of the 1988 series (only the eighth since 1903), and the 13th consecutive World Series game won at home.

```
*Los Angeles Dodgers    000 010 000  –  1  8 1
 Oakland Athletics      001 000 001  –  2  5 0
```
Tudor(1⅓), Leary(3⅔), Pena(3), Howell(⅓) and Scioscia, LA; Welch(5), Cadaret(⅓), Nelson(1⅔), Honeycutt(2) and Hassey, Oak. W– Honeycutt(1–0), L– Howell(0–1). HR– McGwire, Oak. LOB– LA 10, Oak 4. GWRBI– McGwire, Oak. Time: 3h 21m. Att: 49,316.

Game 4: Wednesday 19 October 1988 (LA lead series 2–1) at Oakland Coliseum, Oakland. Start: 8.25pm EDT
An NBC TV commentator made the unfortunate pre-game assessment, seen in the Dodgers clubhouse, that the LA line-up was possibly the weakest in World Series history. Dodgers manager, Tom Lasorda, turned the remark into the rallying cry he needed to grab a telling victory.

Orel Hershiser, 1988 World Series MVP and NL Cy Young Award.

Los Angeles went ahead in the top of the first, when a passed ball got away from Oakland catcher, Terry Steinbach, for Steve Sax to score. Following a fielding error by second baseman, Glenn Hubbard, Mickey Hatcher bustled home on John Shelby's sacrifice. Oakland's worst nightmare was coming true. They were playing catch-up again, at home, against a team whose injury reports had made the team doctor almost as famous as some players.

Jose Canseco grounded out to second but that allowed Luis Polinia to score. In the third, Franklin Stubbs scored for the Dodgers when rookie shortstop Walt Weiss's casual attempt to catch Mike Davis let the ball through his glove into left field for another Athletics error.

In the bottom of the sixth, Dave Henderson scored on a single into right field by Carney Lansford, to reduce Oakland's deficit to 3–2. But almost immediately, Alfredo Griffin scored when Tracy Woodson grounded out to the shortstop.

Dave Henderson belted a double into left field in the bottom of the seventh inning, which allowed Walt Weiss to score from second base. Then got his fourth hit of the game in the bottom of the ninth, with one out. However, Jay Howell was pitching confidently and struck out Jose Canseco, and got Dave Parker to foul out to Jeff Hamilton down the third base line to end the game.

*Los Angeles Dodgers   201 000 100 – 4 8 1
Oakland Athletics   100 001 100 – 3 9 2
Belcher($6\frac{2}{3}$), Howell($2\frac{1}{3}$) and Scioscia/Dempsey, LA; Stewart($6\frac{1}{3}$), Cadaret($1\frac{2}{3}$), Eckersley(1) and Steinbach, Oak. W– Belcher(1–0), L– Stewart(0–1).
Time: 3h 05m. Att: 49,317.

Game 5: Thursday 20 October 1988 (LA lead series 3–1) at Oakland Coliseum, Oakland. Start: 8.39pm EDT
The Los Angeles Dodgers cut-and-paste line-up, with walking wounded and reserves, were within one game of winning it all. Their concern that Canseco and McGwire would break loose was calmed by the reassuring sight of Orel Hershiser on the mound. 'The Bulldog' did not let them down. True, he gave up four hits and yielded two runs, but LA was not complaining. Four earned runs in his last 101 innings (0.35 ERA) gives some indication of the extraordinary pitching streak Hershiser had enjoyed since mid-August. Some commentators have called it perhaps the greatest control pitching in modern times.

Los Angeles got off to another fast start, with a two-run homer by Mickey Hatcher off Storm Davis. Even at this early stage the Dodgers were confident enough for Hatcher to try a mocking Oakland-style forearm bash on his way back to the dugout, adding a feigned grimace of pain as he did so.

Oakland clawed a run back in the third, when Stan Javier's sacrifice fly to left field allowed Carney Lansford to score. But the Dodgers increased their lead in the fourth, with another two-run homer by Mike Davis over the right field fence (on a 3–0 pitch), and again in the sixth, when Davis scored from first base on a double to deep right field by veteran catcher, Rick Dempsey.

Tony Phillips scored on single to centre field by Stan Javier in the eighth, but the Awesome As were not going to deny Hershiser and the crafty, banged-up Dodgers, the latest in a long line of World Series upsets. When Mark McGwire flied out to centre field in the bottom of the ninth, leaving the two 'Bash Brothers' (78 home runs and 340 hits between them in the regular season and ALCS), with just two hits in 36 at-bats, there was nothing more to give.

World Series MVP, Orel Hershiser finished the series by striking out Tony Phillips, his ninth 'K' of the game, and was then engulfed by his delighted teammates. Players with a full share of the postseason pool, received a record $109,740 each.

Before the 1988 Series, many had regarded Tommy Lasorda as more of a windbag than a manager. Now he had the last laugh and the final word. 'This was the 1969 Mets all over again. The Impossible Dream revisited. No one gave us a chance to win the division, the National League, or the World Series, but we did. We won it all. You wouldn't have believed it unless you saw it.'

*Los Angeles Dodgers   200 201 000 – 5 8 0
Oakland Athletics   001 000 010 – 2 4 0
Hershiser(9) and Dempsey, LA; S. Davis($4\frac{2}{3}$), Cadaret(0), Nelson(3), Honeycutt($\frac{1}{3}$), Plunk($\frac{2}{3}$), Burns($\frac{1}{3}$) and Hassey, Oak. W– Hershiser(2–0) LA, L– S. Davis(0–2) Oak.
HR– Hatcher, M. Davis, LA. GWRBI– Hatcher, LA.
Time: 2h 51m. Att: 49,317.

* For explanation of these line scores see page 120

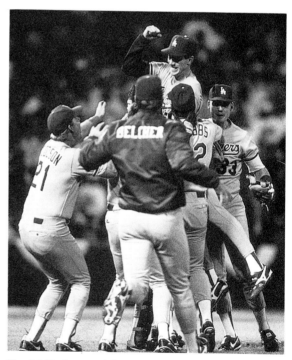

The LA Dodgers celebrate their World Series victory and $109,740 per man payout.

World Series Statistics

WORLD SERIES RESULTS 1903–1988

Year	Winner Games	Loser Games	Attendance
1903	Boston AL, 5	Pittsburgh NL, 3	100,429
1904	No Series		
1905	New York NL, 4	Philadelphia AL, 1	91,723
1906	Chicago AL, 4	Chicago NL, 2	99,845
1907	Chicago NL, 4	Detroit AL, 0 (1 tie)	78,068
1908	Chicago NL, 4	Detroit AL, 1	62,232
1909	Pittsburgh NL, 4	Detroit AL, 3	145,295
1910	Philadelphia AL, 4	Chicago NL, 1	124,222
1911	Philadelphia AL, 4	New York NL, 2	179,851
1912	Boston AL, 4	New York NL, 3 (1 tie)	252,037
1913	Philadelphia AL, 4	New York NL, 1	151,000
1914	Boston NL, 4	Philadelphia AL, 0	111,009
1915	Boston AL, 4	Philadelphia NL, 1	143,351
1916	Boston AL, 4	Brooklyn NL, 1	162,859
1917	Chicago AL, 4	New York NL, 2	186,654
1918	Boston AL, 4	Chicago NL, 2	128,483
1919	Cincinnati NL, 5	Chicago AL, 3	236,928
1920	Cleveland AL, 5	Brooklyn NL, 2	178,737
1921	New York NL, 5	New York AL, 3	269,976
1922	New York NL, 4	New York AL, 0 (1 tie)	185,947
1923	New York AL, 4	New York NL, 2	301,430
1924	Washington AL, 4	New York NL, 3	283,665
1925	Pittsburgh NL, 4	Washington AL, 3	282,848
1926	St Louis NL, 4	New York AL, 3	328,051
1927	New York AL, 4	Pittsburgh NL, 0	201,705
1928	New York AL, 4	St Louis NL, 0	199,072
1929	Philadelphia AL, 4	Chicago NL, 1	190,490
1930	Philadelphia AL, 4	St Louis NL, 2	212,619
1931	St Louis NL, 4	Philadelphia AL, 3	231,567
1932	New York AL, 4	Chicago NL, 0	191,998
1933	New York NL, 4	Washington AL, 1	163,076
1934	St Louis NL, 4	Detroit AL, 3	281,510
1935	Detroit AL, 4	Chicago NL, 2	286,672
1936	New York AL, 4	New York NL, 2	302,924
1937	New York AL, 4	New York NL, 1	238,142
1938	New York AL, 4	Chicago NL, 0	200,833
1939	New York AL, 4	Cincinnati NL, 0	183,849
1940	Cincinnati NL, 4	Detroit AL, 3	281,927
1941	New York AL, 4	Brooklyn NL, 1	235,773
1942	St Louis NL, 4	New York AL, 1	277,101
1943	New York AL, 4	St Louis NL, 1	277,213
1944	St Louis NL, 4	St Louis AL, 2	206,708
1945	Detroit AL, 4	Chicago NL, 3	333,457
1946	St Louis NL, 4	Boston AL, 3	250,071
1947	New York AL, 4	Brooklyn NL, 3	389,763
1948	Cleveland AL, 4	Boston NL, 2	358,362
1949	New York AL, 4	Brooklyn NL, 1	236,716
1950	New York AL, 4	Philadelphia NL, 0	196,009
1951	New York AL, 4	New York NL, 2	341,977
1952	New York AL, 4	Brooklyn NL, 3	340,706
1953	New York AL, 4	Brooklyn NL, 2	307,350
1954	New York NL, 4	Cleveland AL, 0	251,507
1955	Brooklyn NL, 4	New York AL, 3	362,310
1956	New York AL, 4	Brooklyn NL, 3	345,903
1957	Milwaukee NL, 4	New York AL, 3	394,712
1958	New York AL, 4	Milwaukee NL, 3	393,909
1959	Los Angeles NL, 4	Chicago AL, 2	420,784
1960	Pittsburgh NL, 4	New York AL, 3	349,813
1961	New York AL, 4	Cincinnati NL, 1	223,247
1962	New York AL, 4	San Francisco NL, 3	376,864
1963	Los Angeles NL, 4	New York AL, 0	247,279
1964	St Louis NL, 4	New York AL, 3	321,807
1965	Los Angeles NL, 4	Minnesota AL, 3	364,326
1966	Baltimore AL, 4	Los Angeles NL, 0	220,791
1967	St Louis NL, 4	Boston AL, 3	304,085
1968	Detroit AL, 4	St Louis NL, 3	379,670
1969	New York NL, 4	Baltimore AL, 1	272,378
1970	Baltimore AL, 4	Cincinnati NL, 1	253,183
1971	Pittsburgh NL, 4	Baltimore AL, 3	351,091
1972	Oakland AL, 4	Cincinnati NL, 3	363,149
1973	Oakland AL, 4	New York NL, 3	358,289
1974	Oakland AL, 4	Los Angeles NL, 1	260,004
1975	Cincinnati NL, 4	Boston AL, 3	308,272
1976	Cincinnati NL, 4	New York AL, 0	223,009
1977	New York AL, 4	Los Angeles NL, 2	337,708
1978	New York AL, 4	Los Angeles NL, 2	337,304
1979	Pittsburgh NL, 4	Baltimore AL, 3	367,597
1980	Philadelphia NL, 4	Kansas City AL, 2	324,516
1981	Los Angeles NL, 4	New York AL, 2	338,081
1982	St Louis NL, 4	Milwaukee AL, 3	384,570
1983	Baltimore AL, 4	Philadelphia NL, 1	304,139
1984	Detroit AL, 4	San Diego NL, 1	271,820
1985	Kansas City AL, 4	St Louis NL, 3	327,494
1986	New York NL, 4	Boston AL, 3	321,774
1987	Minnesota AL, 4	St Louis NL, 3	387,138
1988	Los Angeles NL, 4	Oakland AL, 1	259,984

WORLD SERIES RECORDS 1903–1988

TEAM RECORDS

AL clubs have won 49 WS, won 272 games, and scored 363 home runs (12 in 1956)

NL clubs have won 36 WS, won 230 games, and scored 256 home runs (9 in 1977 and 1955)

36 teams have won the WS after losing the first game
10 teams have won the WS after losing the first two games
6 teams have won the WS after winning one game but losing three
No team has won the WS after losing the first three games

Most WS played: 33 New York Yankees (won 22, lost 11)
Most WS games: 187 New York Yankees (109–77–1)
Most WS lost: 12 Brooklyn/Los Angeles Dodgers, NL
Latest date WS started: 20 October 1981
Latest date WS finished: 28 October 1981
Most innings (day game): 14 in 1916
Most innings (night): 12 in 1975 and 1977
Longest game: 4hrs 13mins, 1973
Shortest game: 1hr 25mins, 1908
First night game: 13 October 1971, Pittsburgh–Baltimore
All 7 WS games at night: 1985, 1986
Most players used in WS: 26 by Detroit 1945, Boston 1946
Fewest players used in WS: 12 by New York 1905, Philadelphia 1910 and 1913 (13 Baltimore 1966)
Most players in a game: 21 by New York 1947, Cincinnati 1961, Oakland 1973
Largest game attendance: 92,706 LA–Chicago (1959)
Largest WS attendance: 420,784 (6 games in 1959)
Most runs scored by a team: 18 NY Yankees (1936)

BY PLAYERS IN A GAME

Most hits: 5 Paul Molitor 1982
Most runs: 4 (6 players, most recent 1987)
Most RBIs: 6 Bobby Richardson 1960
Most home runs: 3 Babe Ruth 1926 & 1928, 3 Reggie Jackson 1977
Most stolen bases: 3 (4 times, most recent 1968)
Grand Slam homers: 15 (most recent 1988)
Runners stolen home to score: 13 (most recent 1964)
Pitchers have hit homers: 14 (most recent 1974)
Most strikeouts by pitcher: 17 Bob Gibson 1968
Perfect game by pitcher: 8 October 1956 Don Larsen, NYY

BY PLAYERS IN A SERIES OR CAREER

Most WS as a player: 14 Yogi Berra (won 10)
Most WS as a manager: 10 Casey Stengel (won 7)
Most WS as an umpire: 18 Bill Klem (104 games)
Most games: 75 Yogi Berra (WS 1947–63)
Most games by a pitcher: 22 Whitey Ford
 (Ford won 10, pitched 146 Innings, 94 strikeouts)
Most games saved by pitcher: 6 Rollie Fingers
Most times hit by pitch: 3 Max Carey 1925
Most at bats: 259 Yogi Berra
Most hits: 71 Yogi Berra
Most runs: 42 Mickey Mantle
Most RBIs: 40 Mickey Mantle
Most stolen bases: 14 Lou Brock, Ed Collins
Youngest player: 18yrs 10m 13d, Fred Lindstrom 1924
Oldest player: 46yrs 2m 29d, John Quinn 1930
Oldest non-pitcher: 42yrs 6m 2d, Pete Rose 1983
Youngest manager: 26yrs 11m 21d, Joe Cronin 1933
Most years between first and last WS: 22 Willie Mays, Giants 1951 to Mets 1973
Most years in majors before appearing in WS: 21 Joe Niekro, Cubs 1967 to Twins 1987

Donald George Bradman meets George 'Babe' Ruth at Yankee Stadium on 30 July 1932. A few months later, Ruth's Yankees had won another World Series, while Bradman was embroiled in cricket's infamous Bodyline Test Series in Australia.

Off The Pitch

FACTS ABOUT 1988 MAJOR LEAGUERS

Each Major League club produces an annual media guide of up to 200 pages, which gives facts and figures about the franchise and its players, past and present, both on and off the diamond. The following information listed under various headings has been selected from the 26 media guides produced in 1988.

BIRTHPLACES

Of the 874 players invited to Spring Training in 1988, 711 were born in the USA and 163 abroad. The most common US birthplaces were California 252, Texas 69, New York 59, Ohio 57, Florida 56, Illinois 49 and Pennsylvania 44. Mentioned only once were Delaware, Vermont, Arkansas and Alaska.

Foreign-born players came from the Dominican Republic 61, Puerto Rico 37, Venezuela 24, Mexico 9, Cuba 6 and Canada 5. Those from further afield tended to be born overseas to US forces families, or families who emigrated to the USA when the players concerned were young: France 3, Jamaica 3, West Germany 3, Britain 2, Nicaragua 2, Panama 2, Netherlands, Virgin Isles, Dutch Antilles, Colombia, Honduras, Australia. The most remarkable town for developing baseball talent seems to be San Pedro de Macoris, in the Dominican Republic. Twelve of today's Major Leaguers, including 7 shortstops, were born there between 1951 and 1968 (Joaquin Andujar, Pedro Guerrero, Nelson Norman, Rafael Ramirez, George Bell, Juan Samuel, Julio Franco, Tony Fernandez, Juan Castillo, Balvino Galvez, Manny Lee, Juan Bell).

FAMILY AND RELATIONS

102 players have brothers who play (or played) in the majors, and there are 45 sons, 14 cousins, 10 nephews, and 8 brothers-in-law of big leaguers. **Frank Williams**, Cincinnati, is a full-blooded Sheshatee Indian. **Gary Thurman**, KC, has a twin sister and triplet brothers and sister. **Jose Canseco**, Oakland, has an identical twin brother, Ozzie, also with the A's. **Casey Candaele**, Houston, learnt his baseball from his mother who played professionally. **Jackie Gutierrez**, Philadelphia, was born in Colombia. His father threw the javelin at the 1936 Olympics, his brother ran 100 metres in the 1964 Games. **Jose Cruz**, Yankees, has two brothers who played pro-baseball in Japan. **Lee Mazzilli**, Mets, is son of Libero Mazzilli, a former pro-boxer. **Darrell Miller**, California, has a brother with the NBA Indiana Pacers and a sister, Cheryl, who won an Olympic basketball gold medal and now works for ABC Sports. **Bryn Smith**, Montreal, had parents who worked at RKO in Hollywood. They were introduced to each other by Jayne Russell. **Cal Ripken Jr**, Baltimore, and wife Kelly honeymooned in England in 1987.

Players with many brothers and sisters: 13 **Willie Upshaw**, Cleveland; 13 **Antonio Armas**, California; 13 **Dennis Boyd**, Boston; 12 **Eddie Murray**, Baltimore; 11 **Mookie Wilson**, Mets; 10 **Geronimo Pena**, St Louis; 9 **Fred Manrique**, White Sox; 8 **Kirby Puckett**, Minnesota.

Mookie Wilson, Mets, got married at home plate in Jackson, Mississippi, 1978. **Jose Rijo**, Cincinnati, is married to the daughter of Hall of Famer Juan Marichal. **Ray Knight**, Detroit, is married to golfer Nancy Lopez. **Greg Booker**, SD, is managed by his father-in-law, Padres' GM, Jack McKeon. **Tom Niedenfuer**, Baltimore, is married to TV actress Judy Landers. **Billy Hatcher**, Houston, is married to the Astros Director of Special Events. **Dave Magadan**, Mets, is godson and cousin of ex-Yankees manager Lou Piniella. **Carney Lansford**, Oakland, is a direct descendant of sea captain Sir Francis Drake.

HEALTH

Rick Rhoden, Yankees, had osteomyelitis as a child. He could only walk with a leg brace and stick. **Oddibe McDowell**, Texas, sustained a ruptured spleen in a serious car crash in 1979. **Keith Moreland**, SD, a defensive back for Texas at college, broke his wrist on the opening kickoff v. Oklahoma. **Bob Nipper**, Pittsburgh, has to do lengthy daily exercises, as he suffers from spondylitis (inflammation of the vertebrae).

JOBS AND BUSINESS

Ed Olwine, Atlanta, spent the 1987 off-season as a food vendor at NBA Atlanta Hawks games. **Shane Rawley**, Philadelphia, has had his pilot's licence since 1980. **Bob Brenly**, SF, and **Joe Magrane**, St Louis, each host a post-game show on local radio. **Marvin Freeman**, Philadelphia, once worked at shaping and finishing concert violin bows. **Don Mattingly**, Yankees, has a restaurant, 'Mattingly's 23', in his home town of Evansville, Indiana. **Ernie Whitt**, Toronto, is a partner in 15 Mother's Pizza-Pasta Restaurant franchises around Toronto. **Ron Guidry**, Yankees, served for 6 years in the National Guard. **Tim Jones**, St Louis, rode skateboards professionally for Power Flex. **Rene Gonzales**, Baltimore, worked as a Dodger Stadium usher for two years while at Cal State. **Tom Henke**, Toronto, is a bricklayer by trade with a degree in building construction. **Dave Winfield**, Yankees, and **Ron Darling**, Mets, each has a Manhattan restaurant, 'Border Cafe USA' and 'Champions'. **Kevin Seitzer**, KC, has a BSc in industrial electronics. **Jeff Musselman**, Toronto, has a BSc in economics from Harvard University and works as a stockbroker in the off-season. **Lance McCullers**, SD, is involved with 'Pitchers for Pets' – a project to assist responsible pet ownership in San Diego.

INTERESTS/MISCELLANEOUS

Chili Davis, California, born in Jamaica, was given his nickname after a chili bowl haircut when he was 11. **Storm Davis**, Oakland, was given his nickname by his mother before he was born. Dr Storm was a character in a book she read during her pregnancy. **'Oil Can' Boyd**, Boston, comes from Meridian, Mississippi, where beer is called oil. **George Brett**, KC, co-owns with his three brothers two Northwest League clubs. **Paul Molitor**, Milwaukee, graduated in 1974 from Cretin High School, St Paul, Minnesota. **Keith Hernandez**, Mets, appears on radio shows to discuss his deep interest in the US Civil War. **Rick Dempsey**, LA, has become famous for singing and sliding about on the tarp. during rain delays.

De Wayne Buice, California, does a wide variety of cartoon and TV impressions. **Andre Dawson**, Cubs, has had a street named after him in Miami South, and was a guest at the 1983 Japanese World Series. **Craig Shipley**, Mets, born in Parramatta, NSW, is only the second Aussie (after Joe Quinn 1884–91) to play in the majors. He went to college at Alabama. **Tom Waddell**, Cleveland, born in Dundee, is a cousin of former Leeds and Scotland soccer international Peter Lorimer. **Danny Cox**, St Louis, born in Northampton, was the third European-born starting pitcher in the World Series (Bert Blyleven, Minnesota, was the second), and the 13th European-born WS player overall.

SPORT

Bobby Bonilla, Pittsburgh, was spotted by GM Syd Thrift at a 1981 baseball clinic in Europe. **Harold Baines**, White Sox, was noticed as a 12-year-old Little Leaguer by former White Sox owner, Bill Veeck. **Rick Mahler**, Atlanta, played Little League in England before his family returned to Texas. **Marvell Wynne**, SD, was the only player signed from 200 applicants at a Chicago tryout camp held by KC in 1978. **Lloyd Moseby**, Toronto, started as a catcher in Little League but was cut from the team. **Lee Mazilli**, Mets, won 8 age group US speed skating titles 1965–71. **John Candelaria**, Yankees, had trials for the Puerto Rico basketball team to the 1972 Olympics but signed to play baseball instead. **Kirk McCaskill**, California, was an All-American at ice hockey. **Doug Sisk**, Baltimore, was considered for the 1976 US Olympic rifle team. **Paul Mirabella**, Milwaukee, was an expert fencer at high school and college. **Rick Leach**, Toronto, played quarterback for Michigan in 48 NCAA games including 3 Rose Bowls. **Vince Coleman**, St Louis, was punter/place kicker at Florida A&M. His cousin punted for the NFL Vikings. **Rick Rhoden**, Yankees, is a scratch golfer. **Greg Brock**, Milwaukee, earned free use of a car for a year by scoring a hole-in-one at a golf tournament. **Bryn Smith**, Montreal, a 2-handicap golfer, once hit a golf ball out of Olympic Stadium, Montreal. **Chris Sabo**, Cincinnati, played goalie on two ice hockey national junior championship teams. **Kirk Gibson**, LA, scored 24 touchdowns as an All-American flanker at Michigan State. **Bo Jackson**, KC, won the 51st annual NCAA Heisman Trophy and played for the NFL's LA Raiders in 1987–88. **Bo Diaz**, Cincinnati, was just one game from the Little League World Series when an earthquake hit his Venezuelan home town.

MAJOR LEAGUERS BORN IN ENGLAND, WALES AND SCOTLAND

In its earliest years, the impression given was that Major League baseball was dominated by eastern, urbanised Irishmen. Although that was plainly an exaggeration, *The Baseball Encyclopedia* (7th edition) lists 37 players (five of whom later became managers) who were born in Ireland between 1846 and 1891. The Irish overtones were doubtless encouraged by the fact that 14 of these early players survived until over 80 years of age. To date, an equal number of Major Leaguers have been born in Britain. As with the Irish, most were immigrants before the turn of the century and all remained in the USA when their playing careers were over.

The following list of British-born Major Leaguers gives their name, age, birthplace, (position: games played/any managerial experience), the extent of their career (and any World Series appearances), in order of birthdates, from 1835 to 1959.

Harry Wright, 60, Sheffield (OF:2/Man:1,917) 1876–93
Bob Morrow, 60, England (Man:51) 1881
George Hall, 74, England (OF:121) 1876–77
Dick Higham, 54, England (OF:130) 1876–80
Tim Manning, 81, Henley (2B:200) 1882–85
John Conner, 79, Scotland (P.12) 1884–85
Ed Cogswell, 34, England (1B:109) 1879–82
Jim McCormick, 62, Glasgow (P:494/Man:167) 1878–87
Hugh Nicol, 63, Campsie (OF:888/Man:38) 1881–97
Tom Brown, 67, Liverpool (P:12/Man:115) 1882–98
John Foley, England (P:1) 1885
Mac MacArthur, 70, Glasgow (P:6) 1884
Jim Halpin, 30, England (SS:63) 1882–85
Dennis Fitzgerald, 71, England (SS:2) 1890
Pete Hasney, 43, England (OF:2) 1890
Al Lawson, 85, London (P:3) 1890
Marty Hogan, 54, Wensbury (OF:40) 1894–95
Ted 'Parson' Lewis, 64, Machynlleth (P:183) 1896–1901
Mike Hopkins, 80, Glasgow (C:1) 1902
Ed Walker, 73, Cambois (P:4) 1902–03
Al Shaw, 84, Burslem (C:180) 1901/07–09
Harry Smith, 59, Yorkshire (C:343) 1901–10 (WS:1903)
Lou 'Old Dog' Ritter, 77, Liverpool (C:462) 1902–08
David Brain, 78, Hereford (3B/SS:679) 1901/03–08
Jimmy Austin, 86, Swansea (3B:1580/Man:75) 1909–29
Charlie Hanford, 82, Tunstall (OF:232) 1914–15
Walter 'Rosy' Carlisle, 62, Yorkshire (OF:3) 1908
Armstrong 'Klondike' Smith, 72, London (OF:7) 1912
George Chalmers, 72, Edinburgh (P:121) 1910–16 (WS:1915)
Ned Crompton, 61, Liverpool (OF:18) 1909–10
Sam White, 37, Preston (C:1) 1919
Jim Wright, 63, Hyde (P:4) 1927–28
Bobby Thomson,* Glasgow (OF:1,779) 1946–60
Keith Lampard,* Warrington (OF:62) 1969–70
Les Rohr,* Lowestoft (P:6) 1967–69
Tom Waddell,* Dundee (P:113) 1984–87
Danny Cox,* Northampton (P:152) 1983–88 (WS'85'87)
* Still alive in 1988

There are just three British-born (but no Irish) members of baseball's Hall of Fame: Harry Wright (see above), executive and 'pioneer' Henry Chadwick from Exeter, and Manchester-born umpire Tom Connolly (see AL records, page 98).

ABBREVIATIONS

C	– Catcher	ERA	– Earned Run Average
1B	– First Baseman	SOs	– Strikeouts
2B	– Second Baseman	BBs	– Bases on Balls
3B	– Third Baseman	Inns	– Innings
SS	– Shortstop	W	– Won
LF	– Left fielder	L	– Lost
CF	– Centre fielder	RBIs	– Runs Batted In
RF	– Right fielder	HRs	– Home Runs
OF	– Out fielder		
P	– Pitcher		
LH	– Left Handed		
RH	– Right Handed		

Line Scores explained:

Where space allows, American newspapers publish box scores, the equivalent of a scorecard at cricket. More usually they give the all-in-a-line scores used in this book for the 1988 ALCS, NLCS and World Series.

The visiting team always bats first in baseball, so is listed above the home side. The runs scored in each inning (from first to ninth) are listed in sets of three figures. There will be more numbers if teams played extra innings because scores were tied after nine stanzas. An 'x' shows that the home team did not need to bat in the ninth inning, as it had already won the game.

After the dash there is a set of three numbers showing the total runs, hits and any errors by each team. Then follows the starting pitcher followed by any relief pitcher(s) used (with the number and fraction of innings they pitched in brackets), and finally the catcher(s) with the club's name abbreviated. This is done for both teams with each divided by a semicolon.

The winning and losing pitchers are listed with their season or playoff series record, plus any relief pitcher credited with a save.

Next, any home runs hit, the total runners left on base, any game winning run batted in are given, and finally the time the game lasted and the ballpark attendance.

BRITISH-BORN MAJOR LEAGUERS

The Minor Leagues 1988

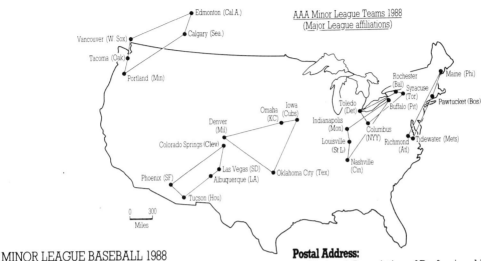

AAA Minor League Teams 1988
(Major League affiliations)

MINOR LEAGUE BASEBALL 1988
(1) = 1988 Champions; (2) = 1988 Playoff Losers
The 160 clubs attracted over 21 million spectators in 1988.

Postal Address:
National Association of Professional Baseball Leagues, Inc., PO Box A, St Petersburg, Florida 33731, USA
Telephone: (813) 822 6937

AAA:
INTERNATIONAL LEAGUE (Int.), since 1884
Eastern: Pawtucket, RI. (Red Sox)
Portland, Maine (Phillies)
Richmond, Va. (Braves)
(2) Tidewater, Va. (NY Mets)
Western: Columbus, Ohio (NY Yankees)
(1) Rochester, NY (Orioles)
Syracuse, NY (Blue Jays)
Toledo, Ohio (Tigers)

AAA:
AMERICAN ASSOCIATION (AmA.), since 1902
Eastern: Buffalo, NY (Pirates)
(1) Indianapolis, Ind. (Expos)
Louisville, KY. (Cards)
Nashville, Tenn. (Reds)
Western: Denver, Col. (Brewers)
Iowa, Ia. (Chicago Cubs)
Oklahoma City, Ok. (Rangers)
(2) Omaha, Neb. (Royals)
(Indianapolis (AmA) then beat Rochester (Int) in the AAA Alliance playoffs)

AAA:
PACIFIC COAST LEAGUE (Pac.), since 1903
Northern: Calgary, Alb., Can. (Mariners)
Edmonton, Alb., Can. (Angels)
Portland, Ore. (Twins)
Tacoma, Wash. (Athletics)
(2) Vancouver, BC, Can. (White Sox)
Southern: Albuquerque, NMex. (Dodgers)
Colorado Springs, Col. (Indians)
(1) Las Vegas, Nev. (Padres)
Phoenix, Ariz. (Giants)
Tucson, Ariz. (Astros)

AA:
TEXAS LEAGUE (T), since 1888
Eastern: Arkansas, Ark. (Cards)
Jackson, Miss. (NY Mets)
Shreveport, La. (Giants)
(1) Tulsa, Okla. (Rangers)
Western: (2) El Paso, Tex. (Brewers)
Midland, Tex. (Angels)
San Antonio, Tex. (Dodgers)
Wichita, Kan. (Padres)

AA:
SOUTHERN LEAGUE (S), since 1904
Eastern: Charlotte, NCar. (Orioles)
Columbus, Georgia (Astros)
(2) Greenville, SCar. (Braves)
Jacksonville, Fla. (Expos)
Orlando, Fla. (Twins)
Western: Birmingham, Ala. (White Sox)
(1) Chattanooga, Tenn. (Reds)
Huntsville, Ala. (Athletics)
Knoxville, Tenn. (Blue Jays)
Memphis, Tenn. (Royals)

AA:
EASTERN LEAGUE (E), since 1923
(1) Albany, NY (Yankees)
Glens Falls, NY (Tigers)
Harrisburg, Penn. (Pirates)
New Britain, Conn. (Red Sox)
Pittsfield, Mass. (Cubs)
Reading, Penn. (Phillies)
(2) Vermont, Vt. (Mariners)
Williamsport, Penn. (Indians)

A:
NORTHWEST LEAGUE (NW), since 1901
North Div: Bellingham, Wash. (Mariners)
Boise, Idaho (Independent)
Everett, Wash. (Giants)
(1) Spokane, Wash. (Padres)
South Div: Bend, Ore. (Angels)
Eugene, Ore. (Royals)
(2) Medford, Ore. (Athletics)
Salem, Ore. (Dodgers)

A:
CALIFORNIA LEAGUE (Cal.), since 1914
Northern: Fresno, Cal. (Co-op)
Modesto, Cal. (Athletics)
Reno, Nev. (Co-op)
San Jose, Cal. (Giants)
(2) Stockton, Cal. (Brewers)
Southern: Bakersfield, Cal. (Dodgers)
Palm Springs, Cal. (Angels)
(1) Riverside, Cal. (Padres)
San Bernardino, Cal. (Mariners)
Visalia, Cal. (Twins)

A:
FLORIDA STATE LEAGUE (FS), since 1919
Eastern: Fort Lauderdale, Fla. (Yankees)
Miami, Fla. (Independent)
(1) St Lucie, Fla. (NY Mets)
Vero Beach, Fla. (Dodgers)
West Palm Beach, Fla. (Expos)
Central: Baseball City, Fla. (Royals)
Lakeland, Fla. (Tigers)
(2) Osceola, Fla. (Astros)
Winter Haven, Fla. (Red Sox)
Western: Clearwater, Fla. (Phillies)
Dunedin, Fla. (Blue Jays)
Port Charlotte, Fla. (Rangers)
St Petersburg, Fla. (Cards)
Tampa, Fla. (White Sox)

A:
NEW YORK-PENN LEAGUE (NY-P), since 1939
McNamara Div: Auburn, NY (Astros)
Elmira, NY (Red Sox)
Little Falls, NY (Mets)
Oneonta, NY (Yankees)
Utica, NY (White Sox)
(1) Watertown, NY (Pirates)
Stedler Div: Batavia, NY (Phillies)
Erie, NY (Orioles)
Geneva, NY (Cubs)
Hamilton, Ont., Can. (Cards)
(2) Jamestown, NY (Expos)
St Catharines, Ont., Can. (BJays)

A:
CAROLINA LEAGUE (Car.), since 1945
Northern: Hagerstown, Md. (Orioles)
(2) Lynchburg, Va. (Red Sox)
Prince William, Va. (Yankees)
Salem, Va. (Pirates)
Southern: Durham, NCar. (Braves)
(1) Kinston, NCar. (Indians)
Virginia, Va. (Co-op)
Winston-Salem, NCar. (Cubs)

A:
MIDWEST LEAGUE (MW), since 1947
Northern: Appleton, Wis. (Royals)
Beloit, Wis. (Brewers)
(2) Kenosha, Wis. (Twins)
Madison, Wis. (Athletics)
Rockford, Ill. (Expos)
South Bend, Ind. (White Sox)
Wausau, Wis. (Mariners)
Southern: Burlington, Ia. (Braves)
(1) Cedar Rapids, Ia. (Reds)
Clinton, Ia. (Giants)
Peoria, Ill. (Cubs)
Quad City, Ia. (Angels)
Springfield, Ill. (Cards)
Waterloo, Ia. (Indians)

A:
SOUTH ATLANTIC LEAGUE (SA), since 1948
Northern: Asheville, NCar. (Astros)
Charleston, WVa. (Cubs)
Fayetteville, NCar. (Tigers)
Greensboro, NCar. (Reds)
Gastonia, NCar. (Rangers)
(1) Spartanburg, SCar. (Phillies)
Southern: Augusta, Georgia (Pirates)
(2) Charleston, SCar. (Padres)
Columbia, SCar. (NY Mets)
Myrtle Beach, SCar. (Blue Jays)
Savannah, Georgia (Cards)
Sumter, SCar. (Braves)

A-Rookie:
APPALACHIAN LEAGUE (Ap.), since 1921
(1) Kingsport, Tenn. (NY Mets)
(2) Burlington, NCar. (Indians)

A-Rookie:
PIONEER LEAGUE (P), since 1939
(1) Great Falls, Mont. (Dodgers)
(2) Butte, Mont. (Rangers)

A-Rookie:
GULF COAST LEAGUE (GC), since 1964
(1) Yankees

(There are a few changes in minor league affiliations after every season.)

MINOR LEAGUE TEAMS 121

NCAA College Baseball

Before the Second World War, the majority of players with ambitions to play in the majors signed for professional franchises when they left high school. After several years playing with the team's minor league farm clubs they might be given their chance to succeed in the big leagues.

Today, things are quite different. Some players (e.g. Don Mattingly) sign straight from school, but well over 60 per cent (e.g. Mike Schmidt) gain a college education before entering the free agent draft.

This trend has helped reduce the number of minor leagues around the country, but has improved the standard of NCAA baseball, and increased public and Major League interest in the NCAA College World Series. Traditional college baseball powerhouses are in the sun belt states of the south and west. Schools such as Texas, USC or Arizona State could each field an 'old boys' team from today's major leaguers. But the most remarkable of the smaller colleges which encourage baseball talent is in fast-growing Florida; Miami-Dade Community Colleges (North & South), in Miami, had 15 former students on 1988 Major League rosters.

The combined attractions of a good education and the chance of representing the USA in international competitions such as the Olympic Games (selected by the USBF), before trying for fame and fortune in the majors, means that NCAA college baseball is becoming increasingly influential. Today's youngsters take heart from the successes of the players listed below who played on the US silver medal winning squad at the 1984 Olympics.

Many notable figures in other aspects of American life have played in the CWS, including US President George Bush, who captained the two Yale teams that reached the final, and Dallas Cowboys former QB, Danny White (Arizona State), the only player to play in the CWS and NFL Super Bowl.

	1984 College	1988 MLB club
Sid Akins	USC	Atlanta
Flavio Alfaro	San Diego State	—
Don August	Chapman	Milwaukee
Scott Bankhead	North Carolina	Seattle
Bob Caffrey	California State	—
Will Clark Jr	Mississippi State	San Francisco
Mike Dunne	Bradley	Pittsburgh
Gary Green	Oklahoma State	(San Diego '86)
Chris Gwynn	San Diego State	Los Angeles
John Hoover	Fresno State	Baltimore
Barry Larkin	Michigan	Cincinnati
Shane Mack	UCLA	San Diego
John Marzano	Temple	Boston
Oddibe McDowell	Arizona State	Texas
Mark McGwire	USC	Oakland
Pat Pacillo	Seton Hall	Cincinnati
Cory Snyder	Brigham Young	Cleveland
B. J. Surhoff	North Carolina	Milwaukee
Billy Swift	Maine	Seattle
Bobby Witt	Oklahoma	Texas

Postal Address: The National Collegiate Athletic Association, Nall Avenue at 63rd Street, PO Box 1906, MISSION, Kansas 66201, USA
Telephone: (913) 384 3220

NCAA COLLEGE WORLD SERIES 1947–1988

Year	Champion	Score	Runner-up
1947	California	8–7	Yale
1948	Southern California	9–2	Yale
1949	Texas	10–3	Wake Forest
1950	Texas	3–0	Washington State
1951	Oklahoma	3–2	Tennessee
1952	Holy Cross	8–4	Missouri
1953	Michigan	7–5	Texas
1954	Missouri	4–1	Rollins
1955	Wake Forest	7–6	Western Michigan
1956	Minnesota	12–1	Arizona
1957	California	1–0	Penn State
1958	Southern California	8–7	Missouri
1959	Oklahoma State	5–3	Arizona
1960	Minnesota	2–1	Southern California
1961	Southern California	1–0	Oklahoma State
1962	Michigan	5–4	Santa Clara
1963	Southern California	5–2	Arizona
1964	Minnesota	5–1	Missouri
1965	Arizona State	2–1	Ohio State
1966	Ohio State	8–2	Oklahoma State
1967	Arizona State	11–2	Houston
1968	Southern California	4–3	Southern Illinois
1969	Arizona State	10–1	Tulsa
1970	Southern California	2–1	Florida State
1971	Southern California	7–2	Southern Illinois
1972	Southern California	1–0	Arizona State
1973	Southern California	4–3	Arizona State
1974	Southern California	7–3	Miami, Florida
1975	Texas	5–1	South Carolina
1976	Arizona	7–1	Eastern Michigan
1977	Arizona State	2–1	South Carolina
1978	Southern California	10–3	Arizona State
1979	Cal St. Fullerton	2–1	Arkansas
1980	Arizona	5–3	Hawaii
1981	Arizona State	7–4	Oklahoma State
1982	Miami, Florida	9–3	Wichita State
1983	Texas	4–3	Alabama
1984	Cal St. Fullerton	3–1	Texas
1985	Miami, Florida	10–6	Texas
1986	Arizona	10–2	Florida State
1987	Stanford	9–5	Oklahoma State
1988	Stanford	9–4	Arizona State

Since June 1950, the NCAA College World Series has been played at Johnny Rosenblatt Stadium, Omaha, Nebraska.

Colleges with the most CWS tournament appearances are: 24 Texas, 17 Southern California, 15 Oklahoma State, 15 Arizona State, 14 Arizona, 10 N. Colorado, 10 Miami (Fla), 9 Florida State.

IBA World Amateur Baseball

The world governing body of amateur baseball is the IBA (International Baseball Association) which has its headquarters in Indianapolis, USA. Sixty-eight national federations, representing countries in every continent, with more than 90,000,000 players worldwide, are already members.

At least a dozen other nations, including the USSR and the Peoples' Republic of China, are rapidly developing their baseball programmes with the aim of producing a broad-based pyramid of participation throughout the country, as well as a national adult squad able to compete for Olympic and World Championship places before the end of the century.

At the highest level the IBA organises biennial World Championships for the best dozen amateur baseball nations (which qualify through their continental tournaments), and, in alternate years, the invitation Inter-Continental Cup. The IBA also liaises with the IOC over Olympic tournaments such as those in 1984, 1988 and the full medal competition in 1992. The strongest amateur baseball nations are: Cuba, South Korea, USA, Taiwan, Japan, Nicaragua, Canada, Italy, Netherlands, Australia, Dutch Antilles, Puerto Rico, and other Latin American countries. The IBA also organises the World Youth Baseball Championships for 16–18-year-olds (AAA) and 13–15-year-olds (AA). The tournaments for 10–12-year-olds (A) will be suspended until after 1992 in order to focus world attention on the development of their exciting new Tee Ball programme which was launched in September 1988.

TEE BALL

Tee Ball is an ideal game for teaching new players the basic skills necessary to advance to baseball or softball, while having fun. Tee Ball's major difference from both games is that there is no pitching. The ball is placed on an adjustable, waist high batting tee just in front of home base (not home plate). The pitcher must stand on the pitcher's plate until the batter hits the ball cleanly off the tee into fair territory.

Apart from providing national federations around the world with the option of various levels of subsidised Tee Ball equipment and coaching instructions, the IBA has produced a simple 32-page colour comic book (in a joint project with the International Softball Federation) called *How to Play Tee Ball*, which explains the game in a concise and interesting way. It is hoped that this programme will appeal to school teachers and youth leaders. In British junior schools, for example, it could soon prove a realistic alternative to rounders or Kwik Cricket.

Postal Address: International Baseball Association,
Pan American Plaza, Suite 490, 201 South Capitol Avenue,
INDIANAPOLIS, Indiana 46225, USA
Telephone: (317) 237 5757
Fax: (317) 237 5405

AMATEUR WORLD CHAMPIONSHIPS 1938–1992

In August 1938, England played the USA in a five test match series. Although the American team was composed of amateur players, it is believed that (except for Sid Bisset of Durex Athletic, Birmingham) the English side was largely made up of Canadians from professional clubs. England won the first game 3–0 at Liverpool, won 8–6 at Hull, lost 0–5 at Rochdale, won 4–0 at Halifax, and won 5–3 at Leeds. At the time, no claims seem to have been made that the series was for any world championship. Indeed, but for the War it might have become a regular event.

For reasons that remain unclear, FIBA later recognised the two team series as the first world championship, and so it remains in the record books.

The 12 nations which competed in the 30th World Championships were: Cuba, USA, Japan, South Korea, Canada, Taipei, Puerto Rico, Nicaragua, Netherlands Antilles, Italy, Netherlands, Spain.

Year	Winner (Nations)		Year	Winner	(Nations)
1938	England	(2)	1965	Colombia	(9)
1939	Cuba	(3)	1969	Cuba	(8)
1940	Cuba	(7)	1970	Cuba	(12)
1941	Venezuela	(9)	1971	Cuba	(10)
1942	Cuba	(5)	1972	Cuba	(8)
1943	Cuba	(4)	1973	Cuba	(8)
1944	Venezuela	(8)		USA	(10)
1945	Venezuela	(6)	1974	USA	(9)
1947	Colombia	(9)	1976	Cuba	(11)
1948	Dominican Republic	(8)	1978	Cuba	(11)
1950	Cuba	(12)	1980	Cuba	(12)
1951	Puerto Rico	(11)	1982	South Korea	(10)
1952	Cuba	(13)	1984	Cuba	(13)
1953	Cuba	(11)	1986	Cuba	(12)
1961	Cuba	(10)	1988	Cuba	(12)

1990   4–19 August, Edmonton, Canada
       31st World Championships
1992   25 July–9 August   Summer Olympics, Barcelona, Spain

INTER-CONTINENTAL CUP 1973–1991

Year	Winner	Year	Winner
1973	Japan	1981	USA
1975	USA	1983	Cuba
1977	South Korea	1985	Cuba
1979	Cuba	1987	Cuba
1989	(16–27 August)	9th ICC at San Juan, Puerto Rico	
1991	(July)	10th ICC at Barcelona, Spain	

Olympic Baseball

Baseball first appeared at the Olympics back in 1904 at St Louis, but the concerted campaign to get the game included as a full medal sport did not begin until the early 1960s. More than 25 years of planning came to fruition in October 1986, when the IOC included baseball as the 25th Summer Olympic sport, with full medals from the 1992 Olympiad at Barcelona, Spain. Baseball history as an Olympic demonstration sport started in 1904, then in 1912 at Stockholm the USA beat the Swedish club, Vasteras, 13–3. In 1936 at Berlin, the US World Amateurs beat the US Olympics 6–5 in front of a capacity, but somewhat puzzled, crowd of 115,000.

The Finns play a game similar to baseball (pesapallo), so it was not surprising that the game was a demonstration sport in 1952 at Helsinki. But only 4,000 were on hand to see the USA beat Finland 19–1 and the Finnish BL beat the Finnish WAL 8–4.

Australia has had a long tradition of playing baseball. Before the War, baseball games were popular curtain raisers before VFL (Aussie Rules) football matches. So a demonstration game (USA 11–5 Australia) at the MCG attracted over 100,000 spectators.

Although Italy has been a European baseball power for many years the game did not appear at Rome in 1960, but the Japanese (with two strong professional leagues and massive public interest) hosted two games at Tokyo in 1964, where USA beat Japan 6–2, then tied 2–2 with a Japan Students team.

The demonstration tournament that sealed baseball's entry to the Olympics was in 1984 at Los Angeles. The 8-nation tournament drew 375,290 fans to Dodger Stadium, making baseball the 4th most popular sport behind soccer, athletics and basketball.

With Cuba, easily the best amateur team in the world, joining the Communist boycott, Japan won the gold by defeating the strongly fancied USA team 6–3 in the final (see page 122). Taiwan beat South Korea 3–0 to take the bronze. Other qualifiers were Italy, Canada, Nicaragua and the Dominican Republic.

In 1988, South Korea (which has strong professional and amateur baseball) hosted the eighth and last baseball demonstration tournament, at Chamshil Baseball Stadium beside the main Olympic stadium in Seoul. Chamshil has a capacity of 30,306 and playing field dimensions almost the same as Royals Stadium, Kansas City. The USA (gold) beat Japan (silver) 5–3 in the final, thanks to Tito Martinez, and one-handed pitcher, Jim Abbott. Puerto Rico (bronze) defeated South Korea 7–0. The other four nations involved were: Taipei, Netherlands, Canada and Australia.

Former Commissioner, Peter Ueberroth, who organised the profitable 1984 Los Angeles Olympic Games.

LITTLE LEAGUE WORLD SERIES WINNERS 1947–1988

(All 14 players per squad must be 11–12 years old)

Little League Baseball is played by 2½ million children in 25 countries. The winning teams from preliminary competitions during July in 8 world regions – USA (Central, South, East, West), Canada, Europe, Far East and Latin America – meet each August at Williamsport, Pennsylvania, for the Little League World Series.

The 8 game championship series draws capacity crowds of 33,000 to Lamade Stadium (all tickets are free), and has been televised by ABC-TV since 1963.

Year	Winner	Year	Winner
1947	Maynard, Penn., USA	1968	Wakayama, Japan
1948	Lock Haven, Penn., USA	1969	Taipei, Taiwan
1949	Hammonton, NJ, USA	1970	Wayne, NJ, USA
1950	Houston, Tex., USA	1971	Tainan, Taiwan
1951	Stamford, Conn., USA	1972	Taipei, Taiwan
1952	Norwalk, Conn., USA	1973	Tainan, Taiwan
1953	Birmingham, Ala., USA	1974	Kao Hsiung, Taiwan
1954	Schenectady, NY, USA	1975	Lakewood, NJ, USA
1955	Morrisville, Penn., USA	1976	Chofu, Tokyo, Japan
1956	Roswell, N.Mex., USA	1977	Kao Hsiung, Taiwan
1957	Monterrey, Mexico	1978	Pin-Tung, Taiwan
1958	Monterrey, Mexico	1979	Chia-Yi-Hsien, Taiwan
1959	Hamtramck, Mich., USA	1980	Hua Lian, Taiwan
1960	Levittown, Penn., USA	1981	Tai-Chung, Taiwan
1961	El Cajon, Calif., USA	1982	Kirkland, Wash., USA
1962	San Jose, Calif., USA	1983	Marietta, Georgia, USA
1963	Granada Hills, Calif., USA	1984	Seoul, South Korea
1964	Staten Island, NY, USA	1985	Seoul, South Korea
1965	Windsor, Conn., USA	1986	Tainan Park, Taiwan
1966	Houston, Tex., USA	1987	Hua Lian, Taiwan
1967	West Tokyo, Japan	1988	Tai-Chung, Taiwan

Amateur Baseball in Europe

Postal Address: CEBA – European Amateur Baseball Confederation, (Confédération Européene de Baseball Amateur), Turnhoutsebaan 66/5, B-2200 BORGERHOUT, Belgium

Ten years ago, there were only 583 affiliated clubs and 18,133 players around Europe. But by 1987, CEBA's official review of its 18 national member federations was able to declare a total of 46,150 players (19,760 seniors and 26,390 juniors) at 1,244 clubs. CEBA figures suggest that the numbers playing baseball in Britain over the past 10 years has increased from just 450 to 1,180.

Today, CEBA governs baseball from Poland in the East, to Spain (and perhaps Portugal before too long) in the West; from Bizerte, Tunisia, to the South, to Skelleften, Sweden (only 200 km from the Arctic Circle), to the North.

Baseball in Europe is at an exciting phase in its evolution; in 1988 the World Championships were in Italy, there is increasing support for baseball in the USSR (CEBA's 19th federation), and the first 8–12 nation competition for full medals will be at the 1992 Olympic Games in Barcelona.

EUROPEAN CHAMPIONSHIPS
Pool 'A' 1954–1991

Year	Winners	(Nations)	Year	Winners	(Nations)
1954	Italy	4	1969	Netherlands	7
1955	Spain	5	1971	Netherlands	8
1956	Netherlands	5	1973	Netherlands	6
1957	Netherlands	5	1975	Italy	6
1958	Netherlands	6	1977	Italy	5
1960	Netherlands	4	1979	Italy	4
1962	Netherlands	7	1981	Netherlands	4
1964	Netherlands	5	1983	Italy	6
1965	Netherlands	5	1985	Netherlands	6
1967	Belgium	5	1987	Netherlands	7

1989 Paris. 21st European Championships 1–11 September (8 teams)
1991 Rome. 22nd European Championships Pre-Olympic Tournament (8 teams)

The rules of baseball seem to have had their roots in various children's stick and ball games of European origin – particularly feeder, rounders, stoolball, cricket and schlagbal (or hit ball) – which had been taken across the Atlantic by migrants to the New World.

In Europe, the tradition of stick and ball games played by children or as folk celebrations of religious occasions (such as Easter, or Islamic festivals in Moorish Europe) is reflected in this marginal picture on the famous manuscript (kept in the Bodleian Library, Oxford) containing *The Romance of Alexander* illuminated between 1338 and 1344 AD. Its Flemish origins make it somehow appropriate that the modern headquarters of European baseball are in Antwerp, Belgium.

Baseball in Europe is governed by CEBA, the European Amateur Baseball Confederation, founded in April 1953 by Belgium, France, West Germany, Italy and Spain. Although growth has been steady, there have been teething troubles. The FEB Congress (it was renamed CEBA in 1972) was held in London in 1960 but bickering between Britain's two baseball organisations meant membership was delayed until the NBA was accepted in 1964. Four years later, the English federation's chairman, Mr K. Clappison, was involved in meetings that brought Italy and The Netherlands back into the organisation.

Britain has participated in just two (Pool A) European Championships. In 1967, in the absence of Italy and The Netherlands, Britain came second, defeating Spain 10–4, Switzerland 3–2, West Germany 11–9, but losing to Belgium 2–13.

However, with both countries returned to the fold it was a different story in 1971. Britain finished 7th, suffering a 0–21 drubbing by Italy and gaining just one victory (Sweden 10–7).

Over 600 years before the Padres joined the NL, a catcher and four infielders crowd a batter trying to bunt?

Things had settled down in Europe, but by March 1972 the squabbling in Britain between the NBL(UK) and the BBL had become so destructive that CEBA Secretary General, Roger Panaye, called a meeting in London to unite the two bodies into the EABF. In 1974, the UK Sports Council recognised the BABSF as the governing body for baseball and softball in this country, and so it remained until recently, when softball broke away, and baseball was reconstituted as the BBF.

In 1975 Britain played a qualifying game for the European Championship but lost 0–13 to West Germany at Southport. In 1982, in the North European Cup at Antwerp, Britain beat Finland 19–3, but lost heavily to Holland 0–25, France 7–17, and Belgium 2–15.

The increasing number of federations affiliated to CEBA, not to mention the variation in playing standards, meant a Pool A and Pool B championships had become essential. In the 1984 Pool B tournament at Hull, Britain came 3rd, beating Finland 10–0, but lost to West Germany 2–12 and San Marino 7–15. Britain came 3rd again in the 1986 Pool B championships in Paris, beating Finland 9–8, Switzerland 14–10, but losing to West Germany 0–10 and France 3–13. However, Britain won the 1988 Pool B tournament at Birmingham (beating Finland 11–0, Switzerland 27–4, and Czechoslovakia 11–0) to qualify for the 1989 Pool A championships for eight nations in Paris in September. This keeps alive Britain's chance of qualifying for the 1992 Olympics.

Postal Address: British Baseball Federation, East Park Lido, HULL, Humberside, HU8 9AW
Ansaphone: (0482) 76169

British Baseball

NATIONAL CUP FINALS

Baseball Association of Great Britain and Ireland
1890 Preston North End Amateurs beat Birmingham Amateurs 42–15 and 42–7

National Baseball Association
1892 Middlesbrough 26–16 St Thomas's Derby
1893 Thespians London 33–6 St Augustine's Darlington
1894 Thespians London 38–14 Stockton-on-Tees
1895 Derby 20–16 Fuller's London
1896 Wallsend on Tyne 16–10 Remington's London
1897 Derby 30–7 Middlesbrough
1899 Derby 14–3 Nottingham Forest
1900 Nottingham Forest 17–16 Derby

British Baseball Association
1906 Tottenham Hotspur 16–5 Nondescripts
1907 Clapton Orient 8–7 Fulham
1908 Tottenham Hotspur 6–5 Leyton
1909 Clapton Orient 6–4 Leyton
1910 Brentford 20–5 West Ham
1911 Leyton 6–5 Crystal Palace

National Baseball Association (2)
1934 Hatfield Liverpool 13–12 Albion Liverpool
1935 New London 7–1 Rochdale Greys
1936 White City London 9–5 Catford Saints
1937 Hull 5–1 Romford Wasps
1938 Rochdale Greys 1–0 Oldham Greyhounds
1939 Halifax 9–5 Rochdale Greys

Baseball Association Limited
1948 Liverpool Robins 13–0 Thames Board Mills Purfleet
1949 Hornsey Red Sox 10–5 Liverpool Cubs
1950 Burtonwood USAF Bees 23–2 Hornsey Red Sox
1951 Burtonwood USAF Bees 9–2 Ruislip USAF Rockets

British Baseball Federation
1959 Thames Board Mills Purfleet 12–3 East Hull Aces
1960 Thames Board Mills Purfleet 6–1 Liverpool Tigers
1962 Liverpool Tigers 8–3 East Hull Aces
1963 East Hull Aces 8–6 Garrington's Bromsgrove

British Baseball Association (2)
1965 Kingston Aces Hull 4–2 Stretford Saints Manchester

National Baseball League (UK)
1966 Stretford Saints Manchester 3–1 Liverpool Aces
1967 Liverpool Mormon Yankees 4–2 Beckenham Blue Jays
1968 Hull Aces 4–1 Hull Royals
1969 Watford Sun-Rockets 8–7 Liverpool Trojans
1970 Hull Royals 3–1 Hull Aces
1971 Liverpool NALGO Tigers 8–3 Hull Aces
1972 Hull Aces beat Hull Royals (official score not known)

British Amateur Baseball Federation
1973 Burtonwood Yanks 23–2 Hull Aces
1974 Nottingham Lions 5–3 Hull Royals
1975 Liverpool NALGO Tigers 5–3 Nottingham Lions
1976 Liverpool Trojans 5–4 Kensington Spirit of '76 London
1977 Golders Green Sox 9–5 Hull Aces

British Amateur Baseball and Softball Federation
1978 Liverpool Trojans 14–12 Crawley Giants
1979 Golders Green Sox 9–7 Hull Aces
1980 Liverpool Trojans 12–1 Hull Aces
1981 London Warriors 23–3 Hull Aces
1982 London Warriors 16–7 Liverpool Trojans
1983 Cobham Yankees London 10–3 Hull Mets
1984 Croydon Blue Jays 9–8 Hull Mets
1985 Hull Mets 10–8 London Warriors
1986 Cobham Yankees 12–0 Hull Mets

British Baseball Federation (2)
1987 Cobham Yankees 6–0 Nottingham S. Hornets
1988 Cobham Yankees 16–1 Burtonwood Braves

BASEBALL ON RADIO

The American Forces Network, Europe, has 30 AM broadcasting stations in West Germany:

    873 AM (1 station) Frankfurt
    1107 AM (5) including Berlin/Munich
    1143 AM (17) including Stuttgart/Bremerhaven
    1485 AM (7) including Garmisch

and 22 FM stations, between 89.2 and 107.7 FM in West Germany, Netherlands (4), Belgium (4).

AFN has sports news roundups from Mon–Fri at 6am, 7am, 12 noon, 6pm and 10pm (Central European Time); on Saturdays at 12 noon; on Sundays at 8.55am and 12 noon; and relays over 100 live MLB regular season games, all play-off and World Series games from AFRTS (Armed Forces Radio and Television Service) late into the night and early morning British time.

In recent years, MLB has been screened nationally by BBC-TV, ITV, Channel Four, and on cable-TV by Screensport. The advent of satellite TV is certain to bring regular, live screenings of MLB to the increasing number of British fans.

CAREER RECORDS SINCE 1900

not included in AL or NL records on pages 98 and 51

Most years in majors: 26 James McGwire
Most clubs in majors: 10 Bob Miller, Tommy Davis, Ken Brett
Most home runs: 755 Hank Aaron
Most years pitched: 25 Jim Kaat
Most games pitched: 1,070 Hoyt Wilhelm
Most innings pitched: 7,377 Cy Young
Most games saved: 341 Rollie Fingers
Most games won: 511 Cy Young
Most games lost: 313 Cy Young
Most strikeouts: 4,775 Nolan Ryan
Youngest manager: 24yrs 4m 8d Lou Boudreau, Cleveland 1941
Oldest manager on debut: 66yrs 2m 18d Tom Sheehan, SF 1960
Most years a manager without a title: 26 Gene Mauch, Phil/Mont/Minn/Cal. 1960–87

MAJOR LEAGUE 1989 REGULAR SEASON FINAL STANDINGS (to fill in)

AMERICAN LEAGUE

WEST	won–lost	Pct.	Games Behind
1.			—
2.			
3.			
4.			
5.			
6.			
7.			

AMERICAN LEAGUE

EAST	won–lost	Pct.	Games Behind
1.			—
2.			
3.			
4.			
5.			
6.			
7.			

NATIONAL LEAGUE

WEST	won–lost	Pct.	Games Behind
1.			—
2.			
3.			
4.			
5.			
6.			

NATIONAL LEAGUE

EAST	won–lost	Pct.	Games Behind
1.			—
2.			
3.			
4.			
5.			
6.			

Possible Fixture Dates	Venue	1989 ALCS		TOTALS Runs-Hits-Errors
1. Wednesday 4 October	at West	E		
		W		
2. Thursday 5 October	at West	E		
		W		
3. Saturday 7 October	at East	W		
		E		
4. Sunday 8 October	at East	W		
		E		
(5. if needed) Mon 9 October	at East	W		
		E		
(6. if needed) Wed 11 October	at West	E		
		W		
(7. if needed) Thurs 12 October	at West	E		
		W		

Winner of 1989 American League:

Possible Fixture Dates	Venue	1989 NLCS		TOTALS Runs-Hits-Errors
1. Tuesday 3 October	at East	W		
		E		
2. Wednesday 4 October	at East	W		
		E		
3. Friday 6 October	at West	E		
		W		
4. Saturday 7 October	at West	E		
		W		
(5. if needed) Sun 8 October	at West	E		
		W		
(6. if needed) Tues 10 October	at East	W		
		E		
(7. if needed) Wed 11 October	at East	W		
		E		

Winner of 1989 National League:

Possible Fixture Dates	Venue	1989 WORLD SERIES	1	2	3	4	5	6	7	8	9	TOTALS Runs-Hits-Errors
1. Saturday 14 October	at AL	NL										
		AL										
2. Sunday 15 October	at AL	NL										
		AL										
3. Tuesday 17 October	at NL	AL										
		NL										
4. Wednesday 18 October	at NL	AL										
		NL										
(5. if needed) Thurs 19 October	at NL	AL										
		NL										
(6. if needed) Sat 21 October	at AL	NL										
		AL										
(7. if needed) Sun 22 October	at AL	NL										
		AL										

Runs scored in each inning

Winner of 1989 World Series: